WITHDRAWN

Politics and Politicians in American Film

Recent Titles in the
Praeger Series in Political Communication
Robert E. Denton, Jr., *General Editor*

Politics, Media, and Modern Democracy: An International Study of Innovations in
Electoral Campaigning and Their Consequences
Edited by David L. Swanson and Paolo Mancini

In Contempt of Congress: Postwar Press Coverage on Capitol Hill
Mark J. Rozell

From the Margins to the Center: Contemporary Women and Political Communication
Patricia A. Sullivan and Lynn H. Turner

Headline Diplomacy: How News Coverage Affects Foreign Policy
Philip Seib

Campaign Craft: The Strategies, Tactics, and Art of Political Campaign Management
Daniel M. Shea

Inside Political Campaigns: Theory and Practice
Karen S. Johnson-Cartee and Gary A. Copeland

Rhetorical Studies of National Political Debates–1996
Edited by Robert V. Friedenberg

Communication Consultants in Political Campaigns: Ballot Box Warriors
Robert V. Friedenberg

Manipulation of the American Voter: Political Campaign Commercials
Karen S. Johnson-Cartee and Gary A. Copeland

Presidential Crisis Rhetoric and the Press in the Post-Cold War World
Jim A. Kuypers

The 1996 Presidential Campaign: A Communication Perspective
Edited by Robert E. Denton, Jr.

Reconciling Free Trade, Fair Trade, and Interdependence: The Rhetoric of Presidential
Economic Leadership
Delia B. Conti

Politics and Politicians in American Film

Phillip L. Gianos

Praeger Series in Political Communication

PRAEGER

Westport, Connecticut
London

Library of Congress Cataloging-in-Publication Data

Gianos, Phillip L.
    Politics and politicians in American film / Phillip L. Gianos.
        p. cm.—(Praeger series in political communication, ISSN
1062–5623)
    Includes bibliographical references and index.
    ISBN 0–275–96071–4 (alk. paper)
    1. Motion pictures—Political aspects—United States. 2. Politics
in motion pictures. 3. Motion pictures—Social aspects—United
States. I. Title. II. Series.
PN1995.9.P6G53   1998
791.43′658—dc21   97–33245

British Library Cataloguing in Publication Data is available.

Copyright © 1998 by Phillip L. Gianos

All rights reserved. No portion of this book may be
reproduced, by any process or technique, without the
express written consent of the publisher.

Library of Congress Catalog Card Number: 97–33245
ISBN: 0–275–96071–4
ISSN: 1062–5623

First published in 1998

Praeger Publishers, 88 Post Road West, Westport, CT 06881
An imprint of Greenwood Publishing Group, Inc.

Printed in the United States of America

The paper used in this book complies with the
Permanent Paper Standard issued by the National
Information Standards Organization (Z39.48–1984).

10 9 8 7 6 5 4 3 2 1

CONTENTS

SERIES FOREWORD

Those of us from the discipline of communication studies have long believed that communication is prior to all other fields of inquiry. In several other forums I have argued that the essence of politics is "talk" or human interaction.[1] Such interaction may be formal or informal, verbal or nonverbal, public or private, but it is always persuasive, forcing us consciously or subconsciously to interpret, to evaluate, and to act. Communication is the vehicle for human action.

From this perspective, it is not surprising that Aristotle recognized the natural kinship of politics and communication in his writings *Politics* and *Rhetoric*. In the former, he establishes that humans are "political beings [who] alone of the animals [are] furnished with the faculty of language."[2] And in the latter, he begins his systematic analysis of discourse by proclaiming that "rhetorical study, in its strict sense, is concerned with the modes of persuasion."[3] Thus, it was recognized over 2,300 years ago that politics and communication go hand in hand because they are essential parts of human nature.

Back in 1981, Dan Nimmo and Keith Sanders proclaimed that political communication was an emerging field.[4] Although its origin, as noted, dates back centuries, a "self-consciously cross-disciplinary" focus began in the late 1950s. Thousands of books and articles later, colleges and universities offer a variety of graduate and undergraduate coursework in the area in such diverse departments as communication, mass communication, journalism, political science, and sociology.[5] In Nimmo and Sanders' early assessment, the "key areas of inquiry" included rhetorical analysis, propaganda analysis, attitude change studies, voting studies, government and the news media, functional and systems analyses, technological changes, media technologies, campaign techniques, and research techniques.[6] In a survey of the state of the field in 1983, the same authors and Lynda Kaid found additional, more specific areas of concerns such as the presidency, political polls, public opinion, debates, and advertising to name a few.[7] Since the first study, they also noted a shift away from the rather strict behavioral approach.

A decade later, Dan Nimmo and David Swanson argued that "political communication has developed some identity as a more or less distinct domain of scholarly work."[8] The scope and concerns of the area have further expanded to include critical theories and cultural studies. While there is no precise definition, method, or disciplinary home of the area of inquiry, its primary domain is the role, processes, and effects of communication within the context of politics broadly defined.

In 1985, the editors of *Political Communication Yearbook: 1984* noted that "more things are happening in the study, teaching, and practice of political communication than can be captured within the space limitations of the relatively few publications available."[9] In addition, they argued that the backgrounds of "those involved in the field [are] so varied and pluralist in outlook and approach, . . . it [is] a mistake to adhere slavishly to any set format in shaping the content."[10] And more recently, Nimmo and Swanson called for "ways of overcoming the unhappy consequences of fragmentation within a framework that respects, encourages, and benefits from diverse scholarly commitments, agendas, and approaches."[11]

In agreement with these assessments of the area and with gentle encouragement, Praeger established the Praeger Series in Political Communication. The series is open to all qualitative and quantitative methodologies as well as contemporary and historical studies. The key to characterizing the studies in the series is the focus on communication variables or activities within a political context or dimension. As of this writing, nearly forty volumes have been published, and there are numerous impressive works forthcoming. Scholars from the disciplines of communication, history, journalism, political science, and sociology have participated in the series.

I am, without shame or modesty, a fan of the series. The joy of serving as its editor is in participating in the dialogue of the field of political communication and in reading the contributors' works. I invite you to join me.

Robert E. Denton, Jr.

NOTES

1. See Robert E. Denton, Jr., *The Symbolic Dimensions of the American Presidency* (Prospect Heights. Ill,: Waveland Press, 1982); Robert E. Denton, Jr., and Gary Woodward, *Political Communication in America* (New York: Praeger, 1985; 2nd ed., 1990); Robert E. Denton, Jr., and Dan Han, *Presidential Communication* (New York: Praeger, 1986); and Robert E. Denton, Jr., *The Primetime Presidency of Ronald Reagan* (New York: Praeger, 1988).

2. Aristotle, *The Politics of Aristotle*, trans. Ernest Barker (New York: Oxford University Press, 1970), p. 5.

3. Aristotle, *Rhetoric*, trans. Rhys Roberts (New York: The Modern Library, 1954), p. 22.

4. Dan Nimmo and Keith Sanders, "Introduction: The Emergence of Political Communications as a Field," in *Handbook of Political Communication*, eds. Dan Nimmo and Keith Sanders (Beverly Hills, Calif.: Sage, 1981), pp. 11-36.

5. Ibid., p. 15.

6. Ibid., pp. 17-27

7. Keith Sanders, Lynda Kaid, and Dan Nimmo, eds., *Political Communication Yearbook: 1984* (Carbondale: Southern Illinois University, 1985), pp. 283-308.

8. Dan Nimmo and David Swanson, "The Field of Political Communication: Beyond the Voter Persuasion Paradigm," in *New Directions in Political Communication*, eds. David Swanson and Dan Nimmo (Beverly Hills, Calif.: Sage, 1990), p. 8.

9. Sanders, Kaid, and Nimmo, *Political Communication Yearbook: 1984*, p. xiv.

10. Ibid.

11. Nimmo and Swanson, "The Field of Political Communication," p. 11.

PREFACE

Film critic Stanley Kauffmann recalled this story (Kauffmann, 1989, 90):

When I was a high school senior, I took a girl named (let's say) Jean Miller to a party, a nice forthright girl who all night long was nice, forthright Jean Miller. I took her home after the party, and at her front door I kissed her good night; and as our faces moved together, I saw Jean Miller become Joan Crawford. It was at that moment, I suppose, that I first became clear about what had been happening in my own daydreams (in which I was usually Richard Dix) and in those of many others. Within every sentient being on the face of the earth—or at any rate so many of them that the claim is tenable—films are a part of his or her dreams and daydreams. This is often true of the arts; it is always true of films.

Ronald Reagan, a man of the movies before he was one of politics, seemed occasionally to be unable or unwilling to distinguish between the world that is in films from the world that is not. He told audiences of a bomber pilot's decision to go down with his injured comrade rather than bail out. The pilot, Reagan said, was posthumously awarded the Congressional Medal of Honor. In 1983, Reagan told the Israeli prime minister of his horror at seeing the Nazi death camps when he visited them after the war as a member of a military film crew.

Neither story was true. The heroic scene in the bomber described by Reagan came entirely from the 1944 picture, *Wing and a Prayer,* and Reagan never served on a film crew in Germany: his whole military career was spent in Los Angeles, making movies. (For accounts of these events and others related to Reagan's film career and his presidency, see Rogin, 1987, chap. 1, Wills, 1987, chap. 17, and Schickel, 1989, 121-36.)

Reagan was hardly the first. In a letter to Orson Welles, Franklin Roosevelt referred to Welles as the "second best" actor in America and to himself as the best. John Kennedy, whose father produced films and had a long affair with film star Gloria Swanson, was fascinated by the film industry and its people, including Marilyn Monroe. Richard Nixon, it was said, repeatedly watched

Patton prior to ordering the invasion of Cambodia in 1970, events some critics were convinced were related. Navy recruiters reported greatly increased business after the release of *Top Gun* in 1986. The proposed Strategic Defense Initiative rapidly came to be called "Star Wars," to the annoyance of its supporters. Robert C. McFarlane, the former national security adviser implicated in the Iran/Contra affair, said that the 1946 Frank Capra classic *It's a Wonderful Life* gave him the courage to go on after his suicide attempt. Newt Gingrich famously and briefly suggested orphanages as a solution to the problem of at-risk children and offered *Boys Town* as his model, and the regularly embattled Bill Clinton said his favorite film was *High Noon*.

But film and politics are related in ways more interesting and subtle than these. Movies do more than provide images and labels to apply conveniently to events or to offer themselves as metaphors for politics. Sports, after all, do the same.

Movies are partly cultural phenomena; likewise, politics. Both grow from the same places, tap the same sources, speak in the same powerful and ambiguous ways. Movies and politics are not the same, but neither are they entirely different. In their fashion, both play to the same audience. And in the United States, films play a unique cultural role. As historian Arthur Schlesinger, Jr., has noted, "Film is the only art where the United States has made a real difference. Strike the American contribution from drama, painting, music, sculpture, dance, even possibly from poetry and the novel, and the world's achievement is only marginally diminished. But film without the American contribution is unimaginable" (O'Connor and Jackson, 1975, x).

This book is about movies—fiction movies—and politics in the U.S. setting. Least importantly, it is about how we may confuse the two. More importantly, it is about how politics and movies inform each other, about what each tells about the other and what both tell about the society from which they come. It is about what films say about politics in America and how they say it. My focus on mass-market, fiction, U.S.-produced films—by no means the only kinds of films worth thinking about in political terms—carries with it the fundamental economic and social biases of such films—biases that follow from films' most basic role as vehicles for profit making, as well as biases of gender, of race, of belief. Those biases, of course, are the point.

My biggest immediate debts are three: to the filmmakers, who made the movies; to the scholars, imperfectly acknowledged in the sources cited, whose work was invaluable; and to many students over the years, whose messages—verbal and nonverbal—variously reflected recognition, confusion, or disagreement. Lee Anderson did wonderful work on manuscript preparation, and Joanne Fawley, likewise, on the index.

My longer-term debts are to my parents, to whom this book is dedicated, who, among many other gifts, dragged me to films I had no desire at the time to see but which have stayed with me since, and who also let me spend, on my own, Saturdays at the Ramona and North Park theaters in San Diego. Badger was with me most of the way on this, and Nancy for all of it. A better home I cannot imagine.

Politics and Politicians in American Film

1

MAKING MOVIES

Movies are produced to make money. They are, in the ugly but honest term of show business, "product." When the product is successful the rewards can be enormous. Urging him to come to Hollywood, Herman Mankiewicz wired writer Ben Hecht in 1925, "Millions are to be made out here and your only competition is idiots" (Hecht, 1954, 466). Hollywood's failures are no less spectacular.

Individual films have made or destroyed entire studios. *Heaven's Gate*, enormously expensive to make and unable to find an audience when it was released in 1980, was blamed for the subsequent collapse of United Artists; *Ghostbusters* was credited with saving Columbia in 1984. And movie history is littered with the stories of individuals who enjoyed great success, or great failure, or, not infrequently, both. (For two case studies of the corporate politics and economics of filmmaking, see Bach, 1985, and McClintick, 1982.)

It is essential to understand that films are a commodity intended to make money to understanding their relationship to politics and of politics' relationship to film. The imperative that films make a profit means seeking large audiences, and seeking large audiences requires caution about a film's subject matter and treatment. As with any other genuinely mass medium, the content and form of films is largely dictated by economic necessities; and filmmaking, even more than other areas of show business, requires caution. Films frequently require at least two years to go from conception to release and their creators thus must anticipate—guess is probably more appropriate—the tastes of an often fickle audience.

Filmmakers must avoid subjects that promise to be fleeting; the audience likely will not be there when the film is released. This includes political events and personalities, in which the public's interest may be intense but brief. Indeed, television, rather than feature films, is the place where such topics are now often addressed, largely because television programs can be produced and aired relatively rapidly. Recent years have seen television movies about Watergate,

Martin Luther King, Jr., Oliver North and the Iran/contra affair, and Richard Nixon's last days in the White House. Similarly, a number of politically relevant social issues have been dramatized on television—the aftermath of nuclear war, child and spousal abuse, and racism. And, for years, shows dealing with police work and lawyers have instructed audiences about the criminal justice system. In order to understand politics and film, therefore, it is necessary to note the implications for filmmaking of the increasingly important role played by television in consuming political material. This does not mean that all the topics addressed by television would necessarily have become feature films, though some probably would have. The more important consequence is that filmmakers are likely to conclude that the mass audience has access to such material at home and does not wish to see more of it in theaters.

If a film project is already well developed or even produced and the market seems unready, the project may be shelved and released later when market conditions seem better. Such a strategy is a common way for filmmakers to hedge their investment in producing or developing a film. This is sometimes responsible for the nearly simultaneous release of several similar films. If the initial film does well, others similar to it, and already available are rushed into production or release. Thus are trends created, which may be misinterpreted as socially meaningful rather than commercial.

Caution is also part of the filmmaker's calculations because making movies is so expensive. Film is the only art form, apart from architecture, that routinely requires financing involving millions of dollars: as Orson Welles noted, a poet needs a pen, a painter a brush, and a filmmaker an army. Film armies—what Welles called "this terribly expensive paintbox"—cost money, which is usually controlled by prudent people seeking a return on their investment. In an era in which many film studios are themselves owned by conglomerates, executives of the parent corporation, perhaps a considerable distance from the film community both geographically and otherwise, may be involved in decisions on the fate of a film. Frequent changes in studio ownership (especially in the 1980s) and the high turnover rate among studio executives also frequently mean the demise of film projects. (For a discussion of the politics of the new Hollywood, see Litwak, 1986, especially chaps. 2-5.) And always in the background is the possibility of organized opposition from interest groups. Films as different as *Mississippi Burning* (1989), *Top Gun* (1984), *Cry Freedom* (1987), *The Last Temptation of Christ* (1988), and *Do the Right Thing* (1989) have drawn fire, though all were nonetheless made. The classic *Citizen Kane* (1941), based on the life of publisher William Randolph Hearst, was attacked in the Hearst press before and after its release, and an effort was made by Louis B. Mayer, after a conversation with Hearst, to buy the film for its $805,000 production costs with the intention of destroying all prints (Brady, 1989, 288.) The prime influence of organized opposition lies in its anticipation by filmmakers and the adjustments they make to avoid objections. Interest groups, too, define the boundaries of the filmmaker.

As in national politics, there are veto groups in the political process of filmmaking that can block a proposed movie. This is especially so because the contemporary political structure of Hollywood is more decentralized than it was during the height of the studio system in the 1930s and 1940s. In the fragmented decision system of current Hollywood filmmaking, to make a film requires that all of many doors be open; one closed door may stop a film. Contemporary moviemaking requires agreements among financiers, agents, stars, producers, directors, writers, studio heads, studio promotion departments, distributors, and exhibitors. The politics of killing a film is vastly simpler than the politics of fashioning the many agreements and commitments necessary to produce one; for that reason, the creation of a film is a frustrating and sharply political process in which nothing happens unless a fragile consensus is built and kept alive. Making movies is an activity in which compromise is inherent. Director Billy Wilder expressed a common view of the contemporary politics of making movies when he noted in an interview, "It's not hard to make a picture; what's hard is to make a deal" (Wilder, 1989).

These things—facts of life in filmmaking, regardless of the subject of the film—make movies a cautious medium. Institutional caution, however, does not mean that movies do not speak to political subjects; they do. But they do it in their own way, as movies.

SUBJECT

The most basic way films speak to politics is through subject. It was producer Sam Goldwyn, the story goes, who made the definitive comment on the matter when he said, "Messages are for Western Union." While overtly political subjects have always been present in films, they have never predominated. The conventional wisdom of the industry is that political subjects are to be avoided.

In largely avoiding explicitly political themes, films deliver their first political messages: politics is neither interesting nor important. What is important and interesting for film purposes are people's immediate circumstances—whether they are happy, whether they are in love, whether they catch the bad guy, how they overcome crises. The personal politics of people's lives is at the heart of most films, not the public, collective activity we usually associate with politics. *Dangerous Liaisons* (1988) is a film about personal sexual politics in which the characters' actions are in the service of amusement and manipulation. Films personalize life and so privatize it. The corollary is that when films do address political topics they personalize them.

There is a way, however, in which virtually all American films are political and that is their role as windows through which to see American society. Those who have grown up in that society may not see it, but others do. A Soviet filmmaker told an American counterpart:

You go see an ordinary [American] film and the telephone rings and somebody runs over and there is a telephone in the middle of the living room. And then you cut and the kid is talking on the telephone in his bedroom. In the hall you see . . . [another] telephone, and there is one in the kitchen. In Russia if you have a telephone it is in the closet so you can go in and close the door so nobody can hear you. Then you open a refrigerator in a film and it is stocked full of food and people are taking things out, spilling things. They are treating food as if it was nothing. My God, that is propaganda. I'll bet that many of the people around the world are looking at that and not even seeing the picture. They are watching the food in the refrigerator . . . cars are smashed up . . . we wait five years to get a car . . . here you have kids driving huge cars. And we say to ourselves, "How much gasoline does that car take to go a mile? This is political. (Quoted in Litwak, 1986, 105-6)

Equally interesting is how a film that is politically explicit may, with time, change in meaning for its audience. As Andrew Sarris notes:

Every movie I have ever seen keeps swirling and shifting in ever changing contexts. On the whole, most movies tend to be more complex than profound, but this makes it all the more difficult to pin down, describe, and categorize for all time. What is particularly fascinating is how the same movie can keep changing its ideological coloration over the years. (Sarris, 1978, 3-4)

But the most fundamental political lesson of virtually all American films regardless of subject is that of the most enduring of all movie conventions, the happy ending: films show that, in the end, things will be all right, love will find a way, the good guys will win. Problems may be encountered—indeed for dramatic purposes must be encountered—but the resolution is nearly always a happy one. That the world is essentially fair and just is a deeply powerful political lesson.

Politics is not consequential; politics is not interesting; happiness is purely an individual matter; things will be all right. That is what virtually all American films tell their audiences.

GENRE

Beyond the subject of a film, the manner in which that subject is treated is central to understanding movies. The analysis of film genre is one way to examine this. The clearest way of understanding genre in films (the term is French for "type" or "class" and is based on the Latin "genus") is to think about television, particularly series television, for contemporary television production with its insatiable appetite for material closely resembles the legendary Hollywood studio system when the production of genre films was at its peak.

Consider the classic "I Love Lucy". Anyone familiar with that series knows the structure of most episodes: Lucy conspires, usually with Ethel Mertz, to get something to which Ricky is adamantly opposed. (Frequently and interestingly, what Lucy wants is a new role in life, which often includes getting into show business, her husband's profession.) Lucy gets into a predicament, usually involving considerable slapstick comedy; she is caught and things end on a note of embarrassed confession on Lucy's part and loving exasperation on Ricky's. All this is observed by Fred Mertz, who is sometimes Ricky's ally but often stands apart as the audience's surrogate by observing and critically commenting on events. "I Love Lucy" is essentially the story of a housewife who tries to break from that role against her husband's opposition, often by aggressively deceiving him.

Seasoned viewers of series television can frequently anticipate a plot twist or the resolution of a conflict in a favorite show or deliver the punchline of a joke before the performer does. In movie theaters, one member of the audience elbows another to predict what will happen before it occurs; a parent with complete certainty reassures a worried child that, no, the dog in the movie will not die, though the parent has never before seen the film.[1]

We know these things because we have seen them before, perhaps hundreds of times. Knowing them lets us feel in control of the film's world; there is a kind of power that knowledge of a genre gives the audience. Knowledge based on familiarity is the essence of film genre, and when our expectations are not met we are surprised: no one expects Bambi's mother to die.

Genre films are those whose settings, characters, and plots have become, through repetition and development, familiar and reassuring. If we refer to a "western" or a *film noir* or a "horror film," the designation tells us much about the movie. In a sense, we have already seen the film many times, and our curiosity is about how skillfully the conventions of the genre are played out.

Genre films evolved during the early days of filmmaking in the teens of the twentieth century and reached their height during Hollywood's "Golden Age," roughly from the 1930s through the 1940s. It was then that the studios dominated not only the production of films but also their distribution and exhibition through what economists call "vertical integration," in which a firm controls the manufacture of a product from raw material through final sale. Until the 1950s the Big Five, or "majors" as they were called (MGM, Twentieth Century Fox, Warner Brothers, Paramount, and RKO), along with "major minors" (Columbia, Universal-International, Republic, and Monogram) not only made films but leased them through their own distribution companies to theater chains they owned or controlled. The majors, while they never approached controlling a significant fraction of all the theaters in the country, dominated theaters in the largest markets, where most of the audience was. At the height of movies' mass popularity in the mid 1940s—the peak was 1946, when average weekly attendance was 90 million, a figure never again reached—the majors controlled or owned nearly eighty percent of the theaters in the country's twenty-five largest markets. It was not until the mid-1980s that the studios, under the deregulation philosophy of the Reagan administration, began again to buy theaters. By the end of the decade of the 1980s, the studios had acquired more than 3,500 of the country's 22,000 theater screens (Kilday, 1989, 65).

While the studios were similar in their corporate structures, each nevertheless had its own cinematic signature due to its leaders, who frequently founded the studio or were related to those who did. MGM was known for its musicals and its receptivity to producers, Paramount as the home of the biggest stars and for its receptivity to directors, and Warner Brothers for making films that dealt with social and political themes and for being the most left/liberal in its films. (For discussions of the corporate styles of the studios, see Mordden, 1988; Schatz, 1988; Gabler, 1989; and Gomery, 1986.)

In 1948, after ten years of litigation, the Supreme Court, in *U.S. v. Paramount Pictures*, ordered the studios to divest themselves of their theater chains. In the two decades prior to that decision the studio system had reached its height and the genre film had flourished. What came to be known as the "Golden Age" of Hollywood filmmaking was based solidly on a mature vertical oligopoly, the executives of whose companies—the legendary movie moguls— exercised as much power as any turn-of-the-century robber baron. (For an analysis of the founding fathers of the Hollywood film industry, see Gabler, 1989; Powdermaker, 1950; and Rosten, 1941.) An assistant to Darryl Zanuck, head of production at Warner Brothers, remembered Zanuck sitting down with a blank piece of paper matching the stars and directors the studio had under contract with the stories it owned: "O.K., we want three Bette Davises, four Cagneys, four Eddie Robinsons, three Bogarts, two Errol Flynns. Who's got a good story for Bogart—anything we can put Bogart in?" (Litwak, 1986, 83). Thus was established an entire year's production schedule for a major studio.

Studio control of theater chains prior to the Supreme Court decision meant a large audience was all but guaranteed; theaters had to show "their" studio's films, good or bad, in compliance with a policy called "block booking" in which theaters had to accept a studio's weak films in order to get its strong ones. The stronger film—the "A" picture—was shown on a double bill with the weaker one—the "B" picture"—along with a cartoon or two, a newsreel, and perhaps a serial. Filmgoing became a weekly habit for two-thirds of the country in this pre-television period, just as television viewing is now. Theaters usually changed their programs weekly, and audiences went regularly to *the* movies rather than to *a* movie, just as many now regularly watch whatever television shows are available rather than a specific program. Woody Allen's 1985 *The Purple Rose of Cairo* evokes the role that films played in people's lives during this time.

The huge movie audience consumed considerable product and the studios supplied it, with some averaging one film produced per week. The studios sought formulas for films that would assure rapid and efficient production. The studio solution was simply to learn—via box office receipts—which films were successful and then make more. This strategy gave us genre films, the movie equivalent of variations on a theme. A mature genre film is recognized instantly by its audience; but to achieve that level of recognition genres must evolve through several stages (Giannetti and Eyman, 1986, 478):

The primitive stage, in which the genre first appears in a form that is crude compared to later incarnations. This is the seed from which the genre grows; its success and potential for elaboration assure that others like it will be made. The 1922 German production of *Nosferatu the Vampire* was such a film in the development of the horror film genre.

The classical stage, in which the genre matures. Its major themes are established and its primary variations developed, as in *Dracula* (1931), *Frankenstein* (1932), and their successors.

The revisionist stage, in which filmmakers extend the genre past its commonly understood boundaries and apply the genre's conventions to new settings. *Rosemary's Baby* (1968) did this with the conventions of the horror film. Pictures of this type are not only an extreme extension of the genre—a mutation—but may be an indication that the genre is close to exhaustion.

The parodic stage, in which the genre, because its conventions are so understood by the audience, becomes the subject of parody, as in *Young Frankenstein* (1974). Mel Brooks has devoted much of his career to film parodies: horror films (*Young Frankenstein*); westerns (*Blazing Saddles*, 1974); silent comedies (*Silent Movie*, 1976); Alfred Hitchcock films (*High Anxiety*, 1977); and the *Star Wars* series (*Spaceballs*, 1987).

Part of the pleasure in viewing and analyzing genre films lies in the variations a genre permits. A mature genre creates and defines a closed, self-referential universe about which much is known by the audience but in which there is room for variations provided they do not stray too far from the genre's conventions. Genres are not straitjackets for creative filmmakers any more than the sonata form is for composers or haiku is for poets. Even a well-defined art form—perhaps especially a well-defined one—invites creativity in the development of variations. As a student of gangster films observed:

For such a type to be successful means that its conventions have imposed themselves upon the general consciousness and become accepted vehicles of a particular set of attitudes and a particular aesthetic effect. One goes to any individual example of the type with very definite expectations, and originality is accepted only in the degree that it intensifies the expected experience without fundamentally altering it. (Warshow, 1962, 130)

While genre films existed to assure the steady flow of reliable commercial product to audiences, they also gave us some of our finest movies: westerns such as *Stagecoach* (1939), *Shane* (1952), and *The Searchers* (1956); and *films noir* like *The Maltese Falcon* (1941), *Double Indemnity* (1944), and *Sunset Boulevard* (1950). (For discussions of genre, see Schatz, 1981; Gehring, 1988; Grant, 1986.)

A film genre exists because a community is established between filmmakers and their audience, a world whose conventions are an accepted and welcome reality. Studying genres tells us about both parts of this community. On the filmmaker's part, the desire is to attract an audience. On the audience's part, the desire is to live briefly in the world the genre defines. To look at a genre is to look at the society that generates and sustains it; genre analysis is as much social as aesthetic. For that reason it is significant that nothing approaching a developed political film genre has ever taken root in the United States, as it has elsewhere.[2] The United States has developed over the years a richer film vocabulary for gangsters, cowboys, and mummies raised from the dead than it has for citizens and presidents.

The strongly nonpolitical tendencies of American film reflect the economics and politics of filmmaking and the norms of American culture. Those who complain that films ought to be more political—including some filmmakers— ignore these realities. Films are much less useful as a means of achieving political ends than they are as a means of tracing a culture's beliefs about politics. To expect films to be vehicles for political change is to be willing to enlist cautious allies in one's cause, though the fiction that one is making a film that makes a political difference—as opposed to a political statement—is hard to resist. It is the nature of a mass medium to support the status quo. The economics and politics of making movies assure that, politically, mass-market fiction films will follow, not lead.

CONVENTIONS

A number of movie conventions have evolved since the inception of the medium, ones that transcend genre and appear in a wide variety of films. Several have particular applicability to political films.

Sugarcoating and Personalizing

Political events are often inherently dramatic because they involve conflict; but conflict brings controversy, something filmmakers usually avoid. One way to take advantage of the drama of political situations is to sugarcoat and personalize the politics. Love stories are the classic way to do this: *Casablanca* (1942), with its background of World War II and its subtext of the morality of isolationism; *Gone with the Wind* (1939) set against the Civil War and Reconstruction; *Coming Home* (1978), which deals with the Vietnam War's effect on both civilians and the military; and *Reds* (1981), which deals with the radical American journalist John Reed (Warren Beatty), are all love stories and may be enjoyed at that level alone. In *The Last Hurrah* (1958), we may understand the story of Frank Skeffington in solely personal terms or in terms of his position of mayor or in terms of the entire generation of politicians he represents. The 1982 film *Missing* may be seen in terms of its personal relationships rather than its actual background of the CIA-backed coup to overthrow the popularly elected Marxist president of Chile, Salvador Allende. *The China Syndrome* (1979), though an obviously anti-nuclear power film, was also an effective thriller. Audiences can enjoy such films whether they agree with the message or are even aware of it.

Allegory

Another way to hide the politics of a film is to structure a story so that it parallels political events and personalities, though at a considerable distance. Inevitably, this also makes the film's politics all but unseen. The classic *The Wizard of Oz* was based on an explicit political allegory that was invisible to its 1939 audience. The 1956 production of *Invasion of the Body Snatchers* was similarly interpretable as either an anti-Communist statement or as an "anti-anti-Communist" film critical of McCarthyism, and the 1978 remake of the same film was a less-thinly disguised attack on cults. In such films there is little or no explicit reference to politics: the audience may make the connections or not.

Safe Topics

There are a number of political topics that by virtue of a consensus developed over time become safe. The spate of Vietnam films dealing both with combat (*Platoon*, 1986) and the war's aftermath (*Running on Empty*, 1988; *In Country*, 1989) are such films, as are *Mississippi Burning* (1988) and *Rosewood* (1997). Some of the topics with which these films deal—brutality against civilians by American troops in Vietnam, the lives of former radicals, the generations left behind by the war, the implication of local officials in racial violence—could not have been addressed in a feature film in a time contemporaneous with the events described; with time they could. Such films are often criticized for rewriting history, however. *Mississippi Burning* was reproached for telling its story from a predominantly white point of view and for portraying the FBI's vigor in investigating racial crimes more favorably than many thought justified. *Cry Freedom* (1987), set in South Africa, was similarly criticized for telling its story from the point of view of the main white character, Donald Woods, rather than of Steve Biko, a black.

The Unlabeled Bottle

A common way to deal with politicians is to avoid being specific about them. In *Mr. Smith Goes to Washington* (1939), we are told nothing about the party affiliation of any character in the film or even the state from which Senators Smith and Paine come. This permits the audience to read its own political views into the characters. It also allows writers to portray political characters negatively without concern about delighting some of the audience but angering the rest.

Ambivalence

A common way to deal with controversy in films, political or otherwise, is to treat the topic ambivalently by "balancing" contending sides so that partisans of any persuasion have something to applaud. In *Do the Right Thing* (1989), director Spike Lee ends the film with two quotations, one from Martin Luther King, Jr., advocating nonviolence and the other from Malcolm X suggesting that violence may be necessary. The audience may take from these what it wishes. The same balancing occurs in *Dead Man Walking* (1995).

A variation on the theme of ambivalence is to use satire to make everyone and everything look equally foolish, as in the Marx Brothers' *Duck Soup* (1933) in which Freedonia's prime minister Rufus T. Firefly (Groucho Marx) declares war for the hell of it; *The President's Analyst* (1967), in which politicians, corporations, the American middle class, and hippies are satirized and U.S. and Soviet spies find themselves to be kindred spirits; and *The Loved One* (1965), a black comedy about American society in general and Southern California in particular. In *Dr. Strangelove, or: How I Learned to Stop Worrying and Love the Bomb* (1964), the president of the United States and the Soviet premier have a phone conversation in which both appear as fools.

AUTEUR

If genre and convention deal with the norms in filmmaking, *auteur* addresses its exceptions. The term as applied to film comes from the seminal French periodical *Cahier du Cinema* (Film Notes), whose editor, Andre Bazin (1918-1958), encouraged a band of young writers during the publication's peak from 1951 to 1958 to explore movies, even seemingly ordinary ones. Its writers included Jean-Luc Godard (b. 1930), François Truffaut (1932-1984), and Eric Rohmer (b. 1920), each of whom went on to become important directors during the French "New Wave" movement of the 1960s. Their articulation of the "auteur policy" was the most influential and controversial post-World War II contribution to the serious analysis of film. (For a discussion of the founding of this school of film criticism, see Andrew, 1978, chaps. 5 and 6.)

If "I Love Lucy" illustrates genre in television, the series of programs created by Norman Lear—especially "All in the Family" and "Maude"—illustrate the idea behind the auteur policy. *Auteur* —French for "author"—asks that we seek the author of a film. Lear's "authorship" of hit comedies with social content and a left-liberal tilt was done as producer within the limits of studio television production. As applied to feature films, the auteur policy's foremost claim is that the author of a film, of the many involved in its creation, is its director. The auteur student looks for recurring themes in the films of a director, regardless of subject or story line. Auteur analysis is thus similar to some forms of literary analysis in its search for the deep structure in a series of films. Woody Allen is probably the best known contemporary director whose work has been explored in auteur terms; the work of Ingmar Bergman and Akiro Kurosawa has been similarly assessed, as has the work of Oliver Stone. But no director has had his films so thoroughly studied in auteur terms as Alfred Hitchcock. (See, among many others, Spoto, 1976; Spoto, 1983; Truffaut, 1983.)

Students of Hitchcock's films argue that the motifs in his work flow from his particular rendering of the idea of original sin, in which all individuals are seen as guilty in the broadest sense of that term. This theme is played out in his films primarily through two mechanisms: the motif of the "wrong man" (the title of a 1957 Hitchcock film) in which an innocent person is suddenly and for no apparent reason caught up in frightening events (*North by Northwest*, 1959; *Frenzy*, 1972), and the motif of the double, in which two characters, one naive and one evil, are presented as though they were conflicting halves of the same person rather than two different individuals (*Strangers on a Train*, 1951; *Vertigo*, 1958; *Shadow of a Doubt*, 1943; and *Rope*, 1948, in which three characters are associated with each other). In the world of the Hitchcock film, the line between good and evil, innocence and guilt, is drawn arbitrarily. All are guilty, though not all are caught.

Among U.S. directors virtually none has developed a reputation for consistently pursing political themes, though several have made enough such films for them to be a significant part of their careers, including D.W. Griffith (1877-1948), Charlie Chaplin (1889-1977), John Ford (1895-1973), Frank Capra (1897-1991), Hal Ashby (1936-1989), Martin Ritt (1920-1990), John Frankenheimer (b. 1930), and Oliver Stone (b. 1946). It is an interesting contrast between European and U.S. directors that the former often devote a major portion of their careers to political films, including Bernardo Bertolucci (b. 1940), Constantin Costa-Gavras (b. 1933), Jean Renoir (1894-1979), and Jean-Luc Godard (b. 1930).

The auteur theory, though often seen in opposition to genre analysis, in fact fits easily within it. Many of the filmmakers analyzed by the Cahier du Cinema writers worked comfortably and with great success within the studio system. Indeed, the French writers were taken with American films in part because of their interest in the way an individual director could assert his own vision within the limits of studio production.   Genre and auteur analysis juxtapose an essentially industrial production model of filmmaking (genre) with a model (auteur) that celebrates the ability of the individual artist to speak above the din of the film factory. In the end, both schools discovered an author: auteur critics found it in the director; genre critics, in the studio.

FORD

The films of John Ford illustrate these points. Ford was one of the giants of the western film genre for decades, yet his work is also studied profitably in auteur terms. The western is the oldest, most powerful, and most productive of all film genres. And westerns, though they were rarely overtly political, were among our richest films in terms of their implicit political themes. In *Stagecoach* (1939), Ford created one of the classics of the western genre, establishing several of its basic conventions. In *The Man Who Shot Liberty Valance* (1962), he placed an undeniably personal stamp on the film by way of saying farewell to the genre. And both films spoke implicitly but clearly about politics.

The twin poles of the classical western are people and the land. Taken together, they represent the forces of civilization and of nature, each existing uneasily with the other.   The structure of most westerns is a series of elaborations on this theme of opposition: sheriff versus outlaw, saloon girl versus schoolmarm, settlers versus wilderness, individual versus community. It is in the conflict between individual and community that westerns most revealingly address politics as they transform the West into the state of nature and instruct the audience about the social contract, law, justice, and the creation of political institutions on the frontier.

In *Stagecoach*, John Ford created two icons of the western: Monument Valley, Arizona, and John Wayne, at the time a relative unknown. *Stagecoach* is what Roger Ebert calls an "ark movie" (Ebert, 1989, 938), in which a small but diverse group of people are thrown together against the setting of a hostile environment. The ark—in this case the stagecoach—represents the boundaries of a society in microcosm and its individual members are models of distinct social types. In the background, literally and figuratively, is the landscape of Monument Valley sweepingly rendered by Ford's camera. The land is at once beautiful and frightening, punctuated with tiny dots of human communities. In this setting, as Andrew Sarris noted (Sarris, 1968, 46-47), it is more than story and characterization that are important to Ford, "it is also the director's attitude toward his milieu and its codes of conduct." The genre code of the western becomes the behavioral code of the West. It tells how people live in a place that only imperfectly mirrors established societies; it is a moral code where law is nonexistent or weak, where justice is more important than law, and where a way of life is being created rather than adapted to.

The opening of *Stagecoach* visually sets the motif of people in the land: the sweep of Monument Valley and the sky are contrasted with civilization via quick cuts, first to the dusty and cluttered exterior of a cavalry camp, then to its interior. Throughout the film the land is juxtaposed with scenes of human communities, most frequently and tellingly with the tiny and frail society of the stagecoach. The land usually is filmed in wide shots, the interiors usually in tight ones.

The film is divided into thirds. The first part takes place in the town of Tonto, an outpost threatened by Geronimo, where we are introduced to the main characters. The second is the stagecoach journey to the town of Lordsburg (as in many films, the names of people and places are worth noting), where the characters and histories of the principals are developed. The final third of the film is set in Lordsburg, where the story's main conflicts are resolved. The story of the film is that of a journey through a beautiful but hostile landscape moving from one outpost of civilization to another, the stagecoach and its passengers being the only constants.

The coach travels to Lordsburg facing not just the threat from Geronimo but also from conflicts among its passengers: Doc Boone (Thomas Mitchell), an alcoholic physician being driven from Tonto by the local Law and Order League; Dallas (Claire Trevor), a prostitute with the requisite heart of gold, herself being driven from Tonto ("There are worse things than Apaches," she says as the camera cuts to the hate-filled face of a member of the Law and Order League); the cowardly and comic stage driver, Buck (Andy Devine); Gatewood (Berton Churchill), an embezzling bank executive; Lucy (Louise Platt), a prim and stuffy pregnant woman traveling to meet her husband (we can easily imagine Lucy as a potential member of the Law and Order League); Peacock (Donald Meek), a timid whiskey salesman; Hatfield (John Carradine), a gambler who is later killed in an attack by Geronimo; and the sheriff, Curly (George Bancroft). Outside of town they are joined by the Ringo Kid (John Wayne), out to avenge the death of his father and brother by the Plummer brothers and his own wrongful imprisonment, from which he has just escaped.

Unlike many "B" westerns, in which the characters are essentially portrayed in black-and-white terms and stay that way, the principals in *Stagecoach* are more subtly and ambivalently crafted by writer Dudley Nichols. While most hold respectable social roles, some are socially marginal. While most display unattractive qualities, they are also given positive ones. The exception is the banker, Gatewood, who has run off with the bank's money leaving his wife, a Law and Order League stalwart, behind. Gatewood is painted uniformly as a deceitful hypocrite.

Significantly, the only explicitly political references in the film come from Gatewood. After he steals the bank deposits, runs from his wife, and sneaks out of town on the stage, he pompously lectures the other passengers on the Civil War, on the obligation the cavalry has to protect honest travelers like himself, and on the necessity of government leaving business alone (he thinks bank examiners are a bad idea and that the country needs a businessmen as president). Thus, in Gatewood are joined wealth, politics, hypocrisy, and deceit.

The characters' positive traits are shown in scenes involving communal activities: simple personal courtesy; the birth of Lucy's baby, in which the alcoholic Doc Boone delivers the child and the prostitute Dallas (who was earlier spurned by Lucy) cares for baby and mother; a scene in which the passengers vote on whether to continue their journey; a group meal. Thus is created a family, one of the most recurrent themes in Ford's films. It is only during the journey, when the travelers leave human settlements for the hostile wilderness, that the temporary family is created.

Ringo is head of the family. He is the only character who joins the party outside of Tonto; we associate him with the land, not organized society. When he gets into the stagecoach, he sits on the floor between the others in the place— literally and figuratively—of a mediator. When the others bicker, Ford's camera cuts from one antagonist to another then to Ringo, who intercedes either by being tough ("Sit down, mister") or conciliatory ("Doc don't mean no harm"). If there is any doubt about Ringo, Ford removes it with a close-up in which Ringo lowers his head and we see the frame filled with his white hat! If the tiny society of the stagecoach has a leader, a government, it is Ringo. Not only does he mediate between the others, he is heroic during an Apache attack on the coach (though the ultimate hero is the cavalry, which rides to the rescue). More than any other character, Ringo, the outsider, is responsible for the stagecoach reaching Lordsburg. His primary ally is Curly, the marshall. Thus the society of the stagecoach is governed by an escaped prisoner and a representative of the law; the latter agrees temporarily to give Ringo his freedom (Ringo is not handcuffed) but only until they reach Lordsburg. The social contract has joined adversaries.

Yet Ringo is also capable of deceit and violence. Before the Apache attack, Ringo tries to escape with Dallas's help, jeopardizing the lives of the others, including Lucy's baby. When the passengers reach Lordsburg, Ringo seeks out the men who killed his father and brother. He tells the sheriff, who has given him a few minutes' time before he takes Ringo into custody (knowing Ringo will use it to seek revenge on the Plummer brothers), "I lied to you, Curly. I got three [bullets] left." Thus we learn that Ringo further jeopardized the lives of the others during the Apache attack by lying when he said he was out of ammunition. Using his three rounds, Ringo kills the three Plummer brothers.

And then as Ringo is about to be taken into custody, Curly gestures to Ringo and Dallas that they may go. Ringo and Dallas, who have fallen in love on the journey, then ride off into the sunset to Ringo's ranch. As they do, Doc Boone, in the film's best-known line says, "Well, they're saved from the blessings of civilization." Ringo, having done what he had to do in getting the stagecoach safely to Lordsburg and in avenging the death of his father and brother, may now leave civilization and return to the land, and he does so with the consent of the law in the person of the sheriff, Curly. There is law and there is justice, and in the classic western, justice wins.

Throughout *Stagecoach* we learn that the wilderness, while harsh, is also the source of a deeper form of civilization than that of Lordsburg, from which Ringo and Dallas flee at the end of the film, and that of Tonto, from which Dallas and Doc Boone were driven at the film's beginning. This is true for all the film's characters. As one writer noted:

Those who live and act naturally and without pretense are the folk heroes of the West: the innocent cowboy, the prostitute with the heart of gold, the friendly marshall, the comic stage driver, the dignified Indians. . . . The further one progresses down the scale (i.e., toward the negative, more "civilized" end), the more one hides his or her essential self behind clothes and poses. (Stowell, 1986, 32)

And as Andre Bazin commented:

[*Stagecoach*] demonstrates that a prostitute can be more respectable than the narrow-minded people who drove her out of town and just as respectable as an officer's wife; that a dissolute gambler knows how to die with all the dignity of an aristocrat; that an alcoholic doctor can practice his profession with competence and devotion; that an outlaw who is being sought for payment of past and possibly future debts can show loyalty, generosity, courage, and refinement, whereas a banker of considerable standing and reputation runs off with the cashbox. (Bazin, 1971, 146-47)

We are left wondering about the future: Lucy's baby, cared for during the journey more by Dallas than by her mother, is brusquely taken from Dallas upon arrival in Lordsburg and given over to a group of women. The group cannot help but remind us of the Law and Order League. The fate of the baby and the others—the "blessings of civilization"—will not be the fate of Ringo and Dallas.

Stagecoach shows three forms of social organization: the society of civilized human settlements, portrayed in terms of its visual clutter and narrow-minded bigotry (these were the people who drove Doc and Dallas out); the microcosmic society of the stagecoach (the social contract), which is a temporary and necessary instrument for survival; and the wilderness itself (the state of nature) from which Ringo came and to which he and Dallas go. Of these, the first is shown in negative terms, the latter two more ambivalently. For most of the passengers the stagecoach journey permits passage to the greater civilization of Lordsburg. For the western hero and his woman, however, it is the opposite: the journey is a way to return to the land once Ringo has settled his own business in—and with—civilization. For most of us the advantages of society are purchased under the terms of a social contract; the hero of Stagecoach does not want it or need it. He practices his own form of rough justice, treats those who deserve it honorably and helps others, but finally goes his own way. The social contract is intended for most of us; the code of the West, or at least the western, is for heroes only.

Stagecoach was John Ford's first great western; *The Man Who Shot Liberty Valance* (1962) was not only one of his last but also his farewell—to the western hero, to the myth of the West, which Ford more than any other filmmaker helped create—and in a sense to the genre itself. It is a mature, rich, and bittersweet film.

We know from the beginning that things are different: the film is shot in black and white at a time when that was unusual; the opening credits appear on a series of wooden signs, except that they are not really signs but obvious drawings. And while we still see the land in the opening shot, this time it is not Monument Valley but a much less heroic landscape, and through it travels not a lone cowboy or a stagecoach but a train.

The train is bringing U.S. senator Ransom (Ranse) Stoddard (James Stewart) and his wife, Hallie (Vera Miles), home to Shinbone for the pauper's burial of Tom Doniphon (John Wayne), whom no one in town seems to know. While her husband is in town, Hallie and her old Shinbone friend, Link (played by Andy Devine; again, the character's name is important), ride outside of town. After Link, once the sheriff of Shinbone, tells Hallie, "I reckon the only one of us from the old days workin' steady is the Senator," they ride outside of town and talk:

Hallie: The place sure has changed. Churches, high schools, shops.
Link: Well, the railroad done that. Desert's still the same.
Hallie: The cactus rose is in bloom.
Link: Maybe, maybe you'd like to take a ride out desert way and maybe look around.
Hallie: Maybe.

Riding to the remains of a burned-out ranch house, they again begin to talk:

Hallie: You knew where I wanted to go, didn't you?
Link: Well, you said you wanted to see the cactus blossoms. There's his house down there, what's left of it, blossoms all around it.
Hallie: He never did finish that room he started to build on, did he?
Link: No. Oh well, you know all about that.
Hallie: There's a lovely one [blossom] there.

After these suggestive exchanges, Hallie rejoins Ranse in town where they are taken to the room where Tom's simple wooden coffin lies. We do not see Tom's body, but Hallie and Ranse are clearly moved. Ranse demands that Tom's boots, spurs, and gunbelt be put back on his body, but he is told that Tom hadn't worn a gunbelt in years. A newspaper editor asks what it was about Tom Doniphon that has brought Senator Stoddard back all this way, and Stoddard, after getting Hallie's assent, begins his story by recalling his arrival years before. As he does so, he walks over and gently wipes the dust off what first brought him to Shinbone years ago—a stagecoach. Thus, with a reference to the film he made nearly a quarter century before, Ford begins a flashback that lasts almost the entire film. Like the opening of *Citizen Kane* (1941)—even including use of the rose motif, in this case a cactus rose—we are introduced to a riddle.

In the flashback, the stage carrying Ranse to Shinbone is attacked by Liberty Valance (Lee Marvin) and his men, Floyd (Strother Martin) and Reese (Lee Van Cleef). The robbery scene is shot in a studio; its artificiality is obvious. It is startling to see the studio lighting, fake rocks, and tight cropping the studio setting dictates. As with the titles and the opening shot of the film, we are reminded that things are different—as we are reminded when we notice that almost the entire film is shot in indoor locations, often at night, with the open land virtually unseen.

Ranse Stoddard is a young lawyer going west to seek his future in Shinbone. Valance, scoffing at Ranse's citified ways, his invocation of the law, and his attempt to protect a woman passenger, brutally beats Ranse and tears apart his law books, a literal and figurative triumph of might over law ("I'll teach you law—western law!").

The beaten Ranse arrives in Shinbone on the back of a wagon and is taken to a restaurant run by hard-working Scandinavian immigrants Peter and Nora Ericson (John Qualen and Jeannette Nolan) and their daughter, Hallie. The man who has brought the injured Ranse to town is Tom Doniphon, and it is here that we first see in life the man in the coffin. The realization is startling: at the beginning of the film Tom is dead, a forgotten pauper; and Ranse is respected, powerful, and a little pompous. Now their roles are precisely reversed. The shock is especially strong when we realize that Tom is played by John Wayne, the paradigmatic hero of the western, especially the John Ford western. The hero is dead and forgotten and the riddle deepened.

The initial contrast between Tom and Ranse upon Ranse's arrival in Shinbone could not be sharper: Ranse is lying down in the restaurant's kitchen, a posture of weakness and defeat, as he was in the wagon that carried him into town and as he was when Valance beat him. Tom stands tall and strong and confident. After Ranse says he is a lawyer and wants Valance arrested, Tom scoffs and tells him Valance respects only a gun: "Out here a man solves his own problems." But Ranse will not yield and tells Tom, "You know what you're saying to me? You're as bad as he is! What kind of community have I come to here?"

In addition to establishing the contrast between Tom and Ranse and what each represents, the initial scenes involving both men also inform us that Hallie is Tom's girl, that Tom expects them to be married, but also that there is some tension and incompatibility between them. During Ranse's first days in Shinbone a triangle develops between Hallie, Tom, and Ranse, but not one of overt jealousy and competition. Rather, a sort of three-sided marriage—another Fordian family—emerges: Tom is the western male; Hallie, the female; and Ranse, the easterner, is portrayed more ambisexually. Ranse is manfully determined to fight Valance using the law as his weapon; yet he is often associated with femininity: we see him wearing an apron, washing dishes in the restaurant's kitchen, and even waiting tables (Ranse is told "no man waited tables before"). Tom represents the Old West; Ranse, its future; and Hallie, its present: what she chooses is pivotal. Their relationship is less a traditional love triangle than a metaphor for the death of old social and political arrangements of the frontier and the transition to new ones.

Ranse teaches Hallie to read and write and starts a school for the people of Shinbone, with a picture of George Washington in the background. He gives civics lessons, emphasizing the importance of the written word and the law—the Declaration of Independence and the Constitution. From the beginning, Ranse is associated with words and Tom with action. As Ranse teaches Hallie and the others (including children, immigrants, and Tom's black hired hand) to read and write, he not only draws them from Tom and what Tom represents, he prepares them for a new set of political arrangements. Ranse's schoolroom is the back of the stagecoach office, and on the blackboard on which the timetable is usually displayed Ranse has written "Education is the basis of law and order." Tom observes this with a mixture of feigned indifference and skepticism tinged with sorrow, as if he knows what will come both to him and to Shinbone.

The strengths of each man are apparent in a scene in which Ranse, waiting tables in the restaurant, is mocked by Valance for doing woman's work. Valance trips Ranse, sends him sprawling, and demands that he pick up the steak that lies on the floor. Before we know what Ranse will do, Tom intervenes, telling Valance that the steak is Tom's and demanding that Valance pick it up. We expect that Tom will kill Valance; certainly that is what Tom wants. But before he can, Ranse picks up the steak and the confrontation ends with Valance and his men lurching out the door. Later, when Tom sarcastically tells Ranse, "Thanks for saving my life, Pilgrim," Ranse explodes, "That's not why I did it. Nobody fights my battles!"

The back-and-forth quality of this scene is deeply revealing of each man: both are determined to fight Valance (who is the epitome of the state of nature at its most brutal) but each in his own way. Each loses and then regains the initiative. What is nominally in dispute—a steak—is also revealing, for the steak represents each man's stake in the community as well as his particular basis for claiming it. (The word "steak" is used repeatedly in the scene by writers Willis Goldbeck and James Bellah.) The action is more a conflict between Ranse and Tom than it is between them and Valance, and its tension rests on the basis that each man uses in making his political claim on the community: force or law. Yet in a later scene we learn that Ranse is not unwilling to use force; he tries to learn to use a gun and, after being shown up as a marksman and embarrassed by Tom, he knocks Tom down. It is easier for Ranse to learn some of Tom's ways than for Tom to learn Ranse's. Like the politician he is becoming, Ranse is flexible as well as determined.

These underlying differences are brought to a head, personally and politically, in the fight over statehood for the unnamed territory in which Shinbone is located. The cattle interests for whom Valance works oppose statehood for economic reasons; ironically it is the villains who are associated with the land and the people of Shinbone who want law and fences and government. The classical contrast in the western between the land and human communities is reversed.

At a meeting in Shinbone to elect representatives to the territorial convention in Capital City which will decide the issue of statehood, Valance tries to get himself elected. Tom prevents him, and after turning down nomination himself (thus rejecting politics), Tom nominates Ranse, who, along with newspaper editor Dutton Peabody (Edmond O'Brien), is chosen to be a delegate. Tom's ironic role in the meeting is a political one—to enforce the rules, including one that the bar be closed during voting. ("This is democracy, isn't it?" he says, sounding not entirely convinced.) Tom watches Ranse's victory in bemusement from the sidelines passively reclining on a staircase, almost lying down, just as Ranse was lying down when we first saw him. Now it is Ranse who stands in control of the fledgling political community he has created with his ideas and his words.

Peabody publishes a story—words—celebrating Valance's defeat and is subsequently beaten by Valance and his men, who also demolish the newspaper office. Valance vows next to go after his other nemesis, Ranse; Valance's enemies now are the men of law and words; Tom, irrelevant now, has disappeared as an adversary. Valance and Ranse meet, both armed, and Valance, toying with Ranse, wounds him in the right arm. With his left hand, Ranse fires at Valance, who staggers and falls into the street, dead, beneath a sign reading "Mass meeting/Elections." "Liberty's dead!" someone shouts, as the people of Shinbone learn of the death of the ironically named villain.

Hallie rushes to Ranse and embraces him. Tom sees this and takes it as a gesture of Hallie's love for Ranse. Tom gets drunk and rides to his ranch house outside of town where he sets fire to it, throwing a lamp into the room he was building for Hallie. It is the house to which Link took Hallie at the beginning of the film when she told him, "You know where I wanted to go, didn't you?"

At the territorial convention, Ranse is attacked in the pompous oratory of a political opponent (played by John Carradine) for having no more qualification for office than having killed a man. Stoddard slips from the meeting room and encounters a drunken Tom:

Tom: Pilgrim, where are you going?
Ranse: I'm going home, Tom. I'm going back east where I belong.
Tom: What is it now, Pilgrim? Your conscience?
Ranse: Isn't it enough to kill a man without trying to build a life on it?

But now Tom asks Ranse to think back to the night Valance died (thus introducing a flashback within a flashback) in which we see that it was Tom, hiding in the shadows, who killed Valance. Thus does Tom not just set the record straight historically, but, in a fashion, morally. Tom describes his actions and motives: "Cold-blooded murder. But I can live with it. Hallie's happy. She wanted you alive. . . . Hallie's your girl now. Go on back in there and take that nomination. You taught her to read and write, now give her something to read and write about."

The convention scene in Capital City is the political culmination of the film. Statehood is debated in a setting contemptuous of politics and politicians. Pompous oratory dominates and one of the candidates' demonstrations is climaxed by the entry into the meeting hall of a man dressed as a cowboy riding a white horse. The cowboy is now a caricature, a cartoon. A political meeting has turned the most powerful of western icons, the cowboy, into a parody of itself.

We leave the flashback and reenter the present. Ranse's story to the editor is a confession that his political successes (he became governor, senator and an ambassador and now has a chance to be vice president) were all built on a lie. Ranse, surprised when the editor crumples his notes and throws them away says, "Well, you're not going to use the story, Mr. Scott?" "No sir," Scott replies. "This is the West, sir. When the legend becomes fact, print the legend."

As Ranse and Hallie leave Shinbone on the train, they talk. Ranse asks if Hallie would mind if they "just up and left Washington" and return to Shinbone. Looking out the window, Hallie replies, "If you knew how often I dreamed of it! My roots are here. I guess my heart is here." She talks of how what was once a desert is now a garden and about "how proud" Ranse must be. There is a long pause and Ranse asks, "Hallie, who put the cactus roses on Tom's coffin?" And Hallie replies, "I did." We know that whatever pride Ranse may feel is mitigated by the truths recalled by his return to Shinbone and perhaps his recollection that many years ago when Tom came courting he brought Hallie cactus roses.

The Man Who Shot Liberty Valance is about the passage of time—history— and how we deal with it, factually and mythically. The center of the story is Tom. In an interview with Peter Bogdanovich, John Ford noted, "Well, Wayne actually played the lead; Jimmy Stewart had most of the scenes, but Wayne was the central character, the motivation for the whole thing" (Bogdanovich, 1976, 99).

Wayne's Tom Doniphon is the Fordian western hero whom time has now passed by; indeed, time has passed by his entire generation ("I reckon the only one of us from the old days workin' steady is the Senator"). Tom is juxtaposed in life—in "fact"—with Ranse in a zero-sum game. What Tom loses, Ranse wins: community leadership, political power, and Hallie. But the "facts" of the case are built on a legend that is a lie—the legend that Ranse shot Liberty Valance, the basis of his political career and his marriage to Hallie. The film thus reverses legend and fact: the "fact" of Ranse killing Valance is a lie, which becomes a legend, which finally becomes a fact. History is written by the winners. ("This is the West, sir. When the legend becomes fact, print the legend.")[3]

John Ford created much of our film-based western legend, and *The Man Who Shot Liberty Valance* is also about the death of that legend, as is suggested not just in Tom's death but in the artificiality of the sets and the references to stagecoaches. But the death of that legend in the film is a grudging one. We know through the motif of the cactus rose that Hallie loved Tom. And, more importantly, we know that the events of the film occur because of Tom: it is Tom who kills Valance, tells Ranse the truth about it, gives up Hallie, and thereby creates Ranse's career (and, indirectly, statehood); it is Tom who refuses nomination and destroys his (and what was to be Hallie's) home. Thus, Tom gives up power, home, love, and finally his way of life so that Ranse may create community through words and law and politics; Tom's every act is one of denial, of sacrifice, almost of suicide. It is nearly Christ-like.

Ranse wins, but at a cost. He learns what he already suspected—that Hallie loved Tom. His trip to Tom's burial reminds him of the foundation of his entire life, of Tom's sacrifice, and perhaps also of what Ranse told Tom: "Isn't it enough to kill a man without trying to build a life on it?" Now, of course, we know that Ranse has built his life and career not just on the killing of a man but on allowing the lie about that killing to stand. Thus does Ransom Stoddard ransom the truth for his career in politics and his marriage to Hallie. Ranse is doubly tainted (rancid?), and Tom, because he told the truth, is shown to be the real hero. Politics, we are told in the convention scene with the entry of the cartoon cowboy and in the deceitful foundation of Ranse's career, is based on artifice and lies.

Yet Ranse is not portrayed simply as a cynical opportunist but rather as what he becomes—a successful politician who brings law and education to Shinbone. He is adaptable (he tries to use a gun, Tom's weapon; he is willing to do "woman's work," even at the price of being humiliated); he teaches others to read and write (and thereby creates the basis of his political career); he refuses to accept Tom's ways ("Nobody fights my battles!"), yet permits just that to happen and also permits the lie about it to survive. While Ranse's silence about the truth lasts most of his life, he is finally willing to let the editor print the truth, and he does finally want to leave Washington to come home to Shinbone with Hallie. Much more so than Tom, Ranse is a subtle and ambivalently portrayed character. This perhaps is what the new west must have in its hero, though accepting it was not in John Ford's heart. In comments as wistful as the film itself, Ford spoke to an interviewer:

Q.: By the end of the picture, though, it seemed very clear that Vera Miles was still in love with Wayne.
Ford: Well, we meant it that way.
Q.: Your picture of the west has become increasingly sad over the years...
Ford: Possibly—I don't know—I'm not a psychologist. Maybe I'm getting older.
(Bogdanovich, 1976, 100)

In *Stagecoach*, the Wayne character, Ringo, and his woman, Dallas, after their brief membership in the social microcosm of the stagecoach, leave it and the "blessings of civilization." In *The Man Who Shot Liberty Valance*, the Wayne character is left with neither woman nor land (he burns his home), and finally there does not even seem to be room for him in Shinbone.

The social contract of *Stagecoach* may be entered and left at will; it is a matter of necessity but also of choice. In *The Man Who Shot Liberty Valance*, society cannot be ignored; Tom sacrifices everything for the sake of the community and its new leader. He does this not so much out of conviction but of necessity, accepting its inevitability quietly and a little uncomprehendingly. The classic western hero controlled his fate; in *The Man Who Shot Liberty Valance*, he does not. In *Stagecoach*, the social contract was optional; in *The Man Who Shot Liberty Valance*, it is binding and finally, for Tom, overwhelming.

Law and justice are also dealt with in radically different ways in the two films. In *Stagecoach*, the escaped prisoner, Ringo, is allowed by the sheriff not only the time it takes to kill the Plummer brothers (thus allowing the code of western justice, with the implicit consent of the law, to be followed) but also to run off with Dallas (thus allowing the convention of the western to be followed). Thus are law and justice and genre convention joined in a happy ending, western style.

In *The Man Who Shot Liberty Valance*, the fractured relationship between justice and law is shown in our seeing two versions of the death of Valance. In the first we see what Ranse (and Hallie) think happened and what everyone is forever allowed to believe: Ranse shoots Valance after first having been shot at himself. Thus law serves (western) justice as the aggrieved Ranse kills Valance fair and square in what would be a conventional western ending. In the second viewing, we see that Tom shoots Valance from the shadows ("Cold-blooded murder," Tom calls his act. "But I can live with it."). When Tom shoots Valance we learn that (western) justice now serves law, as Tom's murder of Valance does Ranse's dirty work for him. Thus, the basis of Ranse's political career is shown to be illegitimate. The ultimate death for John Ford's west lies in the establishment of a social contract the hero cannot leave and in its implication in the death of the real hero, who is replaced by a politician.

Some students of John Ford's films have termed his work right-wing or even reactionary. Andrew Sarris (1975, 180) came closer to the truth when he wrote:

In accepting the inevitability of the present while mourning the past, Ford is a conservative rather than a reactionary. What he wishes to conserve are the memories of old values even if they have to be magnified into legends. The legends with which Ford is most deeply involved, however, are the legends of honorable failure, of otherwise forgotten men and women who rode away from glory towards self-sacrifice.

The western, the most robust of film genres, turns out to be one of the most interesting politically because the frontier, in fact and in film, was a place where some of the most basic issues of politics were played out: law, justice, the nature of the social contract, and the state of nature itself. In the hands of John Ford, these themes are handled with skill and poignancy. These fundamental political issues are placed in sharp relief when political and social institutions are being created. The path from *Stagecoach* to *The Man Who Shot Liberty Valance* is one in which the lone western hero journeys from coexisting with the state of nature and the demands of the social contract to the realization that there is no place for him in either, except in myth.

NOTES

1. Our familiarity with movie conventions is illustrated by some definitions of movie terms by critic Roger Ebert (Ebert, 1989, 938-39):

"Fruit Cart!" An expletive used by knowledgeable film buffs during any chase involving a foreign or ethnic locale, reflecting their certainty that a fruit cart will be overturned during the chase, and an angry peddler will run into the middle of the street to shake his fist at the departing Porsche.

Mistake of the Unmotivated Close-Up. A character is given a close-up in a scene where there seems to be no reason for it. This is an infallible tip-off that this character is more significant than at first appears, and is most likely the killer.

2. A qualified exception to this is the "social problem film," including films like *I Am a Fugitive from a Chain Gang* (1932), which dealt with the criminal justice system in the American South, *Gentlemen's Agreement* (1948), which addressed anti-Semitism, and *Alamo Bay* (1985), which looked at tensions between Vietnamese refugees and Anglos in a fishing community on the Texas Gulf Coast. (For a discussion of the social problem film, see Maland, 1988, 305-29, and Roffman and Purdy, 1981.) This subgenre, however, never approached the development of the more traditional genre, and, as noted above, much of the contemporary raw material for such films is now consumed by television.

3. The theme of time passing someone by occurs in a more overtly political John Ford film, *The Last Hurrah* (1958), in which Spencer Tracy plays Mayor Frank Skeffington, modeled after James Michael Curly of Boston. Skeffington represents the last of a generation of grassroots ethnic politicians overcome by younger candidates and the coming to politics of television.

2

WATCHING MOVIES

Here is a description of *The Man Who Shot Liberty Valance*:

Ranking with *Stagecoach* as one of the greatest of its genre, *The Man Who Shot Liberty Valance* is the modern-day Western to beat all Westerns. John Ford, whose very name is synonymous with "Westerns," directed the ideal cast. Jimmy Stewart plays the bungling but charming big-city lawyer determined to rid the fair village of Shinbone of its number-one nuisance and Bad Man, Liberty Valance (Lee Marvin). And as if that weren't enough, the biggest star that ever aimed a six-shooter plays the Man of the title: John Wayne. Super-sincere Stewart and rugged rancher Wayne share the same love interest (Vera Miles). One gets the gunman but the other gets the gal...and the glory.

Here is another description of the same film: "*The Man Who Shot Liberty Valance*" is a political western, a psychological murder mystery, and John Ford's confrontation with the past—personal, professional, and historical" (Sarris, 1975, 175).

The first description comes from the back of a videocassette box, the second from a film critic. The respective intents of the authors are clear: to encourage purchase or rental of the movie, and to analyze it. The ability of a good film to entertain a mass audience while still providing material for serious analysis—sometimes frame-by-frame analysis—is one of the movies' chief charms, but also a source of some skepticism. Do most of us, even a small minority of the audience, come close to seeing all the things a serious student of a film does? Do we, after we have seen James Stewart and Vera Miles leave Shinbone on the train, talk with our companions about John Ford's confrontation with the past—personal, professional, and historical?

The audience need not know such things to enjoy the film. One of the most beloved of American films, *The Wizard of Oz* (1939), has entertained millions who do not know or even need to know that the film is a quite specific political allegory about the collapse of the Populist movement in the United States at the turn of the century, when L. Frank Baum published the story on which the film was based. The film is one of the best examples of Jean-Luc Godard's observation that when a good film is also popular it is because of a misunderstanding.

"Oz" is the abbreviation for ounce, the standard measure for gold. The yellow brick road is the gold standard along which travel Dorothy (an innocent Everyman), the Tin Woodman (industrial workers), the Scarecrow (farmers), the Cowardly Lion (William Jennings Bryan), the munchkins (the "little people"), all on their way to visit the Wizard (President William McKinley). The Scarecrow has no brain (does not know his own political interests), the Woodman lacks a heart (has been beaten down by his working conditions), and the Lion has no courage (Bryan, the national leader of Populism, is more talk than action). The Wizard turns out to be "making believe" and to be just "a common man" without any wizardly powers. The Wicked Witches of the East (bankers and capitalists) and the West (drought; the witch is killed by water) are killed, and the Woodman is left in charge of the East (the worker now controls his job) and the Scarecrow of Oz. This fantasy of the political triumph of workers and farmers—the core goal of the Populist movement—is never to be realized, however, as the Lion (Bryan) retreats into the woods. Does not knowing any of this diminish our pleasure in the film? Does knowing any of this increase it?

Going to the movies is essentially a social event, not an intellectual one: a reward at the end of the week, a place to take—or deposit—the kids, the classic place for a date. We go to have a good time; if we talk about the film afterwards it is usually to ask the standard question, "How'd you like it?" Casual observation at theaters would seem to show that further discussion about the film usually ceases there. The next time the film comes up for discussion will probably be in conversation with a friend who wants to know if the film is worth seeing.

Movies are a highly intentional art form: they are written, planned and produced with great care and in great detail. Anecdotes abound about filmmakers lavishing time and money on details few will notice but which will add to the effectiveness of the film. In preparing for a short scene in *Vertigo* (1958) shot in a flower store, Alfred Hitchcock worked with a staffer on the arrangement of flowers in the store window and interior. The staffer recalled:

Mr. Hitchcock was very particular about the customers in the store and the traffic outside. He spoke with the police, and then he picked out each car and truck that passed outside—the color, the size—he selected each one. The mirrors were hung with black drapes to prevent reflections, and the lights caused such intense heat in the store that the sprinkler system went on. An artificial door was constructed at the rear of the store, through which James Stewart could look in at Kim Novak, as if from a rear alley—which the actual store does not have. That artificial door was not used after all, because the art director miscalculated and it was too large. That moment was recreated back in Hollywood.... Everyone in the crew worked for twelve hours that day for only about a minute of film. (Spoto, 1976, 296-97)

Hitchcock meticulously planned his films scene by scene on a storyboard. It was said that he found the actual shooting of a film boring and anticlimactic, for the film in a sense had already been created. Charlie Chaplin, on the other hand, created his films on the set, rehearsing and creating as he went, usually filming everything. But even this improvisational style was meticulously done: in outtakes from Chaplin's *City Lights* (1931), we see a film record of Chaplin taking Virginia Cherrill, playing the blind flower girl, through literally hundreds of takes so she will raise a flower the way Chaplin wanted it done. Among contemporary directors, Woody Allen is noted for frequently reshooting scenes and even recasting his films after shooting has begun until he has what he wants.

Yet most of us see a film only once. Much of what is so carefully put in a film by its creators surely must be lost. How can films be so powerful if the experience of viewing a carefully crafted work is so casual?

EXPERIENCE

Movie advertising has long invited us to "experience" this or that film. But what is the movie-going experience?

It is, first, usually social and special. A film, even viewed at home, is more of an event than watching a television program; it usually takes at least a small amount of time, money, and planning. Even a trip to the video store, however quick, is not as easy as turning on the television. Movie going is usually the result of activity; television viewing, of passivity. A movie is something of an occasion.

Then there is the theater, a public place whose sole purpose is to show movies. It is a revealing aspect of films that many film lovers remember a theater with as much affection as they do the films they saw there. (Video stores sell popcorn and candy and display cardboard marquees to remind us of the theater experience.) There in the dark and surrounded mostly by strangers (we are voyeurs in a theater), unable to stop the film when we want to and—most important—looking at the big screen that dominates our consciousness the way no television screen could, we watch a movie. Part of the experience is that we simply pay more attention to a movie and part is that we know we may never see it again.

The very craft that goes into a well-made film deepens the experience. Typically a motif is reinforced repeatedly or a character carefully developed. This is a luxury in a feature film not possible in television because of time limitations or because the budgets of television programs, even longer ones, do not permit the planning and attention to detail possible in a feature film. The experience of a well-made film is based on relatively detailed information from a number of sources. As Stanley Kauffmann observed:

[Film] manages to make poetry out of doorknobs, breakfasts, furniture. Trivial details, of which everyone's universe is made, can once again be transmuted into metaphor, contributing to imaginative art. A complementary, powerful fact is that this principle operates whether the film-maker is concerned with it or not. In any film except those with fantastic settings, whether the director's aim is naturalistic or romantic or symbolic or anything else, the streets and stairways and cigarette lighters are present, the girl's room is at least as real as the girl—often it bolsters her defective reality. Emphasized or not, invited or not, the physical world through the intensifications of photography never stops insisting on its presence and relevance. (Kauffmann, 1966, 417)

The sheer size of the screen itself allows the filmmaker to show us details we simply cannot see on a television screen (we cannot easily look away from a movie theater screen), and the quality of the film image of light projected through celluloid is always superior to a video image regardless of screen size. The sound system of a theater likewise enhances the experience of movie going, allowing us to be surrounded by the sound track and to hear it in greater clarity and detail—and at greater volume—than we could at home. As Steven Spielberg noted, "The difference between looking at *Mrs. Miniver* (1942) on videotape and looking at *Mrs. Miniver* on 35-millimeter good black and white film is the difference between observation and inspiration" (Rosenfield, 1989, 8). The technology of filmmaking allows the audience more fully to experience the details of a well-made film, which means the force of those details is greater.

The movie experience is a total one in which our expectations are high and our attention focused. Watching movies, we are receptive to the tools available to skilled filmmakers. A properly crafted film or even a single scene of it may utilize—indeed, must utilize—several of these tools. If one tool is not effective, perhaps another will be. As viewers, we respond to the complete experience, which is much more than the sum of its parts. But to understand films it is necessary first to separate these elements of movie craft one from the other in order to appreciate how they function together.

ELEMENTS

Title

The title of a film, as with everything else about it, is a marriage of art and commerce. Usually titles are brief, direct, and sufficiently broad so as not to drive away potential audience members. More than one dispute has occurred between those who want a title that is descriptive and evocative of the film and those who want one that sells.

The best titles do all this and are subtly suggestive as well. The title of *Coming Home* (1978) evokes warmth and the literal return home from Vietnam of the soldier played by Bruce Dern, but it also suggests that the war too has come home. *Meet John Doe* (1941) suggests at least three meanings: the specific character played by Gary Cooper, who adopts the name; the mythical John Doe (Everyman); but the title also invites us to meet ourselves. *Casualties of War* (1989) suggests a broader meaning to casualties beyond just those in battle and *WarGames* (1983) implies that there is something dangerously infantile about adults seriously planning for nuclear war.

Dialogue

This is the most directly accessible element of a film, but its use can vary enormously. Some screenwriters place unmistakably direct and clear speeches into their characters' mouths. Paddy Chayefsky (1923-1981), who was a playwright as well as a screenwriter, was known for writing such dialogue. In *Network* (1976) he has the disgruntled broadcaster played by Peter Finch give the famous "I'm as mad as hell and I'm not going to take this any more" speech, a phrase that has entered the language. In Chayefsky's *The Americanization of Emily* (1964) the characters played by James Garner and Julie Andrews have a series of eloquent but implausible verbal battles about war, courage, cowardice, survival, life, and death. Little is left in doubt in such dialogue.

Woody Allen often gives dialogue to characters who explain, often in a didactic way, the meaning of events in his films. Sometimes this is done by voice-over (*Annie Hall*, 1977, in which Allen's character Alvy Singer provides the running commentary outside of the film's events) and other times by the introduction of a character directly into the film (as in *Crimes and Misdemeanors*, 1989, in which the character of Professor Levy appears throughout the film).

Intense and articulate dialogue of the kind Paddy Chayefsky wrote is the exception, however. Often it does not ring true; people are not that eloquent. Long speeches also can be visually static and they forgo the use of more dynamic visual and aural ways of communicating. To say a film is talky is no compliment. "Dialogue" may also be nonverbal. The legendary sexually charged eating scene in *Tom Jones* (1963) has no dialogue; the desires of the characters played by Albert Finney and Joyce Redman and directed by Tony Richardson are communicated by their actions and expressions, by the symbolism of eating, and by the masterful use of the sounds of the meal being consumed.

Dialogue may also be used in counterpoint to other information provided in the film. A character may say one thing but intend another. A line of dialogue followed by a quick cut to the speaker's eyes—especially if they shift quickly— is a sure sign the speaker is lying. A cut to an object or person about whom a character is speaking may confirm or belie the words spoken.

In political films, dialogue often "balances" things. In *Seven Days in May* (1964), which deals with an attempted military coup against the U.S. government led by a right-wing general, the film's sympathies are clearly on the side of civilian authorities. Yet there are several brief speeches by the general, played by Burt Lancaster, which articulate his views in a way that not only tell us about the character but also doubtless mollify those in the audience sympathetic to Lancaster's character. Dialogue in *The China Syndrome* airs different views on nuclear power despite the clear antinuclear sympathies of the film. Such dialogue, easy to slip into a script, functions as a sop to a portion of the audience, allowing it to leave happy with a memorable phrase or two. Using dialogue this way exploits the phenomena of selective perception and selective retention in which a viewer tends to perceive and remember things consistent with already established beliefs.

Dialogue used at the beginning of a film is often especially important. Usually its purpose is simply expository, to tell us what we need to know about characters and circumstances. This is often done in a scene in which several people talk, one of whom plays the role of the audience's surrogate and is uninformed about background information. (The most ignorant person in a film, to whom all is explained, is there for the sake of the audience.) Often, however, early dialogue provides a subtle means of preparing the audience for things to come. When Link tells Hallie, in *The Man Who Shot Liberty Valance*, that the only one of the old Shinbone hands "working steady" is the senator, he is telling us about the passage of a generation. The most celebrated use of dialogue in American film, however, is the use of the single word "Rosebud" in *Citizen Kane* (1941). The search for the meaning of this single word motivates all the film's subsequent action

Names

As in literature, names in films, whether they are names of characters, places, or things, may carry considerable meaning. Names are unusually efficient vehicles for this; in their names we learn much about Longfellow Deeds in *Mr. Deeds Goes to Town* (1936) or Jefferson Smith in *Mr. Smith Goes to Washington* (1939). In the 1941 production of *The Great Dictator*, Charlie Chaplin plays Adenoid Hynkel of Tomania and Jack Oakie is Benzino Napaloni of Bacteria. In *Wall Street* (1987), Michael Douglas's character is named Gordon Gekko (a gecko is a lizard). Charlie Sheen's younger character, who wants to be a rich and canny financier like Gekko, is named Bud Fox.

Other names are more subtle. The computer HAL in *2001: A Space Odyssey* (1968) becomes IBM if one goes one letter further into the alphabet for each letter in HAL's name. There are names that are richer in their connotations. "Ransom Stoddard" suggests the character's steadfastness (Stoddard/solid/stolid) but also later developments (ransoming the truth) and perhaps even aspects of his character (Ranse/rancid). Liberty Valance is likewise a suggestive name. Liberty is ironic, since the character is portrayed as a mindless, violent psychopath, the essence of lawless license, a kind of exaggerated liberty. When the shout "Liberty's dead!" is heard we may also understand it as the death of a wild and "free" part of the frontier tradition, which is no longer possible in the new Shinbone. The word valence (Valance) refers to the capacity of something to react or unite with something else; thus for the violent character of Liberty Valance, "the valence of liberty depends on force, which is why order and liberty are not identical" (Gallagher, 1986, 392). And in the same film Link is, of course, a link with the past.

In *Coming Home* we see an interesting variation on the use of names in Jane Fonda's character. Her married name is Sally Hyde, and initially she hides from much of the world as a traditional young military wife. After her husband Bob (Bruce Dern) leaves for Vietnam and she meets Luke Martin (Jon Voight), we learn that her maiden name was Bender, and indeed she begins to bend to the new circumstances, political and personal, in which she finds herself. Names given to places and things are likewise often signals from filmmakers. In *Strangers on a Train* (1951) a murderer stalks his intended victim in an amusement park, following her into a tunnel of love on a boat called *Pluto*, the name for the god of the underworld in Roman mythology.

Characters

Films are most obviously "about" what characters do. *Stagecoach* is "about" a group of people thrown together in a hostile landscape, but it is also "about" who those characters are as types. Films, in common with other narrative works, must concentrate the varied and subtle reality of human beings and human experience into a few characters with whom we spend only a few hours.

The standard way to do this is through stereotyping. Put a sneer and a black hat on a cowboy and you have a bad guy; put a trenchcoat and a fedora on Humphrey Bogart and you have Sam Spade, private eye. It is the nature of stereotypes that we know them immediately; the stereotyped character is one of the essential conditions for the existence of a film genre.

Consider how often a politician is portrayed as male, white, at least middle-aged, overweight, self-important, surrounded both by sycophants and those who really control him, not terribly bright, not terribly well informed, and with a cigar. Frank Capra often portrayed politicians this way, as in Governor Hopper (who does just that for his master) of Jefferson Smith's home state in *Mr. Smith Goes to Washington*. Another common convention in portraying politicians is to depict them as decent but ineffectual, as in President Merkin Muffly (Peter Sellers) in *Dr. Strangelove* or the president for much of *The American President* (1996).

A character often represents not just that specific individual but a type— politicians, not a politician. A character may also represent an entire group or social class. In *Lifeboat* (1944) the passengers represent not just different nationalities (the United States, Britain, Germany) but different social classes (a middle-class journalist from a working-class background, a capitalist, a working-class machinist) and different political views (moderate, conservative, and radical).

Politically, the most malleable characters are those empty vessels into which the audience may readily pour its preconceptions. The 1956 version of *Invasion of the Body Snatchers*, in which seedpods from outer space take over the bodies of humans and turn them into soulless replicas, is the classic example. We may choose not to see the pods in political terms at all; if we do, we may readily see them as metaphors either for the advance of communism or the advance of McCarthyism, both of which were on the minds of audiences in 1956. The 1960 production of *The Little Shop of Horrors*, with its voracious plant, Audrey, Jr., is the spiritual descendant of the pods. Audrey's greedy cry of "Feed me!" can be enjoyed for itself, or one may decide that Audrey is really capital or labor or anything else.

A related and effective mechanism in explicitly political films is to omit political identifying marks from a character. Partisanship, a character's ideological orientation, or even the home state are often unspecified. Thus we may project our own views onto the character: liberals are as certain the evil senator is a conservative as conservatives are of the reverse.

The use of characters to represent something beyond just themselves raises a particularly interesting problem in political films. Most students of politics place great emphasis on institutions. Students of American politics, for example, regularly celebrate the role of the Constitution. How does one make a set of institutions or a document a character in a film? In *Seven Days in May* the opening and closing credits are shown with the Preamble to the Constitution in the background, and the film has repeated references to the document in its dialogue. But the demands of filmmaking make it very difficult to deal effectively with such abstractions.   The nature of the medium limits the consideration that can be given to precisely the kinds of topics that for many students of politics are the real "heroes of the piece." The only practical way is to represent institutional subjects in the person of an individual, as in the character of the president played by Fredric March in *Seven Days in May* and the by-the-rules military man played by Kirk Douglas.

Props and Wardrobe

In *The Graduate* (1967), Dustin Hoffman's character, Ben, is given a car by his parents as a graduation gift. He uses it first to court Elaine (Katharine Ross), then destroys it in a series of trips from Los Angeles to Berkeley to win her back. By the end of the film the car is a useless wreck, and Ben and Elaine ride off into their future in a bus. Boy gets girl, loses car, and rejects materialism for love and public transportation.

In the same film Ben is given a wetsuit as a gift and we see him awkwardly flopping across the patio to jump into the family pool and try it out in front of a fawning audience of his parents and their friends. Water is a traditional symbol of life, and the scene and props are designed to tell us that Ben's parents want to make his passage into life (the pool) as protected as possible (the wetsuit). Even the water is contained in the safe confines of the pool. Later we see Ben spending days idly floating in the pool on a raft, pondering his future, floating on the surface of life.

Mirrors are frequently used props.   In *Apocalypse Now* (1979), Martin Sheen's character, Captain Willard, confronts himself in a broken mirror at the beginning of the film and cuts himself with it: revenge of the shattered self. Often mirrors are used to tell us that someone is uncertain or confused by showing the character and a reflection of the character in the same shot. This can also be a signal that the character is deceitful (two-faced). Both these meanings occur in a shot of Madeleine/Judy (Kim Novak) as she looks into a mirror in a scene toward the end of *Vertigo*.

The use of props is often reinforced with dialogue or camera work or both. In *Mr. Smith Goes to Washington* (1939) we learn via dialogue that Jefferson Smith's hat is associated with his revered father. Later, when he is being deliberately diverted from Senate business by the daughter of Senator Paine (Claude Raines), he fumbles with the hat and finally drops it. (Director Frank Capra lets the camera linger on the action.) When Smith later faces a crisis and wants to quit he removes the hat; when he is convinced to persevere he puts it on.

In another Capra film, *Meet John Doe* (1941), we see the villain, a protofascist industrialist with grandiose political ambitions, behind a desk on which sits a statue of Napoleon on horseback. We see him in another scene inspecting his private corps of motorcycle-mounted police, the modern equivalent of horses. The scene also brings to mind similar footage of Nazi motorcycle troops in Leni Riefenstahl's Nazi documentary *Triumph of the Will* (1935).

A recent and altogether lamentable phenomenon is the obvious placement of products and product logos in movie scenes. The reason is financial: product placements are paid for—indeed, they are negotiated for by companies that specialize in such activities. Between 1982 and 1989, Columbia Pictures was controlled by the Coca-Cola Company. Columbia films of that time were replete with references to Coke, almost always in ways that distracted the audience. *Back to the Future II* (1989) is filled with product references. *Rocky III* (1982) showcases Coca-Cola, Sanyo, Nike, Wheaties, TWA, Marantz, and Wurlitzer and shows Rocky Balboa endorsing Nikon, Harley-Davidson, Budweiser, Maserati, Gatorade, and American Express. As Miller notes (1990, 48), such blatant commercials not only destroy film narrative by essentially halting the movie while the product is displayed but "through the partial transfer of creative authority out of the hands of filmmaking professionals and into the purely quantitative universe of the CEOs."

Clothing and grooming, especially for women characters, is another way to send signals to the audience. Jane Fonda's character, Sally, in *Coming Home* changes her clothing and hair styles after her husband Bob leaves for Vietnam. When they reunite briefly while he is on leave, she covers her new hair style with a bandanna and is shown avoiding eye contact with him by obscuring her face with a camera. In *Stagecoach* the socially proper Lucy has dark hair and the prostitute with the heart of gold, Dallas, is blonde. Because of the convention associating darkness with malevolence we have a clue as to which is the "better" of the two women.

Beyond props and wardrobe, filmmakers are also concerned with the overall "look" of a film, the way in which all the design elements work together to advance the film's themes. This is the task of the production designer (the older term is art director), whose job it is to orchestrate color, wardrobe, props, and sets. Richard Sylbert, the production designer of *Chinatown* (1974), directed by Roman Polanski, recalled some of the design elements of that film:

It's about a drought in 1937 in Southern California. All the buildings in this picture will be Spanish except one. And they'll all be white. The reason they're white is that the heat will bounce off them. And not only will they all be white, they'll be above the eye level of the private eye [Jack Nicholson]. Above eye level means for the private eye that he has to walk uphill. It is always harder emotionally to walk uphill. (Sylbert, 1989, 22)

Sound

In *The Candidate* (1972), background and foreground noise constantly overwhelm the ability of the characters to hear each other or for the audience to hear them. The sound becomes a form of dialogue between the characters, almost a separate character. Eventually the audience may realize the purpose of the noise is to tell us something about political campaigns. The aural chaos is reinforced visually and through dialogue, as in several scenes in which candidate Bill McKay (Robert Redford) must escape into a bathroom, an airliner cockpit, or an elevator to talk. Never in the film are we told in words that a political campaign makes it impossible to talk or listen or think, but we can hear it.

Ambient noise is used effectively but subtly in Hitchcock's *Rope* (1950), all of which is set in a New York apartment where a murder is committed and eventually discovered. With the exception of the opening shot outside the apartment building, all the action occurs indoors. In the opening exterior shot we hear the noises of the city. As the camera enters the interior the noises recede. When the murder is discovered a window is opened and the sounds of the city—of reality—are again heard. In the 1972 film *Frenzy* Hitchcock similarly uses street sounds to drown out the sound of a murder being committed: as the camera slowly and sadly withdraws from the door behind which the crime is committed and backs out into the street, the noise of the city become increasingly audible. The slow withdrawal of the camera and the street noise leave us feeling that no one knows or cares that a life has been taken.

In *Citizen Kane*, Orson Welles uses a "dead screen" to force the audience to listen. In a sequence in which Susan Alexander Kane is singing an opera aria—very badly—the camera follows several curtain cables toward the ceiling. The shot is visually dead and we are forced to listen, really hearing how awful her singing is. When the camera reaches the upper reaches of the theater, a stagehand who has heard what we have wordlessly holds his nose.

Music

Film music is as old as the first piano that accompanied a silent film. Then and now, music's role was to expand upon other aspects of a film. Usually this is done by associating a character or setting or emotion with a musical theme, as in "Lara's Theme" in *Doctor Zhivago* (1965), or "Somewhere over the Rainbow," "We're Off to See the Wizard," and "If I Only Had a Heart" in *The Wizard of Oz*. And it is impossible to think of *Casablanca* without thinking of "As Time Goes By."

One of the more common and effective movie music conventions is to reprise a theme with different instrumentation, at a different tempo, or in a major or a minor key so as to modify its effect. A song performed in a minor key has a more melancholy emotional effect than when played in a major key. When a theme reappears, the manner in which it is played will signal the filmmaker's intent, which may to be reinforce its earlier appearance, to signify a change in the person associated with the music, or to remind the audience of a character who is not on-screen. A common convention is for the ambient noise in a scene to be reduced and replaced gradually by the theme for a character, especially when two people first meet. Many characters fall in love this way.

A basic distinction in film music is between music written specifically for the film and music that already exists. Composers who specialized in creating original music for films, like Bernard Herrmann (1911-1975) and Nino Rota

(1911-1979), functioned not unlike opera composers with the screenplay and director's intentions serving as the libretto. Herrmann scored *Citizen Kane*, *The Day the Earth Stood Still* (1951), *Psycho* (1960), *Vertigo* (1958), and *Taxi Driver* (1976), among many others.[1] Rota scored nearly all of Federico Fellini's films and *The Godfather* (1972). Already existing music plays an important role in the soundtrack of *American Graffiti* (1973) and *Coming Home*, both of which use popular songs contemporaneous with the time in which the film is set in order to establish a sense of time.

Popular song lyrics are additionally useful because they can be juxtaposed against actions and characters, as is done constantly in *Coming Home* when the lyrics of songs by the Rolling Stones and the Chambers Brothers, among others, reinforce the story. Similarly, in *Manhattan* (1979), Woody Allen uses the music of George Gershwin to reinforce the beautiful black-and-white photography of Gordon Willis and evoke an idealized conception of Manhattan past against which are contrasted characters in Manhattan present.

Music can also be sharply ironic: in the opening of *Dr. Strangelove, or: How I Learned to Stop Worrying and Love the Bomb* (1964), Stanley Kubrick shows an Air Force bomber being refueled in mid-air to the lushly played "Try a Little Tenderness." At the end of the film, after a nuclear bomb has been dropped triggering the Soviet Doomsday Machine and, thus, the end of the world, we hear Vera Lynn sing "We'll Meet Again." In *The Front* (1978), set against the background of the blacklist period in the entertainment industry, the popular song "Young at Heart" opens and closes the film. Its lyric, "fairy tales can come true, it can happen to you," serves as counterpoint to the film's final scene. The reference to fairy tales in the lyric tell us that the final defiant scene in which Allen's character, Howard Prince, stands up to an investigating committee is a wish-fulfilling fantasy.

There is finally the option of not using music at all, as in Hitchcock's *Rope*, or using it sparingly, as in *Testament* (1983). In the latter case, music appears only over the radio and then not frequently. Its relative absence alerts us to its importance when it does occur, as in a scene when a mother and her son, who know they will die in the wake of nuclear war, dance to a popular song from the mother's generation. In addition to binding the two generations together, the music suggests that the son will never have his own songs to pass on.

Lighting

The visual component of film is based on photography and the essence of photography is light. One does not so much film a person as the light falling on that person. Effective lighting is especially clear in black-and-white films where the absence of color removes an entire visual dimension and where the nature of black-and-white film stock permits the use of greater variation in lighting schemes. (Color film, especially that used in the 1940s and 1950s, required considerable light for proper exposure and did not accommodate great contrast between highlight and shadow areas; as a result many films from that era have a uniformly bright and flat look.)

In a famous scene from *Citizen Kane*, renowned for its black-and-white cinematography by Gregg Toland, a young Charles Foster Kane (Orson Welles) shows his newspaper colleagues his "Declaration of Principles." As he bends over a table, he moves from light into darkness, anticipating his later retreat from principle. In a later scene in the film, Kane silences a complaining Susan Alexander Kane (Dorothy Comingore), whose face is cast in Kane's shadow as he does so. Because she is shot from a high angle, the shot combines power with malevolence.

Roger Ebert describes the telling use of lighting in another black-and-white film, Alfred Hitchcock's *Notorious* (1946):

There is a moment when Ingrid Bergman walks slowly through a doorway toward Cary Grant. He is listening to a record of secret testimony which proves she is not a Nazi spy. At the beginning of the shot, Grant thinks she is guilty. In the middle, he does not know. At the end, he thinks she is innocent. Hitchcock begins with Bergman seen in backlit silhouette. As she steps forward, she is half light, half shadow. As the testimony clears her, she is fully lighted. The lighting makes moral judgments. (Ebert, 1989, 920)

A similar moment occurs in the Hitchcock black-and-white film *Strangers on a Train* when Guy Haines (Farley Granger) considers murdering the mother of Bruno Anthony (Robert Walker). As Guy wavers, his emotions are mirrored cinematically by his movement back and forth between darkness and light.

Film noir ("black film"), often set in cities at night, provides some our most memorable film images: harsh, high-contrast lighting with impenetrable shadows; cigarette smoke that glows because it is backlit; neon signs flashing against rainy streets; the shadows of window blinds on walls. A similar lighting style defines many classic horror films of the 1930s. When we first encounter Count Dracula in his castle, we notice his eyes because they are lighted more than the rest of his face.

Color

As with many things in movies, the advent of color (its use, via a process involving coloring after the black-and-white film had been shot, began in the early 1920s) turned a technological innovation into an aesthetic decision. The most widely known use of color is, of course, in *The Wizard of Oz*, in which the fantasy scenes are shot in color and the "real" ones in black and white. The association between monochromatic films and seriousness and color films and entertainment still persists. A contemporary black-and-white film like *Schindler's List* (1993) is an event.

When we see a contemporary film shot in black and white we assume it to be more serious and less "commercial" than one shot in color. *Manhattan* and Martin Scorcese's *Raging Bull* (1980) are but two recent examples of films that signal their intent through monochromatic photography. A variation is to shoot a film on color filmstock but to make its colors more muted either for the whole film or for parts of it. This can be done via lighting, filters on the camera lens, or by manipulating the film during or after processing. In *Deliverance* (1972), director John Boorman muted the colors of the woods in which the film is set by printing a black-and-white image onto color filmstock. In *Sophie's Choice* (1982), the scenes in a concentration camp are rendered by Alan Pakula in less deeply saturated color. In both cases more vibrant colors would be inappropriate.

Within a more conventionally shot color film colors themselves can be a motif. In *Vertigo*, red and green appear throughout. Donald Spoto describes the color motifs in the characters of Scottie (James Stewart) and Madeleine (Kim Novak):

The camera generally photographs them separately, yet the two are associated by the use of color. Scottie's green sweater links him with Madeleine because of her green car and the green stole she wore in her first appearance. The red of Scottie's robe is repeated as the predominant color in Gavin's [a character who sets Scottie off on the mission that leads him to Madeleine] office and club, and in the McKittrick Hotel [where Scottie looks for Madeleine], in the flowers Madeleine and Carlotta [a woman in a portrait whose "blood is in Madeleine"] carry, and in Scottie's front door. A green ice bucket is seen on the credenza behind the red robe and, in counterpoint, red drapes hang behind the green-sweatered Scottie. The red and green traffic lights which blinked at the opening scene, and which will accompany Scottie's later nighttime stroll homeward continue the color scheme. The lights are also associated with motion halted and resumed, and with the verticality of an elevator's directional signals. Through the frequent use of yellow filters, James Stewart's eyes often appear bright green; the real color of Judy Barton's [the real Madeleine] hair is red. (Spoto, 1976, 316-17)

Color also has broader emotional effects: blues and greens—cooler colors— are restful and peaceful; reds and yellows—warmer colors—are more vigorous. By juxtaposing red and green in Vertigo, Hitchcock not only makes an explicit association between colors and characters but establishes deeper emotional contrasts suggesting a number of dichotomies: stop/start, approach/avoidance, reality/fantasy, life/death, and love/hate.

The controversy over "colorizing" black-and-white films takes on an added dimension when seen from this point of view. The entire design of a film— especially lighting and set and wardrobe design—may be heavily influenced by whether the film is shot in color or black and white. While the National Film Preservation Act of 1989 took a small step in the right direction by permitting the designation of twenty-five films per year as "national treasures," its only practical effect was to require that such films, if colorized, carry a disclaimer saying they were altered without the maker's consent.

Camera Movement

Perhaps the most radical aspect of the fledgling film medium beyond the capacity to photograph movement was the ability to move the camera. D.W. Griffith's *The Birth of a Nation* (1915) was one of the first films to exploit the ability of a camera to move, thus allowing the viewer to see things previously unavailable to the audiences of stage plays: the audience as well as the actors could now move. Ironically this ability was temporarily lost with the arrival of sound because the noisy cameras had to be enclosed in sound-proof boxes to permit audio recording.

Among contemporary directors Martin Scorcese is noted for the movement of his camera. In *The Color of Money* (1986), he photographs a pool game with the camera constantly circling the table and the players, the movement of actors and camera complementing one another and becoming a dance. In Scorcese's segment "Life Lessons" in *New York Stories* (1988), a painter (played by Nick Nolte) is filmed as he works on a canvas, with the camera again constantly moving, as it also does, though more slowly, in almost every scene in the film. A quite different approach to camera movement may be seen in Woody Allen's *Manhattan* in which the camera is usually stationary and the characters move into and out of the frame. Visually the film has the feeling of a series of formally composed black-and-white still photographs.

Camera movements are usually accomplished smoothly. Tracking shots, in which the camera moves forward or backward, are usually done on a dolly placed on tracks; pans, in which the camera sweeps horizontally, are done while the camera is firmly supported; crane shots, in which the camera may move simultaneously vertically and horizontally are likewise done with a firm camera support. The advent of the Steadicam permitted hand-held camera work while the camera is gyroscopically steadied. All these smooth camera movements are what we expect from a feature film.[2]

The jerky camera movement we associate with *cinema verité* (literally, "film truth"), a film style popularized in Europe in the 1950s using portable cameras and sound equipment, occasionally appears in American feature films. Since we associate this visual style with documentaries and documentaries with reality, a feature film contrasting smooth camera movements with the more ragged visual quality of a hand-held camera may be especially effective. Most of *The Candidate* is shot in standard feature-film style; but in the scenes set in political rallies, a hand-held camera is used and we are placed in the middle of the crowd and jostled along with the camera—we appear to be watching a documentary, not a feature film starring Robert Redford. Quite apart from what the camera is photographing—the framing and composition—the presence or absence of camera movement carries its own meaning about the pace of the film. As critic Jean Mitry observed:

Thanks to the mobility of the camera, to the multiplicity of shots, I am everywhere at once...I know that I am in a movie theatre, but I feel that I am in the world offered to my gaze, a world that I experience "physically" while identifying myself with one or another of the characters in the drama—with all of them, alternatively. This finally means that at the movies I am both in this action and outside it, in this space and outside this space. Having the gift of ubiquity, I am everywhere and nowhere. (Mitry, 1963, 179; quoted in Affron, 1982, 7)

Camera movements may also serve as a measure of the emotional state of the characters. In the 1962 political thriller *The Manchurian Candidate*, director John Frankenheimer shows a group of brainwashed American soldiers being displayed to communist observers in an amphitheater, but we also see what the soldiers believe is occurring: that they are listening to a garden club lecture. The camera circles the scene, mixing the gentle garden club women with harsh-looking observers, echoing the bewilderment of the brainwashed men.

Composition

The great still photographer Edward Weston (1886-1958) defined composition as "the strongest way of seeing." A film is literally a series of still pictures filmed and projected at twenty-four frames per second. What is and is not in the frame and how the objects in the frame are arranged are fundamental to filmmaking.

Indeed, the nature of the frame itself is fundamental. Films are photographed and viewed in a horizontal rectangle whose standard format (called Standard aperture) is in a width-to-height ratio of 1.85:1.[3] Unlike the still photographer, the film director must deal with a format that cannot be changed to vertical or to different proportions. For the audience to see what it is supposed to see we must look at the director and cinematographer's *mise-en-scène* (French for "to be put into the scene"). The most common way to experience *mise-en-scène* is to watch a film in video format with the audio off: to do so is to respond to the film purely in visual terms.

In the relatively few seconds a particular shot is on the screen, a properly crafted film can speak volumes about characters and situations. The most famous example is found in *Citizen Kane* in which we see the deterioration of the marriage of Charles Foster Kane and his first wife, Emily (Ruth Warrick). In less than three minutes the individual shots and their relationship to each other tell us all we need to know even without dialogue (though the dialogue adds to the effect). In each of five shots the two are seated progressively farther apart at the breakfast table and, in the last, they do not speak at all while Kane's wife defiantly reads a copy of the opposition newspaper. Later in the same film we see Kane and his second wife, Susan, at Kane's estate, Xanadu, both placed to show them isolated from each other and utterly dominated by the house, which has become a prison. In *Dr. Strangelove*, the scenes in the War Room are composed by Stanley Kubrik to show the men sitting around the table dominated by the technology of the room itself. Above them is a ring of light, which not only provides other-worldly illumination but looks suspiciously like a halo.[4] In *Being There* (1979), director Hal Ashby usually keeps the camera some distance from the human characters, thus allowing their physical environment—one of wealth and power—to dominate them and make them appear less powerful than they believe themselves to be. The framing has the effect of making the people look interchangeable, visually reinforcing one of the main themes of the film.

A host of other compositional techniques permit the *mise-en-scène* to be manipulated. In addition to the size of a person or object in the frame, lighting can obscure or highlight an object, as can the presence or absence of movement. Frequently a director can draw the audience's attention by relying on the human tendency to avoid looking at out-of-focus objects. An object out of focus and in the foreground—often this is done with a lamp—can effectively cut the frame in half and temporarily turn the screen's horizontal format into a vertical one.

Camera Placement

The most basic decision about camera placement is establishing from whose point of view a scene is shot. The most common position is the equivalent of what a theater audience sees, called the "objective" point of view, photographing through the "fourth wall" of a room (we see the other three walls but not the one through which we are looking) or from the point of view of an observer outdoors. Consider a scene in which a murderer is stalking a victim: do we see this from the point of view of the murderer, the victim, or through the "fourth wall"? Each alternative has different emotional effects on the audience.

Often such camera placement introduces a sequence of shots beginning with an "establishing shot" to show us the relative placement of characters and setting in a scene, then "two shots" (showing only two characters), and finally close-ups. Often these follow-up shots are subjective in nature, showing us the action from one or more characters's points of view. (Such shots are also called POV shots, for "point of view.") The emotional difference between "objective" and POV photography are great: the former places the audience in the role of an outside—and more detached—observer whereas the latter invites us literally to see the world as a character sees it.[5]

If the norm in camera placement is the "objective" one, typical also is the placement of the camera at eye level. Even a small change in camera height makes a significant emotional difference. Again *Citizen Kane* is a prime example. Much of the film is shot from a low camera placement, requiring that we look up at the characters. Such an angle usually has the effect of making the characters and circumstances larger-than-life. A higher than usual camera placement usually has the opposite effect, making the characters appear weak or defenseless. Tilting the camera to one side tells a visual story of disorientation, whether it is from a character's point of view (perhaps the character has just awakened) or in an establishing shot, when, for instance, a house is shot with a tilted camera to tell us that strange things occur inside.

Editing

While *mise-en-scène* is concerned primarily with individual shots, editing—"cutting"—involves relationships between shots. Editing can radically change the meaning of an individual shot. Alfred Hitchcock described a common example:

If you [film] the man looking, you do his closeup—say it's Mr. [James] Stewart. He looks. And now you cut to what he sees. And you show a woman holding a baby in her arms. Then you cut back to him and he smiles. Now take away the middle piece of film, have his closeup and, instead of cutting to a woman with a baby, cut to a girl in a very risque bikini. Now you see the same smile, but you've changed him from the benevolent gentleman to a dirty old man only by changing one piece of film. (In Schickel, 1975, 285-86)

Older techniques of cutting from one scene to another—the best known is the "wipe," in which one shot appears to push another off the edge of the screen—have largely given way to the instantaneous cut, though older methods of transition are still used in special cases to evoke older films and times past, as in the editing style of *Pennies from Heaven* (1981).

Director Jean-Luc Godard, whose aesthetics as a director were as radical as his politics, claimed that shifting from the usual editing convention of cutting from one character to another in favor of showing all the characters in the same deep-focus shot (where all characters, foreground or background, were in sharp focus) was more democratic. The standard practice of cutting back and forth, called montage, was, Godard claimed, manipulative and a filmmaker could thus "preach liberation in his content, and yet practice repression in his form" (Sarris, 1968, 67).

Probably the most subtle but significant effect of editing, however, is its role is establishing the pace of a film. Brief shots followed by cuts to equally brief shots are a hallmark of most contemporary films. Influenced by the demands of television, which must attract and hold an audience armed with remote controls, commercials have developed an editing style in which many individual images are seen for only a few seconds or less. Films have followed suit. A comparison with older films is instructive in this regard: a great many film classics slowly build to one climax, often in the last scene, as in the airport scene in *Casablanca* or the burning of the sled in *Citizen Kane*. The duration of individual shots, scenes, and the overall pacing of these films are languorous compared to contemporary films, which tend to be constructed as a series of climaxes, both visually and in terms of plot. This often has the paradoxical effect of leaving us pleased with individual scenes but unsatisfied with the film as a whole.[6] The crossover of directors and editors from music videos, commercials, and feature films has exacerbated this: the visual style of many feature films now strongly resembles that of commercials and music videos rather than the reverse. As more than one observer has noted, more and more, movies have come to have a cartoon-like quality, as in the hit *Independence Day* (1996).

All these elements of film craft combine in the experience of film viewing. The attentive movie buff as well as the serious film student (who will view the film a number of times) have much to analyze; the more casual film goer will assimilate greater or lesser portions of the filmmaker's art and craft and come away with a more holistic response to the film without necessarily thinking consciously about props or music or POV shots. It is always useful to recall, however, that it is easy to overanalyze a film, as in the following exchange between two film buffs in Woody Allen's 1980 film *Stardust Memories*:

Character 1: What do you think the significance of the Rolls-Royce was?
Character 2: I think that represents his car.

AUDIENCE

Film has been called the "democratic art" (Jowett, 1976). The first movie houses, called nickelodeons because of their admission prices, charged significantly less than did their chief competitors, vaudeville theaters. Largely set up in storefronts in large cities, they catered to a predominantly working-class audience. As Arthur Schlesinger, Jr., noted, movies "emerged three-quarters of a century ago as a dubious entertainment purveyed by immigrant hustlers to a working-class clientele in storefront holes-in-the-wall scattered throughout the poorer sections of the industrial city" (O'Connor and Jackson, 1975, ix). Not for several years did the size of this audience become clear.

The creation of a huge and largely working-class audience was not an altogether happy development for some members of the middle class. Not for the first or the last time, such a development was viewed with concern, especially by social and political reformers. As Robert Sklar observes:

To these guardians of public morality, the movie theaters were one more example of corrupt institutions and practices that had grown up in the poor and immigrant districts of the new industrial city; they belonged in the same class as brothels, gambling dens and the hangouts of criminal gangs. In a way, they were worse, for the movies appeared to some merely as harmless amusements and thus were an even more insidious trap for the unwary....What was most galling to many in well-to-do city districts, suburbs and small towns was the idea that workingmen and immigrants had found their own source of entertainment and information—a source unsupervised and unapproved by the churches and schools, the critics and professors who served as caretakers and disseminators of the official American culture. (Sklar, 1975, 18-19)

The rise of movies raised questions about the nature of the film audience, about the effects of films on that audience, and finally about efforts to persuade or coerce filmmakers to alter the content of films. The last of these questions will be dealt with in chapter 3; the first two deserve treatment here.

The most significant change in the film audience since the inception of movies is an inversion of its demographics. While the first film audiences were working class and relatively uneducated, the contemporary audience is the opposite, though not extremely so. One-quarter of frequent 1988 moviegoers (those who viewed at least one film per month in the preceding year) had at least some college education; the comparable figure for those with less than a high school education was seven percent (Motion Picture Association of America, 1988, 5). Roughly two-thirds of the audience is thirty years of age or younger, though since the mid-1980s there has been a slight increase in the over-forty segment of the audience, and males still tend to see films more than females. The number of moviegoers of whatever frequency has remained relatively unchanged in recent years; the total movie audience, regardless of frequency of attendance, was 123 million in 1988 (Motion Picture Association of America, 1988, 1).

While this latter figure seems impressive, it must be contrasted with the peak years during and immediately after World War II when average weekly attendance approached ninety million. Beyond its sheer size (in part bolstered by military personnel, who saw movies during their time in the service and continued the habit after), this audience was a more genuinely mass one than its contemporary counterpart. Such a large and loyal audience meant a greater variety of films could be produced with the assurance they would have an audience, if only as the second feature. It meant also that the sheer number of films made could be—had to be, to meet demand—greater. It meant finally that, given the coincidence of the "Golden Age" of Hollywood with the Great Depression, World War II, and the first stirrings of the Cold War, more politically relevant topics were potentially available as raw material for the film factories.

This period saw the height of the movies' influence. As Arthur Schlesinger, Jr., notes of the 1930s:

During that moment, films mattered in American life....A great popular art requires a committed popular audience. That is what existed in the United States in the Thirties....The film had for a moment a vital connection with American life—more, I think, than it ever had before; more certainly than it has had since. The movies were near the operative center of the nation's consciousness. They played an indispensable role in sustaining and stimulating the national imagination. (In Mast, 1982, 420)

And then came television. The demise of the studio system was hastened not just by the Supreme Court's antitrust ruling in 1948 but by the availability of free programming at home, a not unwelcome phenomenon to the post-war generation of parents busy begetting the Baby Boomers.

As the size of the movie audience declined and the studio-as-film-factory waned, filmmakers found themselves dealing with not only a smaller audience but one that could get its entertainment at home for free. In the studios' glory days a box office failure could reasonably be expected to be made up for by a success; not so in the new environment. Much more was at stake and filmmakers became even more cautious out of economic necessity. As Steven Spielberg observed, "Careers begin or end based on one movie. Your membership in the club is extended or denied based on one picture. There's no room for naivete now. Everything has to succeed—or else" (Rosenfield, 1989, 79).

EFFECTS

The concerns expressed in the early days of movies over their allegedly deleterious effects were not expressed in terms of social control or the fear of working-class people congregating in their own places for their own entertainment but instead on the content of the films themselves. Early critics viewed with alarm film portrayals of crime or sex, convinced that such subjects could not but contribute to undesirable behavior. They could cite such films as *The Trapeze Disrobing Act* (1901), *The Pouting Model* and *Water Nymphs* (both 1902), and such 1903 productions as *The Corset Model*, *The Physical Culture Girl*, and *From Showgirl to Burlesque Queen* as examples of the sort of unwholesome films to which the growing movie audience was being exposed.[7]

The new film medium also attracted the attention of the equally new enterprise of social science. One study in 1919, based on an intensive examination of Toledo, Ohio, assessed movies by placing them in a broader setting of alternative entertainment opportunities. Particular attention was paid to the effects of films on children. While the study's author, Reverend John Phelan, noted "moral dangers" that might accompany film-watching, his research was most notable for establishing how dominant a medium movies had become and for its recognition of the context—community and family—in which film attendance occurred (Jowett, 1976, 231-15).

In 1931, Walter Pitkin, an innovator in the field of reading techniques, published an article in which he argued that movies had a considerably greater "psychic intensity" than other media, by which he meant that the stimuli in movies was much greater than, especially, in print media. Pitkin viewed this with alarm and with an obvious class bias: "One minute before the screen excites them [the 'hypersuggestibles'] more than a week of reading crime stories" (quoted in Jowett, 1976, 218). Pitkin expressed particular fear of the effect of movies on the illiterate: "These same people constitute the bulk of the movie fans; they attend the pictures more frequently than our superior classes. From the screen they derive nearly all the joy, the excitement, the sexual thrill, and the underworldly wisdom which they ever acquire" (Pitkin, 1931, 414; quoted in Jowett, 1976, 218). Pitkin's arguments, though they are couched in what now seems quaint language, are not in principle different from contemporary concerns about the mass media, with the exception that the emphasis has shifted to include television and popular music lyrics.

The best known and most ambitious study of movies' effects conducted during Hollywood's "Golden Age" was the Payne Fund Studies, named after the organization that supported them. The research was multi-disciplinary, used a variety of research designs, and, like the Toledo study, examined films in a broad social setting. The most basic finding was that the effects of film on its audience was highly individualized. As the authors concluded in a summary volume:

That the movies exert an influence there can be no doubt. But it is our opinion that this influence is specific to a given child and a given movie. The same picture may influence different children in distinctly different opposite directions...the movies tend to fix and further establish the behavior patterns and types of attitudes which already exist among those who attend most frequently. (Shuttleworth and May, 1933, 93; quoted in Jowett, 1976, 223)

The studies of this era are interesting not just because they represent an attempt to apply the still relatively new techniques of social science to a topic of public concern but because they are snapshots of the period when movies as a mass medium were near their peak of influence.[8]

It is even more difficult to assess the effects of certain types of films on their audience than it is to do the same for films in general. It is one thing for a member of an audience to conclude that a love story is or is not "realistic": most of the audience has its own experiences along such lines. When films address politics the topic is much further removed from the direct experiences of the viewer. But the more overt the politics of a film the less likely an apolitical viewer is to see such a film. That is why the implied politics of films is so important, for it is precisely the kind of political communication most likely to be seen by the less politically aware. Exposure—perhaps inadvertent—to more overtly political films is probably most effective on a less politically aware audience precisely because it lacks alternative points of reference.

In the end, however, attempts to assess the effects of film on its audience must fail. Much more so than in the days of the Payne Fund studies, American culture provides so many messages from so many sources that attempts to disentangle one from the others must at best be uncertain and at worst wildly misleading. If we conclude that *The Graduate* (1964) or *The Big Chill* (1983) somehow epitomize an era, it is useful to recall that these are retrospective judgments and that many other films, produced at the same time with equal attention to the audience and with equally high hopes, fell from our collective memory. Films do not in any meaningful way predict, nor do they in any meaningful way "cause" later similar events; at best they anticipate and they epitomize.[9] We watch movies to be entertained; but as with any other experience in our lives, what we take from them, individually or collectively, tells us more about ourselves than it does about the film.

NOTES

1. Many of Bernard Herrmann's scores were written for Hitchcock films. In the 1956 version of *The Man Who Knew Too Much* (Hitchcock also directed another version of the same story in 1934), the director honored his longtime collaborator in a scene at the Royal Albert Hall in London showing a poster reading "Bernard Herrmann Conducting the London Philharmonic" and giving Herrmann close-ups on the podium.

2. In at least one case, slow camera movement uncovers a clever visual reference. In the opening sequence of *Back to the Future* (1985), director Robert Zemeckis has the camera pan slowly over the workshop of the scientist played by Christopher Lloyd, showing us equipment and timepieces to establish the science fiction and time-travel theme of the film. For the briefest of times, we see one piece of equipment labeled "CRM 114," which is the name of the decoder aboard the bomber in *Dr. Strangelove, or: How I Learned to Stop Worrying and Love the Bomb.*

3. Silent films were shot with a format, called the aspect ratio, of nearly 1:1. In the 1930s and 1940s, the ratio (called Academy aperture) was 1:1.33. The difference in aspect ratio between film and television screens has led to the practice in home video of either chopping off part of the film image or "panning and scanning," in which the video image is comprised of sweeps across the original film image. The most effective way of dealing with the problem thus far is "letterboxing," in which the entire original film image is placed inside the television screen, complete but smaller. Another response has been to alter the composition of movie shots by placing more elements toward the center of the frame, permitting them to be more easily contained within the frame of a television screen.

4. In a scene in *The Candidate* there is an example—intended or not—of a visual pun based on composition. Robert Redford stands before a wall covered with wallpaper in a stylized sunburst pattern. Shot from a slightly lower than usual camera position, Redford appears to wear the pattern as though it were a crown and looks, briefly, like the head of the Statue of Liberty.

5. Alfred Hitchcock's *Rear Window* (1954) is an especially interesting example of the objective versus subjective camera position. James Stewart's character, L.B. Jeffries,

spies on his neighbors across a courtyard by looking into their windows, sometimes with the help of his camera's telephoto lens. It is hard not to see this as an amusing but telling commentary on both movie directors and the audience: the windows into which Jeffries peers look like movie screens, each showing its unique film.

6. Consider Ebert's (1989, 941) definition of the "Self-Repeating Inevitable Climax": "In the age of the seven minute attention span, one climax per movie will no longer do. Thus movies like the *Friday the 13th* series are constructed out of several seven-minute segments. At the end of each segment, another teenager is dead. When all the teenagers are dead (or, if you arrived in the middle, when the same dead teenager turns up twice), the movie is over."

7. It is important to recall that many of the reformers of this period were largely on the political Left, and not, as is the case with many contemporary critics of film and television, on the Right. Much of this turn-of-the-century reformist zeal combined traditional middle-class and nativist concerns about propriety, convention, and adaptation to U.S. society with outrage at economic exploitation of newly arrived immigrants, especially children.

8. Movies' biggest competitor was radio, whose influence in this period should not be forgotten: recall the legendary 1938 broadcast by Orson Welles's Mercury Theater of H.G. Wells's *The War of the Worlds*, which convinced thousands the earth was being invaded by Martians. The power of radio was acknowledged by theater operators when they broadcast the popular Amos 'n' Andy program in theater lobbies.

9. An interesting example of this sort of analysis is Siegfried Kracauer's *From Caligari to Hitler* (1957), which argued that the rise of Hitler could be inferred from German films of the 1920s. While the study illustrates the ease with which cultural evidence can be marshalled in support of subsequent events, it nonetheless underscores the importance of attempting to assess the variety of themes that may be present in a culture at a particular time.

3

POLITICS AND THE FILM INDUSTRY

The history of movies is clear on one point: people in and out of the industry have behaved as though movies make a difference, as though they are powerful. From the beginning, movies were the target of attempts from without to control their content; these were succeeded by efforts from within to do the same. In one case, movie executives directed a campaign, using film as a weapon, to defeat a candidate in an election in the movies' home state of California. And of course there was the blacklist, the best known episode in the history of politics and film.

CENSORSHIP

Movies are politically unique: they are the first genuinely mass entertainment medium whose perceived influence stimulated political action but whose legal status, as it related to the First Amendment, was unclear. The result was a spate of attempts to censor the content of movies.

The initial arena was local. Both Chicago and New York City, the largest markets in the early years of the medium, saw local reformers organize against films. In 1907, Chicago passed an ordinance enabling the police department to issue permits for the exhibition of movies. In the same year the mayor of New York, George McClellan, revoked the licenses of all of the roughly 550 movie houses in the city, generating an immediate response by exhibitors, who successfully sought an injunction against the action. A local board of review was created as a compromise. In both cities those in favor of censorship were a coalition of secular reformers and religious leaders, the latter concerned not just because of their belief that movies damaged the public morals but because movies damaged church attendance: Sundays were the biggest moviegoing day.

Despite the legal ability to enact municipal censorship ordinances most cities chose not to do so: a 1929 survey found that only 100 of 2500 cities with over

2500 inhabitants had any type of censorship board or official (Jowett, 1975, 114). Those that did usually ceded the power to their police departments; the remainder created local censorship boards, though these were often also under the control of the police.   Most of the boards that did exist did nothing. Monitoring films in a time when theaters changed their programs weekly and showed several films per program was difficult at best. Other ordinances, like one in New York that mandated that no one under sixteen years of age attend a film without an adult, were impossible to enforce, especially when exhibitors helpfully provided adults to accompany the young through the door. As with many other such efforts the prime political function of creating local censorship boards was to placate those who demanded them.

Municipal censorship was therefore largely a fiction—not widespread and impotent where it did exist. Censorship at the state level was another matter. The potential economic loss to the industry was much greater if a film was banned in an entire state, and it was in the states that the industry made its most vigorous legal stands and where it suffered its worst legal defeat.

Ohio created the second state film censorship board in 1913 (the first was Pennsylvania in 1911) and other states quickly followed. The Ohio law was challenged by a Detroit film distributor, and in 1915 the United States Supreme Court ruled in *Mutual Film Corporation v. Ohio* that the Ohio law creating the state's censorship board—essentially permitting prior censorship of films—was constitutional and that the First Amendment did not apply to films. The Court held:

It cannot be put out of view that the exhibition of moving pictures is a business pure and simple, originated and conducted for profit, like other spectacles, not to be regarded, nor intended to be regarded as part of the press of the country or as organs of public opinion. They are mere representations of events, of ideas and sentiments published or known; vivid, useful, and entertaining, no doubt, but...capable of evil, having power for it, the greater because of their attractiveness and manner of exhibition. (Quoted in Jowett, 1976, 120)

The decision was based on what would now be seen—and was seen by some in 1915—as spurious grounds. Acknowledging that movies were a business in justification of exempting them from First Amendment protection was irrelevant: publishers, protected by the First Amendment, also made money. The second basis—that movies were "spectacles" and not part of the press—reflected more about public attitudes toward films than it did about the quality of the films themselves, for by this time the medium had produced its share of serious work as well as froth, just as had the print medium. The final argument—that films were "capable of evil"—likewise failed to distinguish films from any other form of communication. It was not to be until the 1952 decision in *Burstyn v. Wilson* that the Supreme Court ruled that films were covered by the First Amendment.[1] It is a telling commentary on the politics and economics of the film industry that both the 1915 and 1952 cases were brought by small film distribution firms, which economically could ill afford censorship. The major studios were satisfied with the legal status quo: their economic interests still safe, they were not interested in the First Amendment status of films.

The fear that the Court's decision would open the door for more censorship efforts led the industry to attempt to forestall further government action.[2] One such effort was the "Seabury Proposal," named after William Seabury, general counsel to the National Association of the Motion Picture Industry, a trade group. Seabury proposed that films be defined and regulated as public utilities under federal law, thus insuring that "better" films would be produced and, not incidentally, providing a stable economic environment for filmmakers. Few, however, took the Seabury proposal seriously.

A more important response, prior to the 1915 *Mutual Film* case, was the creation in 1909 of the National Board of Review (the name, changed a few years after its creation, originally used "censorship" in place of "review"). The board was an outgrowth of the censorship board created in New York City in the aftermath of Mayor McClellan's order closing the city's theaters. The Board, while never an official industry organization, was financed by film producers. Rather than operate as a national censorship board—which it lacked the mandate and the resources to do in any event—the Board instead emphasized public relations, creating in 1916 the National Committee for Better Films, which published lists of Board-approved films, such as "Pictures Boys Want and Grown-Ups Endorse" and "Motion Picture Aids to Sermons" (Jowett, 1976, 128). Politically the Board was a qualified success: its activities served to deflect legislative efforts at censorship while it was at the same time more liberal in its treatment of films than were most state censorship boards. Though it seemed a fine solution for the industry, it was not enough. As the United States entered the Roaring Twenties and the Prohibition Era, criticism of the movies increased.

Much of this criticism again came from religious groups and much of it was focused on sex in movies, a subject not unknown in films but one which critics now believed was getting too much attention with the arrival of the 1920s version of the emancipated woman, the flapper, and the coming of Prohibition in 1920. A flurry of sensational cases, widely reported in the press, reinforced the reputation of Hollywood as a den of iniquity. The most sensational involved silent film comedian Roscoe "Fatty" Arbuckle, who was tried in 1921 for the rape and murder of a young actress after a party. That Arbuckle was ultimately acquitted after several trials was little comfort to the industry. A final consideration was the economics of the movies: by 1918 the brisk but chaotic early growth of the industry had abated and stabilization and consolidation were desirable. The film industry of the early 1920s faced economic stagnation, a poor public reputation, and political assault.

HAYS

Into this breach stepped Will H. Hays, postmaster general under President Warren G. Harding. Hays, an elder of the Presbyterian Church and a solid Republican, was a highly public symbol of the industry's desire to regulate itself before government did.

A skilled administrator and philosophically opposed to censorship, Hays faced a hostile political environment: thirty-two states were considering censorship legislation when Hays was appointed president of the newly created Motion Picture Producers and Distributors of America in 1922. One of his first tasks was one of his most important—opposing a film censorship referendum in Massachusetts. Hays, aided by the substantial financial resources a nervous industry provided, meticulously organized a campaign to fight the referendum, which lost by a margin of more than two to one. Hays also spent considerable time lobbying in the states to ward off censorship legislation as well as regularly urging the virtues of restraint on filmmakers.

Much of Hays's work involved public relations, a strategy based on the hope that a favorable public opinion climate would buy the industry time to sort itself out with the public, with government, and with an increasingly nervous financial community. In these efforts Hays was never entirely successful. His powers were limited at best, but his primary liability was presiding over a fiercely competitive, vertically integrated industry run by men—the studio heads—who brooked little opposition. The arrival in films of Broadway star Mae West, legendary for her aggressively sexual stage persona and her double entendre dialogue (she sang songs entitled "A Guy What Takes His Time" and "I Wonder Where My Easy Rider's Gone" in the 1933 film *She Done Him Wrong*), only fueled the drive to clean up films. Nor did it help that Claudette Colbert took a suggestive milk bath in *Cleopatra* (1934); that Hedy Lamarr swam nude in the Czech import *Ecstasy (1933)*, or that a group of young actresses in *Murder at the Vanities* (1934) praised the pleasures of "sweet marijuana." The zeal with which movies portrayed the newly discovered world of the gangster (the 1932 *Scarface* was one of the best such films and also one of the most attacked for its violence) only added to the pressure.

In 1934 the politics of film censorship reached a watershed when Roman Catholic bishops created the Catholic Legion of Decency to review films, a particularly worrisome development to movie people because, while Roman Catholics were not necessarily more censorious of films than members of other religions, they were far better organized. The new organization quickly received support from some Protestant and Jewish groups. Members of the Legion of Decency were asked to sign a pledge reading in part:

I wish to join the Legion of Decency, which condemns vile and unwholesome moving pictures. I unite with all who protest against them as a grave menace to youth, to home life, to country and to religion....Considering these evils, I hereby promise to remain away from all motion pictures except those which do not offend decency and Christian morality. I promise further to secure as many members as possible for the Legion of Decency. (Jowett, 1976, 250-51)

At this same time the Payne Fund studies were being published in a series of volumes. While their findings about the effects of films were for the time cautious and reasonable, the first volume in the series, *Our Movie Made Children* published in 1933 by Henry James Forman, received the most attention despite being correctly denounced as intellectually unsound and inflammatory.

This book, widely read and discussed, only added to the pressure to do something about the movies.[3] In his book, Forman told the story of the fictional Jack and Joan who are going to the movies, attracted by a "honey of a poster" featuring a "highly colored lithograph of a man embracing and kissing a girl":

Both Jack and Joan are lovely children, for are they not yours and your neighbors? You want them to enjoy themselves, but there may just be a faint uneasiness in our mind. Those movies! You cannot help wondering whether they are wholly good or wholly profitable for the young people. Of course, you yourself go to the movies, but then you are a mature adult and understand that much of the stuff is just so much hokum. It is different with the children, so eager and naive, so inexperienced in life. (Forman, 1933, 28)

By 1933, the year prior to the Legion of Decency's creation, the film industry also faced new economic problems: audiences and revenues had declined for five successive years. Weekly attendance figures were down forty percent from 1929. In 1932, Paramount and RKO were in receivership, and Universal and Fox seemed to be next. No one in the industry felt secure. While much of this was the result of the Great Depression, the threat of a well organized national boycott, never attractive, was now unthinkable. The industry sued for peace. Will Hays offered the victorious critics the Production Code Administration, an industry creation whose job it was vigorously to enforce the Motion Production Code, which had already existed for several years.

CODE

The enforcement of the Code was a political response from the industry intended to assure the public and government that film people were ready to regulate themselves. The industry's need for a more detailed code (a vestigial predecessor created in 1927 was called the "Don'ts and be Carefuls," and prior to that there was an even briefer guideline called "The Formula") was based in part on fears that in the post-Depression economic decline the movies' fortunes would spawn more films with themes of sex and crime, leading in turn to more demands for government regulation. The Code was drafted with Hays's approval by Martin Quigley, a publisher of movie trade papers and magazines and a prominent Catholic layman, and Daniel Lord, a Jesuit and professor of Dramatics at St. Louis University (Moley, 1945, chap. 5). That these men were invited by Hays to draft a code reflected Hays's political judgment that religious figures would be useful, perhaps essential, allies. The creation of the Code by Quigley and Lord and the role of the Catholic Legion of Decency in pressing the issue of its enforcement through the Production Code Administration placed in sharp relief a fact that had long characterized the politics of movies: a disproportionately Jewish industry (particularly with respect to studio ownership and management) was under attack from Protestant and especially Catholic critics. This tension was to resurface later during World War II and the blacklist era.

The word "moral" or its derivatives appeared nearly thirty times in the text of the Code: "sin," "evil," "good," and "bad" were also prominently featured. The premise of the industry's critics became the premise of the Code: movies were unique and powerful and in consequence had a moral responsibility to society: "In general, the mobility, popularity, accessibility, emotional appeal, vividness, straight-forward presentation of fact in the film make for more intimate contact with a larger audience and for greater emotional appeal" (Motion Picture Producers and Distributors of America [MPPDA], 1930; in Mast, 1982, 324.) The Code's premises also echoed the Supreme Court's reasoning in the *Mutual Film Corporation* case that movies were a uniquely powerful medium and reflected the Catholic auspices under which it had been written in its reference to natural law, a prominent feature of Roman Catholic theology.

Three general principles underlay the Production Code:

1. No picture shall be produced which will lower the moral standards of those who see it. Hence the sympathy of the audience shall never be thrown to the side of crime, wrong-doing, evil or sin.
2. Correct standards of life, subject only to the requirements of drama and entertainment, shall be presented.
3. Law, natural or human, shall not be ridiculed, nor shall sympathy be shown for its violators.

                                              (MPPDA, 1930, in Mast, 1982, 324-25)

In its specifics the Code was largely negative: it told filmmakers what they could not do. In addition to sections dealing with general topics, the Code addressed a number of details, including the following:

[Crimes] shall never be presented in such a way as to throw sympathy with the crime as against law and justice or to inspire others with a desire for imitation.

The technique of murder must be presented in a way that will not inspire imitation.

The illegal drug traffic must not be portrayed in such a way as to stimulate curiosity concerning the use of, or traffic in, such drugs; nor shall scenes be approved which show the use of illegal drugs, or their effects, in detail (as amended September 11, 1946).

Excessive and lustful kissing, lustful embraces, suggestive postures and gestures are not to be shown.

Miscegenation (sex relationship between the white and black races) is forbidden.

Obscenity in word, gesture, reference, song, joke, or by suggestion (even when likely to be understood only by part of the audience) is forbidden.

Indecent or undue exposure is forbidden.

Dances which emphasize indecent movements are to be regarded as obscene.

No film or episode may throw ridicule on any religious faith.

The history, institutions, prominent people, and citizenry of all nations shall be represented fairly.

                                              (Quoted in Mast, 1982, 328-31)

Responsibility for administering the Code was given to Joseph Ignatius Breen, a Catholic layman and former newspaperman who had worked under Will Hays. Breen, recruited for the position by Code coauthor Martin Quigley, quickly became identified with his position and the Production Code Administration soon became known as the Breen Office. The term was not just as matter of convenience: the language of the Code was open to interpretation and the interpretation was Breen's. The Breen Office was to govern movies for the next three decades.

The Breen Office's role in the film industry was comprehensive: it extended from discussions with producers about proposed films through detailed examinations of scripts to the screening of films. Films that did not meet the Breen Office's standards were changed. Failure to comply resulted in denial of the Production Code Administration's seal, which essentially denied theatrical release to a film.[4] Failure to comply could also result in a maximum fine of $25,000, though there is no record that this high a fine was ever assessed. (The best known use of a fine was for the "Frankly, my dear, I don't give a damn" delivered by Rhett Butler in *Gone with the Wind* (1939), which cost producer David Selznik $5000. The suggested revision was "Frankly, I don't care.")

Hollywood legend is filled with examples of deletions demanded by the Breen office: that a dissolve in a film (the fading of one scene into another) be eliminated because the technique suggested that a husband and wife were about to have sex; that kissing never be horizontal; that cows' udders not be shown; that scenes in bathrooms not show toilets; that a fight scene substitute gypsies for Mexicans because gypsies, lacking a home country, would not violate code restrictions on casting aspersions on nationalities.

Inevitably filmmakers found ways to work around the Production Code. Again the examples are legendary. Because the code, as administered, permitted kisses of only three seconds' duration, Alfred Hitchcock directed Ingrid Bergman and Cary Grant in a scene from *Notorious* (1946) in which they kiss for three seconds, barely to separate their lips, kiss again, nibble each others' ears, kiss again, talk (about food!), then kiss again. The scene wonderfully violated the spirit of Code while complying with it. The discrete lowering of window shades, the first kiss—usually in the final scene—are hallowed movie conventions. Absent the Production Code, we surely would have seen fewer of them. (For a brief history of the Code and its enforcement, along with case studies of some of the most famous cases involving the Code, see Leff and Simmons, 1990.)

Such gambits illustrate one of the appeals of movies made under the Code: filmmakers were forced to express covertly what they could not express overtly. The Code mandated subtlety if not outright subterfuge, and in doing so, challenged filmmakers to make movies whose indirection we still find clever and charming. But life under the Code had a much more profound and elusive effect on films. Anthropologist Hortense Powdermaker studied Hollywood in the late 1940s as though she were studying a foreign culture, which, in a fashion, she was. Her characterization of the nature of the Code and the reasons for its existence are apt:

The Hollywood taboos embodied in the self-imposed Production Code have the same psychological origin as do those of primitive man, fear. But they differ in that they do not represent the actual beliefs, values, or behavior of the people practicing them. Taboos in Hollywood apply not to the personal lives of the makers of movies, but to the content of movies, and the fears are not of the supernatural, but of a quite specific threat in this world, censorship. (Powdermaker, 1950, 55)

The Code-imposed taboos are significant less for the kinds of films that were made under the eye of the Breen Office than for the kinds of films that were not. The height of the Breen Office's greatest power coincided with the aftermath of the Great Depression, the coming of the New Deal with its profound political and economic changes, the rise of fascism and militarism in Europe and Japan, with the isolationism debate in the United States, the Cold War, and the early stirrings of the civil rights movement. The height of the Breen Office's power also occurred precisely during the time moviegoing became a national habit, when the studios were at their peak, and when the mass audience was most fully acquiring its film vocabulary—its sense of what movies were like and what they were about. Precisely because the Breen Office was a constant during this time, it is easy to underestimate or even to forget its comprehensive importance. Whatever sense of reality—whatever lessons—we draw from the films of the "Golden Age" of Hollywood are conditioned not only by the commercial constraints of film production but by the political reality that for nearly thirty years all films made in the United States were censored. That this censorship was self-imposed makes it no less real. At the core of the Code lay hypocrisy: movies ignored or sugarcoated realities known to all in their audience. Part of the reason that movies are described in terms of escapism and of fantasy must be traced to the effects of censorship and not simply to the inherently wish-fulfilling nature of mass entertainments.

The Code, based on conservative Roman Catholicism and secular middle-class notions of propriety, mandated that the world be portrayed always as a just place (wrong-doing must always be punished); that there be no direct (or even many indirect) references to sex, even among married couples; that no references be made to birth control (anathema to the devout Breen, who called it a "paganistic-Protestant viewpoint"); that no country or its leaders be placed in an unattractive light. The Breen Office virtually legislated the happy ending and also denied filmmakers a huge range of social and political topics at a time when they were not only available but widely presented in other mass media. Social and political subjects, never prominent, dropped sharply in number after the Breen Office came into existence (Koppes and Black, 1987, 15).

As Powdermaker (1950, 78) concluded, "The Code simply does not belong to this world." And she went on to observe:

Many people in and out of Hollywood have made the Code, the Legion of Decency, and other pressure groups into stereotyped villains. Perhaps they are not so much villainous as unintelligent and ineffectual in dealing with the important problem of morality. Neither they nor Hollywood would appear aware that the biggest taboo in the making of movies is an unwritten one. It is a taboo against man. (Powdermaker, 1950, 81)

While we can never assess what movies might have been like without the Code, its presence helps explain the number of costume dramas, biographical films, family melodramas, musical and dance movies that Hollywood produced under the gaze of the Breen Office. To attempt to read a society's sense of politics from its films requires that we be aware that a society, through politics, may limit what those films say. The successive cycles of criticism, threat, and response culminating in self-regulation that the film industry experienced were not unusual in American history; all the mass media have gone through some variation of them.

SINCLAIR

If the industry bowed to political pressure, however, it was also willing to exercise it, if not in the service of artistic freedom then in the service of its economic interests and the political preferences of its most powerful men. Upton Sinclair was a muckraking writer and a socialist. His political proclivities and his profession united in his novel *The Jungle*, which graphically portrayed the sanitation conditions and exploitation of workers in the meat-packing industry of Chicago. The novel generated public outrage, which led to legislation designed to improve the situation. Between books Sinclair ran unsuccessfully as the Socialist party candidate in California for the House and Senate. He also wrote the novel that was the basis for the 1932 film *The Wet Parade* (a tale of Prohibition) produced, ironically, by one of the most politically conservative of the studios, MGM. (Irving Thalberg, head of production at MGM, told story editor Sam Marx to "Keep that Bolshevik [Sinclair] away from me" [Gabler, 1988, 312].)

By 1934, Sinclair had become an enthusiastic supporter of Franklin Roosevelt's New Deal, and he switched his allegiance to the Democrats and ran successfully for the Democratic nomination for governor. His Republican opponent in the general election was the incumbent governor, Robert Merriam, a colorless conservative.

Socialist past or not, Sinclair had a chance. He was an affable and unassuming man, not easily painted as a bomb-thrower, and he was running in the afterglow of the arrival of the New Deal in a state in economic trouble. In 1934 twenty percent of the residents of Los Angeles County survived on welfare at a rate of $16.20 per month per family (Ceplair and Englund, 1983, 90). In the preceding year, California's large agricultural sector saw widespread strikes by workers throughout the San Joaquin Valley. Forces of strike-breakers, financed by agricultural employers, broke up strike meetings and attacked union headquarters.

Sinclair represented a threat—an electable threat—to established economic interests with his share-the-wealth "End Poverty in California" (EPIC) program. The film industry was no less opposed than any other large business to Sinclair's income redistribution proposals, but it also had its own unique reason for wanting Sinclair defeated, for Sinclair had played a major role in an episode that embarrassingly exposed Hollywood's political and economic infighting.

In 1932, Sinclair had been approached by William Fox, the recently deposed head of Fox Film Corporation. Fox had risen from nickelodeon operator in 1904 to owner of Fox Film by the end of the 1920s, then had purchased a controlling interest in Loew's, Inc., the parent company of MGM. Fox was on the verge of becoming the most powerful man in movies when the stock market crash of 1929 and government antitrust action forced him to sell his shares in Loew's to a group of bankers for $18 million. Fox was convinced that Nicholas Schenck, a top executive at Loew's; Louis B. Mayer, the top man at MGM; and banking interests had destroyed him (Gabler, 1989, 313).

Fox wanted Sinclair to hear his grievances and vent them in a book. Three times a week Fox and his lawyer, the latter armed with documents, came to Sinclair's home in Pasadena. Sinclair asked questions as Fox bitterly attacked his own industry and a stenographer recorded it all. After completing an initial draft of the book, Sinclair sent it to Fox, who had returned home to New York; Sinclair heard nothing for several weeks. As he later wrote in his autobiography, he learned "that Fox was using the threat of publishing my manuscript in an effort to get back some of the properties of which he had been deprived" (Sinclair, 1962, 276). After Sinclair verified this, he immediately notified his publisher to put the book into print. Fox's demand that Sinclair not publish came too late.

"When those beautiful yellow-covered books hit Hollywood," Sinclair later wrote, "it was with a bang that might have been heard at the moon if there had been anybody there to listen" (Sinclair, 1962, 276). Beyond exposing the corporate politics of the film industry and painting an ugly picture of the men at the top of it and the bankers who financed it, Sinclair's book, entitled *Upton Sinclair Presents William Fox* (1933), offered such proposals as nationalizing the film industry and the suggestion that the State of California make movies and run theaters in competition with private producers and exhibitors. These proposals were anathema to the industry. At Fox Pictures, the word went out that anyone caught with the book would be fired immediately. The former Socialist and foe of big business had now earned the deep enmity of the film industry, and the industry was quick to respond. Joseph Schenck, founder, with Darryl Zanuck, of 20th Century and soon to become chairman of the new 20th Century-Fox company threatened, "I'll move the studios to Florida, sure as fate, if Sinclair is elected" (quoted in Gabler, 1989, 314).

Both the movie and publishing interests went after Sinclair. The *Los Angeles Times*, at the time a strongly conservative and anti-union paper, published photographs in October of 1934 purporting to show a freight car filled with hobos happily heading to California to live off EPIC's generosity. The Hearst-run *Los Angeles Examiner* published a similar photograph. Neither picture was legitimate. The *Examiner* photograph was staged, using actors hired by the studios; the *Times* picture was a still from the Warner Brothers movie *Wild Boys of the Road* (1933), a "social conscience" film from the most liberal of the Hollywood studios.

The studios responded to the Sinclair threat with money: producers "asked" that all employees making more than $90 per week contribute a day's pay to the Merriam campaign. Writers, regardless of their politics, protested immediately. The newly created Screen Writers Guild passed a resolution condemning the coercion implicit in the request (Ceplair and Englund, 1980, 92; see also

Mitchell, 1992). The studios nonetheless raised an estimated half million dollars against Sinclair.

More importantly, the studios enlisted their own medium in the campaign against Sinclair, producing a series of short films called *The Inquiring Reporter* that looked like the newsreels shown as a regular part of movie programs. One showed the inquiring reporter asking a sweet and frail old woman standing in front of her house—an actress playing a role, as it turned out—whom she was supporting for governor. "I am voting for Governor Merriam," she said in a quavering voice. "Why, Mother?" "Because I want to have my little home. It is all I have left in the world."

Lest the point be lost, another showed a whiskered and disheveled man speaking heavily accented English telling the reporter, "Vy, I am foting for Seenclair." Why? "Vell, his seestem vorked vell in Russia, vy can't it vork here?" The legitimate Metrotone News newsreel showed clean and upright Californians expressing support for Merriam, while "the Sinclair advocates were unshaven poorly dressed and obviously uneducated" (Ceplair and Englund, 1980, 91).

In one description of the faked newsreels, the Sinclair people "…scratched themselves as they spoke. They were dishevelled, bleary-eyed, shabby and scrofulous, They stammered or lisped or spoke in squeaky voices. They proclaimed that they were for Sinclair because he meant soft jobs and easy money. A few openly admitted they they were Communists" (quoted in Fielding, 1972, 268).

Samuel Marx, head of the MGM story department and the man whose job it had been to "keep that Bolshevik" Sinclair away from Irving Thalberg, later admitted that footage of "respectable people" who supported Sinclair "ended on the cutting room floor along with shots of tramps who supported Merriam" (Ceplair and Englund, 1980, 91).

Sinclair lost, though to attribute that loss to the efforts of the film industry would be incorrect. Audiences, for one thing, often responded to the phony newsreels with derisive laughter. Far more important, however, was the presence on the ballot of a Progressive party candidate who criticized Sinclair more than he did Merriam and who split the Democratic/Left vote with Sinclair. Given a clear field and then-current economic conditions, Sinclair had a chance despite the fabrications of newspapers and movies. But if anything led to his defeat it was, ironically, the presence of economic conditions that encouraged two leftist candidates to enter the race and divide the vote.

More interesting than the effects the film campaign might have had on the election was the eagerness with which the industry entered electoral politics at the same time it was so gingerly handling the issue of censorship. The industry's preferences and tactics were certainly no secret. The trade paper *Variety* reported in October of 1934, "Trailers attacking the candidacy of Upton Sinclair for governor are being prepared at several of the studios, for screening in theatres throughout the state during the remaining two weeks preceding the November election" (*Variety*, October 13, 1934, quoted in Ceplair and Englund, 1980, 91). Another trade paper, *The Hollywood Reporter* happily reported, "This campaign against Upton Sinclair has been and is dynamite. When the picture business gets aroused, it becomes AROUSED, and boy, how they can go at it. It is the most effective piece of political humdingery that has ever been effected" (quoted in Gabler, 1988, 314).

After the election, in a heated discussion at a Hollywood party about the ethics of the industry's fake newsreel campaign, actor Fredric March was told by Irving Thalberg that Thalberg had created the fake newsreels. "But it was a dirty trick! It was the damndest unfairest thing I've ever heard of!" the strongly liberal March said. "Nothing is unfair in politics," Thalberg replied calmly. "We could sit down here and figure dirty things out all night, and every one of them would be all right in a political campaign." Recalling the childhood speeches he gave for the Socialist party in New York City that were broken up by Tammany Hall workers, Thalberg told March, "Fairness in an election campaign is a contradiction in terms. It just doesn't exist" (quoted in Gabler, 1988, 315).

That a youthful Socialist might change his politics is not surprising; that he might act in his economic self-interest is likewise not unusual; that he would deliberately prostitute his own medium is perhaps less easily justified. Thalberg's admission illustrated a long-standing political tension within the film industry: profound conservatism in its topmost echelons less widely shared by others, especially writers, directors, and performers. In this the movie business was no different from other industries: one expects the ownership and management of business to have different interests than labor, even if the labor is as well paid as movie labor. This is what happened in the California election of 1934. Rightist writers like Morrie Ryskind and leftist ones like Dorothy Parker united in opposition to the studios' demands that they "donate" some of their pay to the Merriam campaign. The political alliances formed during the 1934 campaign, especially among writers, were to persist long after the votes were counted and would surface again during the blacklist period. While these alliances were largely organized along Left-Right ideological lines, there was also an additional and not always parallel management-labor dimension.

The campaign against Sinclair tells much about another aspect of the politics of the film industry that goes beyond questions of economic interest or political ideology. As Gabler noted:

At its topmost levels, Hollywood was a reactionary enclave of Jews wearing the fashions of American gentility and giving no quarter to anyone who threatened their pretensions to prestige. Politically, genteel fashion dictated fealty to the Republican party, though until the late twenties *most* of the Eastern European immigrant Jews had affiliated with the Republicans, largely because most of them had emigrated during a Republican administration early in the century and wanted to express their gratitude to the party in power, but also because most German Jews, who served as models for Eastern Europeans, were Republicans. Adolph Zukor said he became a Republican "because all the people I knew were Republicans"....Of course there was an economic as well as a psychological basis for their Republicanism. By the mid-thirties nineteen of the twenty-five highest salaries in America and forty of the highest sixty-three went to film executives. (Gabler, 1988, 315)

The political realignment that had begun in 1928 with the Democrats' nomination of New York governor Al Smith, the first Roman Catholic to be nominated for president, and that culminated in the election of Franklin Roosevelt in 1932 moved large numbers of the urban poor and ethnic groups into the Democratic party, establishing the basis of American party politics for the next half-century. But as Gabler notes;

The Hollywood Jews never realigned, and most felt little real affinity with the forgotten men of the Depression—at least most of them never wanted to exhibit any affinity...The Hollywood Jews were after acceptance from those they regarded as their betters, and they saw their community of interests lying with the rich and the powerful of Los Angeles—a conservative lot in a deeply conservative place. (Gabler, 1988, 315)

And as Otto Friedrich observed about the same phenomenon:

In America...Jews clung to their belief in assimilation, the belief that if one behaved like everyone else, then one would be considered to *be* just like everyone else, a good American. In Hollywood, stars assumed neutral names like Fairbanks or Howard or Shaw; actresses underwent plastic surgery; some made a point of going to Christian churches or donating money to Christian charities. This was not so much a denial of Jewishness—though it was also that—as an effort to make Jewishness appear insignificant, too unimportant to be criticized, or even noticed. (Friedrich, 1987, 48)

There is in the history of movie censorship and the Sinclair campaign at least these small ironies: that an industry damned for the licentiousness of its product and its people should be run by deeply conservative men eager to be accepted; that an industry preeminently American in its mythology should be run largely by East European immigrants or their heirs, who seemed to understand the dreamscape of the United States better than those who were native-born; and that much of the politics and economics of this hard-headed and massively profitable industry should finally turn on religion.

BLACKLIST

With the significant exception of World War II, the film industry's next major confrontation with politics came during the period now called the blacklist era, beginning in the immediate aftermath of the war and extending to the beginnings of the cold war. On the surface post-World War II America was a happy place, victorious in war and enjoying the economic benefits of pent-up consumer demand. *Time, Life,* and *Fortune* publisher Henry R. Luce called the twentieth century the "American Century," so certain was he that American political and economic institutions would eventually predominate around the world. A number of American intellectuals, observing that the United States had avoided the tragic excesses of German, Italian, and Japanese fascism and militarism and Stalinist communism, proclaimed the "End of Ideology" and the triumph of American technology, politics, and economic institutions. (For a discussion of this movement, see Waxman, 1969; and Rejai, 1971.)

Below this surface there were signs of unease, however. Maverick academics and social critics, such as William H. Whyte, David Riesman, and C. Wright Mills, wrote books decrying conformity and finding American social and political institutions to be less than advertised in what Mills sneeringly called "The American Celebration" (see Mills, 1956). In the arts, novelists found men in grey flannel suits living quietly unhappy lives; the Beat poets mocked middle-class values; and photographers like Robert Frank showed images (Frank, 1979) of 1950s America far different from those we were to see in the advertisements of the period or that were later recalled in television programs like "Happy Days."

The anti-Communist impulse that began in the late 1940s took root in a society that defended itself with an awkward mixture of ferocity and an uncertainty that belied expressions of pride in American society. The rise of the Soviet Union as the other great superpower in the postwar world, for reasons both substantive and symbolic, came to be the focus of this uncertainty for many Americans. The anti-Communist impulse was to express itself not only in foreign and military policy but also in a fear of domestic subversion—less in a fear of the Soviet Union than of disloyal Americans.

That such uncertainty should be so deeply present in a country busily telling itself that all was well is a major irony of the post-World War II era and helps explain the intensity of the anti-Communist impulse of which the blacklist was a part. In contrasting nineteenth-century rightist movements with their postwar successors, historian Richard Hofstadter noted this difference:

The spokesmen for those earlier movements felt that they stood for causes and personal types that were still in possession of their country—that they were fending off threats to a still well-established way of life in which they played an important part. But the modern right wing...feels dispossessed: American has been largely taken away from them and their kind, though they are determined to try to repossess it and to prevent the final destructive act of subversion. (Hofstadter, 1967, 23)

The post-World War II United States faced a new role and new responsibilities as the only Allied nation to emerge intact from the war yet uncertain and fearful about the rise of the Soviet Union and what was then called Red China. In the aftermath of the war, homefront social relationships changed fundamentally as families separated by the war reunited and new lives were begun, a phenomenon addressed in the 1946 film *The Best Years of Our Lives*, which was concerned particularly with the effects of the war on its women characters. The unity brought by the war now was replaced by uncertainty.

The movie industry was an attractive target for the uncertainties generated: the industry had always been vulnerable to attack—if not outright scape-goating—based on the belief that movies were deeply influential; and the leadership of the industry demonstrated in its accommodation both to censorship and regulation and in its actions in the Sinclair election that it was strongly conservative and anxious to please. There was an additional reason: beginning in the 1930s, there was a small but not insignificant community of leftists, Socialists and Communists in the film industry.

The origins of the organized Hollywood Left were in part rooted in the Great Depression and the general rise of leftist and liberal sentiment that accompanied it; in part in the frustration many felt because of the industry's timidity in opposing, earlier and more forcefully, the rise of fascism in Germany, a timidity largely attributable to studio concern over losing markets in Europe and the Breen Office's reluctance to offend foreign countries; and in the rise in Hollywood of unions. In all this 1930s Hollywood was not particularly unusual; similar trends were present through the country. What was unusual was that Hollywood was a uniquely tempting target, and this finally made all the difference. If there was a single point of origin in Hollywood for what later became the blacklist it was the founding of the Screen Writer's Guild (SWG). As Victor Navasky noted, before film people were asked if they were now or had ever been members of the Communist party, they were first asked a similar question about the Guild (Navasky, 1980, 174).

The Guild was created in 1933, born of frustration by writers who felt economically exploited by producers, especially in the post-Depression era when pay reductions were common. The founders of the SWG were ten in number—the first but not the last "Hollywood Ten." One of them was John Howard Lawson, who one year later would announce publicly that he had joined the Communist party, not a particularly startling admission for the time but one which, like many other political associations, would be raised later to great effect. (For a history of the creation of the Guild, see Ceplair and Englund, 1980. chap.2. and Schwartz, 1982.)

Some of the writers' grievances against producers were similar to those of other workers trying to build unions, foremost the desire for more money; others were reflective of the peculiar nature of the film business. Screenwriters were at the mercy of the producers who hired them. Beyond the frustration at having to write what they were told to write—a role they nonetheless chose and for which they were paid much more than other writing assignments would fetch—most writers were hired on a piecework basis; their job security was nonexistent. There were also the unique circumstances and frustrations writing for films presented. Movie writing was looked down upon by writers as a form of prostitution, though many accepted it by rationalizing scriptwriting as a way to make quick money to support more serious work.[5] Yet writers were exquisitely aware that, however well paid they were, they made much less than did others, a particularly galling situation because writers believed themselves to be intellectually superior and more serious as artists than others in the movie business, many of whom the writers believed had achieved their success through good connections, good looks, or good luck. Leo Rosten, a keen observer of Hollywood and a political moderate, noted of the writer's lot:

For two decades [1921-41], the movie writers in the low salary brackets (of whom there are plenty) were not given the protection of minimum wages or minimum periods of employment. They were discharged with no advance notice; their employment was sporadic and their tenure short-lived. They were laid off for short-term periods, under contract but without pay....Their right to screen credits was mistreated by certain producers who allotted credit to their friends or relatives or—under pseudonyms—to themselves. (Rosten, 1941, 318)

Despite the existence of a two-level system of screenwriters—the proletariat of whom Rosten spoke and the upper echelon, which had stable and lucrative relationships with producers—both were able at least to agree on the desirability of forming a Screen Writers Guild in their common interest. The SWG developed its own factions, however—a left wing and a right wing. The former was comprised of younger, less established and less well paid writers, the latter of older writers with much stronger and more profitable ties to the studios. The latter group was also the least militant.

The SWG confronted an industry, led by MGM and Irving Thalberg, which wanted it killed outright. This the industry attempted to do by offering writers the alternatives of "studio unions" and employment or SWG membership and unemployment. The SWG conservatives began resigning, some going on to form the studio-sanctioned Screen Playwrights, Inc. While most writers failed to join the Screen Playwrights (its docility as a studio creation was soon apparent), many more simply left the SWG and the organization nearly ceased to exist.

With the 1937 Supreme Court decision upholding the Wagner Act (which gave unions the right to exist and established the National Labor Relations Board [NLRB] to hear complaints against employers of unfair labor practices), the SWG was revived. In 1938 the NLRB certified the SWG as the sole bargaining agent for screenwriters, establishing in law as well as in fact the union presence in Hollywood.

The SWG not only pioneered Hollywood unionization, however; its creation established and sharpened political cleavages along economic and ideological lines. The remnants of the defeated Screen Playwrights went on to create in 1944 the strongly right-wing Motion Picture Alliance for the Preservation of American Ideals, which was to play a prominent role in the blacklist period. The SWG for its part became increasingly involved in union politics, siding in 1946 with left-wing labor leader Herbert Sorrell's Conference of Studio Unions in opposition to the corrupt International Alliance of Theatrical Stage Employees (IATSE) in the greatest labor dispute in Hollywood history (Navasky, 1980, 176). The founding of the SWG was to be a seminal event for the film business, for it was to become the foundation of the organized Left and Right in Hollywood.

The next major marker on the road to the blacklist was the period prior to the outbreak of World War II, roughly 1936-39, when the coming of fascism to Germany, Italy, and Spain created in the United States its own proxy war between isolationists and interventionists and served further to polarize the film industry as it was polarizing the entire country. The Hollywood community in the 1930s became highly politicized. This came in part from the impetus provided by the founding of the SWG but more importantly by external events and by the changing composition of the Hollywood community.

The Depression and the coming of the New Deal were no less important in Hollywood than they were elsewhere, and though Jack Warner organized an elaborate pageant for Franklin Roosevelt's 1932 campaign, it took Upton

Sinclair's EPIC campaign, occurring at the same time the SWG was being born, to tie movie politics with partisan electoral politics and with even broader political concerns. The expanding scope of political conflict deepened the developing political consciousness of filmmakers.

Beyond Hollywood and California, the United States experienced its own form of home-grown reactionary politics: the economic dislocation of the Depression spawned or revivified the Ku Klux Klan, the American Nazi party, the German-American Bund, the followers of Gerald L.K. Smith (a neo-Nazi) and Father James Coughlin (a demagogic right-wing Catholic priest with a large national radio audience). At the same time, the world outside Hollywood and the United States was swamped with political change. In 1936, Francisco Franco led a militray coup against the elected Republican government of Spain, bringing fascism to that country. Adolf Hitler began his rise to state power in Germany, as did Benito Mussolini in Italy. (Harry Cohn, easily the most vulgar, tyrannical, and flamboyant of the studio heads, visited Mussolini in Italy and was so taken with the dictator's office that he had his own at Columbia Pictures redesigned as an exact copy.) The nascent political community of filmmakers faced an extraordinary range of political issues extending far beyond the boundaries of Hollywood.

Overnight it seemed, Hollywood became a cosmopolitan town as hundreds of refugees fled Europe to seek safety and employment in the film industry: actor Peter Lorre; composer Max Steiner; directors Billy Wilder, Otto Preminger, and Fritz Lang; and writers Bertolt Brecht and Thomas Mann, among many others. (For a detailed examination of the emigre phenomenon, see Taylor, 1983, and Friedrich, 1986.) These refugees, deeply politicized by events in their lives, helped to politicize their new home. By 1938, Thomas Mann's daughter Erika wrote in her diary: "All of [the German and Austrians] are working hard, all of them are learning English furiously, and all of them have exactly two topics in which they are really interested—film and politics" (quoted in Ceplair and Englund, 1980, 96).

The result was an explosion of political groups: The Hollywood Anti-Nazi League (founded in 1936 by writers Donald Ogden Stewart and Dorothy Parker, director Fritz Lang, actor Fredric March, and composer Oscar Hammerstein); the Motion Picture Artists Committee to Aid Republican Spain (writers Dashiell Hammett and Donald Ogden Stewart, actors Paul Muni, Melvyn Douglas, Fredric March, and John Garfield, and director John Ford, among others); the Joint Anti-Fascist Refugee Committee (largely the same people as the Committee to Aid Republican Spain); and the Motion Picture Democratic Committee. (For a more detailed discussion of these and other groups, see Ceplair and Englund, 1980, chap. 4.) These and other groups formed alliances and shared members, forming a relatively unified but not seamless front—in the phrase of the time a "Popular Front"—opposed to fascism at home and abroad but also supportive of traditional left/liberal goals.

In this the Communist party of the United States (CPUSA) played a role, as it did, to a greater or lesser extent, in a number of leftist political movements in the 1930s. Driven underground and limited to a small membership by the "Red

Scare" of the 1920s and the illegal raids of U.S. Attorney General A. Mitchell Palmer (the "Palmer Raids"), the forces of the 1930s that energized the non-Communist Left also energized the CPUSA. The party came closest to the mainstream of Hollywood politics with the founding of the Screen Writers Guild, several of whose founders were acknowledged CPUSA members or were to join later. In so doing the party operated as all political groups operated—forming coalitions with others. The Great Depression, the first stirrings of labor organization in Hollywood, and the rise of fascism offered the CPUSA opportunities for alliances with unions and the assortment of anti-Fascist groups that proliferated in 1930s Hollywood. Such alliances meant that paths crossed on the political Left: anti-Communist liberals, Democratic Socialists, New Deal Democrats, and even anti-Fascist Republicans were members of groups that also contained CPUSA members, a few of whom were hard-line Stalinists whose main political interests were in supporting the Soviet Union, particularly at a time when it was threatened by its chief opponent, Adolf Hitler. The political associations thus established would come to haunt many.

The CPUSA had an enormous moral advantage: it was there first. The party had long championed the causes of the urban working class, of migrant farmworkers, of blacks, and had been at the forefront in warning of the dangers of German fascism, sworn enemy of the Soviet Union. Indeed, during the blacklist period some were attacked by the House Committee on Un-American Activities for engaging in the novel error of "premature anti-fascism"—that is, opposing fascism before it was legitimate to do so. Though small—estimates of its peak membership in Hollywood in 1937 place its membership at around 300 (Ceplair and Englund, 1980, 65)—the party operated reasonably effectively by capitalizing on the commitment and experience of its members. The dilemma of Hollywood politics for the CPUSA, however, was that without non-CPUSA allies the party's members were ineffective; with them, they were forced into moderation and compromise.

Assessments of the party's effects on the Hollywood community agree that it was minimal. The greatest success of its members was in the establishment of the SWG, though the party's role diminished rapidly as the Guild attracted more moderate members. In coalition with other groups, CPUSA members often played their traditional vanguard role, but the constant necessity to work with others—predominantly anti-Communist liberals and bread-and-butter unionists whose interests in ideology were nonexistent—required party members to adopt the classic position required of any coalition member, that of accommodation. But the greatest concerns voiced about the CPUSA were reserved for fears about movie content, for the vast majority of party members and sympathizers were writers.

Considerable attention has been paid by scholars and was paid by blacklist-era legislators to assessing "subversive" messages in films presumably placed there by cunning CPUSA writers and sympathizers. The subject was also of interest to other CP members outside the film industry and to students of Marxism, for the Hollywood Communists were in an unprecedented position by virtue of their jobs: accomplices in the mass production of fantasy and escape.

Screenwriters were simultaneously creative artists and factory workers—and very well paid ones at that. What was their role? To organize the movie proletariat? While there was such a thing, the studio workers who comprised it rapidly organized in unions largely bereft of CP influence. There was a basic contradiction in the role of Communist screenwriter, as Ceplair and Englund noted:

They did not believe that the professional goal of writing a "good" or "shootable" and financially successful script and the political goal of changing society were incompatible. The radical screenwriters were like some many Penelopes: in the daytime, at the office, they unraveled the efforts of their evenings and weekends as political activists, for the movies they wrote reinforced the reigning cultural ethos and political-social order. (Ceplair and Englund, 1980, 49-50)

Radical screenwriters faced a sharp disjunction between their work and their politics, one which was finally too great to bridge. If it is true that the most important political decision most people make is what they do for a living, radical movie writers, to the extent that any had serious hopes of infusing their work with their politics, sealed their political fate when they went to Hollywood to work. Hollywood won. Indeed, many of the most socially conscious films of the period were written not by CPUSA members but by garden-variety liberals, as in *The Grapes of Wrath* (1940), written by the politically moderate Nunnally Johnson and directed by "conservative" John Ford. Conversely, Sidney Buchman, a CPUSA member, wrote *Mr. Smith Goes to Washington*, a film seen by most as a celebration of American institutions. And as many observed, CPUSA writers were as capable as anyone of turning out scripts with racial, ethnic, and sexual stereotypes.

The search for "subversion" in films became a rather subtle thing, supremely open to interpretation as one's political agenda dictated. The most obvious examples of "subversion"—in retrospect at least—were films that celebrated the Soviet Union, but these films were produced at a time when the Soviet Union was a U.S. ally in World War II and were made at government behest as part of the war effort. As for other films, the evidence was thin for those who sought subversion. As Schickel notes there is "the legend of the screenwriter managing to work some lines from La Pasionara into a football coach's pep talk into one of his scripts. And then there's the one about the actor who, asked to improvise some business to cover a pause in a scene, whistled a few bars of the 'Internationale'" (Schickel, 1989, 103).

Those who examined the screen credits of CP writers found movies both good and bad, successful and unsuccessful, but none whose "subversions" were so evident that they seemed to catch anyone's attention when the film was released. CP writers wrote movies much like those of non-CP screenwriters, and many CP writers' films earned praise from the movie rating system established by the vigilant and stridently right-wing Daughters of the American Revolution, in addition to surviving the scrutiny of the Breen Office and the Legion of Decency.

As Charles Champlin observed of the period:

The irony, the blackest irony of all, was that no more rigorously and devoutly capitalist and patriotic endeavor exists than the Hollywood motion picture studio. From the start, the industry was a temple of rambunctious free enterprise....The movies' economic life rests on the consent of the entertained, and the wider and less disturbed the audience is, the more solid the consent. Film's First Commandment is "Thou shalt not worry the customers." (Champlin, 1987, 2)

The final truth is that if one removed all the films written by CPUSA members, the contours of American movies would be essentially unchanged. But to say the CPUSA's influence on films was nil is finally and fundamentally beside the point. The blacklist was not remotely a serious debate over the subversive content of films: it was an occasion for playing out the new realities of postwar U. S. politics. Movies were not the subject: they were the excuse.

What is commonly thought of as the blacklist era began in 1947 with the October hearings in Washington, D.C., of the House Committee on Un-American Activities (the proper acronym for the committee would thus be HCUA; the long-standing practice, however, has been, instead, to use HUAC, and this will be followed here). The committee, chaired by J. Parnell Thomas of New Jersey, was out to investigate Communist influence in the film business, encouraged by the promise of cooperation from Eric Johnston, president of the Producers Association. The committee had held closed hearings in Hollywood in May of 1947 where, among others, actor Adolph Menjou, Ginger Roger's mother, Lela, and director Sam Wood, president of the Motion Picture Alliance for the Preservation of American Ideals, divulged the names of real, imagined, and suspected Communists. Armed with this and other information, the committee subpoenaed 43 witnesses, friendly and unfriendly, to testify in the October public hearings in Washington.

Most of the friendly witnesses (the term was Thomas's) were well known: actors Robert Montgomery (later to be Dwight Eisenhower's television coach), Gary Cooper, Robert Taylor, Ronald Reagan, and George Murphy (later to be elected U.S. senator from California in 1964 and defeated for reelection in 1972), producers Jack Warner and Walt Disney and writer Ayn Rand.

The tenor of the committee's questions was reflected by freshman representative Richard Nixon of California, who asked Jack Warner of Warner Brothers a convoluted one-sentence, 150-word question whose thrust seemed to be whether Warner thought he had a duty to oppose totalitarian infiltration into the movies:

Warner: I am for everything you said.
Nixon: You agree with that statement?
Warner: I agree wholeheartedly.
Nixon: The statement was a little long.
Warner: It was a very good statement; it was the statement of a real American, and I am
    proud of it.

(Ambrose, 1987, 158)

Ronald Reagan, then president of the Screen Actors Guild (and already at the time a prolific secret informer for the FBI, with the code name "T-10"), acknowledged there was a "small clique" within SAG that was "suspected of more or less following the tactics we associate with the Communist Party." But Reagan went on to say, "I never want to see our country become urged, by either fear or resentment of this group [Communists], that we ever compromise with any of our democratic principles through that fear or resentment" (Moldea, 1986, 72). Reagan's comments nicely captured the general tenor of the "friendly" witnesses: an acknowledgment from within the industry that "subversive" elements existed but that the fight against them should not abrogate the rights of citizens. This hopeful compromise was not to be realized.

The unfriendly witnesses (the term was from the right-wing trade publication *Hollywood Reporter*), nineteen in number, had publicly expressed opposition to HUAC. The Hollywood Ten began with the Hollywood Nineteen. The Nineteen were a mixture of writers (Alvah Bessie, Lester Cole, Richard Collins, Gordon Kahn, Howard Koch, Ring Lardner, Jr., John Howard Lawson, Albert Maltz, Sam Ornitz, Waldo Salt, and Dalton Trumbo); directors (Edward Dmytryk, Lewis Milestone, and Irving Pichtel); writer-directors (Herbert Biberman and Albert Rossen); writer-producer Adrian Scott; playwright Bertolt Brecht and one actor, Larry Parks.

Why these particular men were singled out has never been adequately explained. Howard Koch, never a CP member, was subpoenaed because Jack Warner had blurted out his name in the closed hearings in May, perhaps because Koch had written the screenplay for the pro-Soviet *Mission to Moscow* (1943), though the film was produced by Warner's own studio at the behest of Franklin Roosevelt; yet Casey Robinson, the writer of the equally pro-Soviet *Days of Glory* (1944) was not called, perhaps because he was a member of the board of the Motion Picture Alliance. The Hollywood Nineteen likely were chosen because they had at least these factors in common: all lived in Hollywood and were associated with movies; sixteen were writers; all had been actively involved in pro-Soviet or anti-Fascist activities (before the war especially, the two were close to the same); only one was a war veteran (Ceplair and Englund, 1980, 262).[6]

Writers were especially important because the committee was convinced that screenplays were "the principal medium through which Communists have sought to inject their propaganda" into films (quoted in Dick, 1989, 6), and it was writers who were the first of the unfriendly witnesses to testify. It was probably not accidental that a committee politically adept enough to hold a camera rehearsal prior to the hearings was also aware that writers were the most vulnerable people in movies, if for no other reason that their names were not well known (though Dalton Trumbo was at the time the highest-paid writer at MGM).

The Nineteen were political radicals whose opposition to the committee's investigation—indeed to its very existence—was profound. In planning strategy with their attorneys, they considered but rejected invoking the Fifth Amendment's protection against self-incrimination, in part because it might compromise possible subsequent legal appeals but also because it was not deemed wise in public relations terms. They also rejected admitting and defending their political associations. The Nineteen settled on a dual strategy of invoking their First Amendment rights to freedom of speech, but also of responding to the committee's questions without really saying anything. This last gambit was a major strategic error, for under the committee's rules once a witness answered one question he was obligated to answer others or risk being cited for contempt of Congress. Further, any witness could be ruled out-of-order at the discretion of Chairman Thomas. The circumstances of the hearings, now having taken on an adversarial and even prosecutorial tone, placed the unfriendly witnesses at a distinct disadvantage; their legal strategy only exacerbated their situation by relegating the First Amendment defense to a secondary role. Wanting both to make a political point and yet anxious not to destroy their careers, they chose a strategy that did neither and played into the hands of the more politically skilled committee.

The Nineteen were at another disadvantage: previous legislative expeditions into Hollywood had foundered either because of indifference or because producers were resistant, not because they were politically sympathetic to leftists or were committed civil libertarians. (Louis B. Mayer: "Nobody can tell me how to run my studio.") That had changed by 1947; anticommunism was an increasingly efficient way of riding into office, as HUAC member Richard Nixon had already learned and was to exploit further in 1950 when he defeated Helen Gahagan Douglas, wife of actor Melvyn Douglas, for the U.S. Senate. Perhaps it was the ability of Eric Johnston of the Producers Association to sense these changes in postwar political dynamics that led to his offer of cooperation with the committee. Whatever the reason, Johnston's offer was the first sign that HUAC might succeed in getting Hollywood to battle itself.

The first unfriendly witness called was John Howard Lawson, a founder of the SWG and a CPUSA member. As drama his testimony was a high point; as the opening shot in the Nineteen's defense, it was a disaster. Lawson insisted on reading an opening statement, something Chairman Thomas had allowed the friendly witnesses to do. Thomas refused permission after reading Lawson's statement, a bitter denunciation of the committee. Upon being asked the "Are you now or have you ever been" question, Lawson verbally fenced with the committee, never answering the question and being repeatedly gaveled into silence by Thomas whenever he attempted to deliver his opening statement. Over the din of supporters and opponents, a shouting Lawson told the committee that *it* was on trial, that its inquiry was in no way related to communism but rather an attempt by Congress to control the country's movie screens and invade people's rights. After a half hour of jousting, Lawson was cited by Thomas for contempt of Congress and ordered off the witness stand. Shouting, Lawson was forcibly removed by a sergeant-at-arms.

By the time the hearings ended, nine other witnesses had been cited for contempt of Congress: Ornitz, Cole, Biberman, Maltz, Bessie, Scott, Dmytryk, Lardner, Jr., and Trumbo. These were the Hollywood Ten. Some, like Alvah Bessie, sustained the opposition and contempt first articulated by Lawson.

Bessie, a veteran of the Spanish Civil War, told the committee:

The understanding that led me to fight in Spain for the Republic, and my experiences in that war, teach me that this Committee is engaged in precisely the identical activities engaged in by un-Spanish committees, un-German committees and un-Italian committees which preceded it in every country which eventually succumbed to fascism. (Quoted in Ceplair and Englund, 1980, 287)

Though Chairman Thomas promised to resume the hearings soon, he never did. The next such hearings were not held until 1951. Perhaps the committee lost interest, or felt it had done its job, or was responding to limited but intense press criticism.[7] The response of the industry was to issue the famous "Waldorf Statement," named after New York's Waldorf-Astoria hotel, where a group of producers met shortly after the HUAC hearings ended. Under attack in the wake of the hearings from groups like the Veterans of Foreign Wars, the American Legion, the Daughters of the American Revolution, and the Hearst press, and facing threats of boycotts, the industry again sued for peace. The Waldorf Statement pledged "forthwith to discharge without compensation and . . . not re-employ any of the Ten, until such time as he is acquitted, or has purged himself of contempt and declared under oath that he is not a Communist" (quoted in Dick, 1989, 8). By 1950, after a series of unsuccessful appeals, all of the Ten were serving prison sentences. It was in prison that one of the Ten, Ring Lardner, Jr., was to meet HUAC chairman Thomas, himself serving time on charges related to padding his office payroll and taking kickbacks from his employees. (To speak of the Ten as a group, as is usual, is to ignore much of the story. For a more detailed discussion of each as individuals, see Dick, 1989.)

Beyond serving as a stage on which to play out cold war politics, the HUAC hearings displayed again the subtexts of religion and ethnicity in the politics of the film industry—in this case, anti-Semitism. John Rankin, a committee member and notorious race-baiter and anti-Semite, had this to say on the House floor about some prominent members of the Committee for the First Amendment, organized to oppose the hearings:

I want to read you some of these names [of CFA members]. One of the names is [actress] June Havoc. We found...that her real name is June Hovick. Another one was Danny Kaye, and we found out his real name is David Daniel Kaminsky....Another one is Eddie Cantor, whose real name is Edward Iskowitz. There is one who calls himself Edward [G.] Robinson. His real name is Emmanuel Goldenberg. There is another here who calls himself Melvyn Douglas, whose real name is Melvyn Hesselberg. (quoted in Ceplair and Englund, 1980, 289)

Lest his point be lost, Rankin concluded by lamenting what the Communists had done to the "unfortunate Christian people of Europe."

The blacklist grew, ultimately spreading to radio and television production, finally encompassing roughly two thousand people, driven by such publications as *Red Channels* and *Aware*, both of which purported to publish names of Communists and their sympathizers. For many, the blacklist ended careers;

others were to work under assumed names, and some—years later—were finally to work again, making movies.

The blacklist found its way into movies and television, sometimes directly and sometimes subtly. In television, Edward R. Murrow wrote and narrated an episode of his "See It Now" program in 1954 in which he attacked the chief spokesman for the forces of which the blacklist was a part, Senator Joseph R. McCarthy of Wisconsin, even as television engaged in blacklisting.

More typical, however, was the rush to produce films designed to convince audiences that the film industry was unambiguously anti-Communist. Between 1947 and 1954—the latter being the year in which Senator McCarthy was censured by the Senate—Hollywood produced several dozen anti-Communist films. Virtually all were straight formula films in which the standard villain was simply replaced by a Communist. In 1948, the trade papers reported that anti-Communist films were the current hot subjects for films. At the same time, other social and political topics declined.

In 1949, Hollywood produced *The Red Menace*, *The Red Danube*, and *I Married a Communist*, all failures at the box office. In 1954, Leo McCary, a political conservative, directed one of the most interesting of these films, *My Son John*, in which a college student (played by Robert Walker) returns home for a visit and makes fun of the American Legion, of which his father (Dean Jagger) is a devoted member. John's worried mother (Helen Hayes), defends her son, though her faith in him is tested when they are visited by the FBI. To reassure her, John affirms his loyalty on his mother's Bible. Father and son argue after the son makes comments critical of the United States, the father hitting the son with a Bible. Ultimately, the mother learns her son is indeed a spy and turns him into the FBI, begging him, a rosary in her hand, to confess and inform on others. John escapes the FBI, then recants and agrees to become an informer, only to die—on the steps of the Lincoln Memorial—in a car crash. His tape-recorded confession is played for his college graduating class. With its celebration of the FBI, family, and religion and its condemnation of communism and college, the film epitomized Hollywood's anti-Communist impulse better than any other film.

Of much greater interest, however, were other—and better—films that addressed the same issues. *High Noon* (1952, directed by Fred Zinneman, screenplay by Carl Foreman), is the story of the courageous sheriff Will Kane (played by the conservative Gary Cooper) surrounded by cowardly townspeople unwilling to help him stand up to a band of killers. For more than a few, the film was about Hollywood's own cowardice—the film is set in "Hadleyville"—and, indeed, writer Foreman said the film was avowedly left-wing in its political stance. In *12 Angry Men* (1957, directed by Sidney Lumet, screenplay by Reginald Rose), a single juror in a murder trial, played by Henry Fonda, bravely holds out against the majority and finally persuades the remaining eleven of the innocence of the young minority-group defendant. In both films, we are told, the majority is wrong and easily stampeded but can be resisted by courage and intelligence.

The most interesting film record of the period, however, is seen in *On the*

Waterfront (1954) and the events leading to its production. Its background tapped not just the anti-Communist impulse and the ethics of informing but also interest in labor racketeering, fueled by Senate investigations by Senator Estes Kefauver of Tennessee. *On the Waterfront* drew upon all these.

Playwright Arthur Miller had written a screenplay, titled *The Hook*, based on events in Brooklyn involving the death of a young longshoreman trying to organize his fellow workers against organized crime control of his union. Miller and director Elia Kazan, offered the script to Harry Cohn of Columbia. Because the script involved union politics, Cohn showed it to Harry Brewer, chairman of the American Federation of Labor (AFL) Film Council and the most powerful union man in the film industry. Brewer characterized the script as a lie because it suggested there were ties between unions and organized crime. Brewer passed the script along to the FBI and told Miller no loyal American could have written it. Having given Brewer the power of veto over the script, Cohn told Miller that all the writer had to do was to rewrite the script, "so that instead of racketeers terrorizing the dockworkers, it would be the Communists" (Sayre, 1982, 153).

On the Waterfront, using the same general setting as *The Hook*, was written by Budd Schulberg. Schulberg and director Kazan, both briefly Communist party members in the 1930s, had been friendly witnesses before HUAC. Kazan had volunteered sixteen names; Schulberg fifteen. Arthur Miller never was a party member. *On the Waterfront* is the story of Terry Malloy (Marlon Brando, in probably his best performance), who is urged by his girlfriend (Eva Marie Saint) and a priest (Karl Malden) to inform on the corrupt activities of a union boss (Lee J. Cobb, who off-screen was a friendly HUAC witness, as was Leif Erickson, who plays a government investigator). Torn between conflicting loyalties, Malloy's choice is ultimately sealed when the mob kills his brother, played by Rod Steiger.

More than most films of the era that addressed the ethics of informing, *On the Waterfront* confronts the pain such decisions bring, ones which Kazan faced in his own life and which he went on to address in 1971 when he told an interviewer:

I don't think there's anything in my life toward which I have more ambivalence because, obviously, there's something disgusting about giving other people's names. On the other hand...at that time I was convinced that the Soviet Empire was monolithic....I don't say that what I did was an entirely good thing. What's called a "difficult decision" is a difficult decision because either way you go there are penalties, right? But I would rather do what I did than crawl in front of a ritualistic Left and lie the way those other comrades did, and betray my own soul. I didn't betray it. (Quoted in Navasky, 1980, 208)

The heart of the film is Terry's decision. The forces that push him toward informing are personal (his girlfriend), but are also reflective of the political forces then at work on the anti-Communist front, most especially the Catholic priest. All of these become secondary, however, when the racketeers kill Terry's brother, Johnny, whose death transforms Terry's dilemma from one of ethics to one of kinship. In the end, Terry's decision to inform is inevitable.

On the Waterfront was a hit both with critics and the audience, winning eight

Academy Awards, including best picture and a best performance by an actor Oscar for Brando. Beyond the film's sheer quality as a piece of movie-making, its portrayal of the pain involved in choosing to inform made it a considerably more subtle exercise than others like it. Like *High Noon* and *12 Angry Men*, *On the Waterfront* had at its heart the dilemma faced by an individual's lonely confrontation with the majority. The only difference politically is how these films characterize the rightness of the majority's position.

In 1976, twenty-two years after *On the Waterfront* was released, Hollywood addressed the blacklist and the ethics of informing more directly in *The Front*, written by Martin Bernstein and directed by Martin Ritt, both of whom had themselves been blacklisted. Woody Allen plays Howard Prince, a cashier and small-time hustler, who agrees to put his name on the scripts of his blacklisted writer friend Alfred Miller (Michael Murphy) in return for a percentage of the proceeds. (Interestingly, Murphy's character writes for television, not the movies.) Essentially apolitical though vaguely upset that the blacklist exists, Allen's character nonetheless agrees to front for even more writers, thus becoming a cold war profiteer. Prince makes considerable money and meets and falls in love with television producer Florence Barrett (played by Andrea Marcovicci) who initially is attracted by what she believes to be Howard's writing. Howard begins to confuse who is the writer and who is the front: "My name is on this," he tells a writer whose work he finds not up to "his" standards.

The suicide of comic Hecky Green (Zero Mostel, also blacklisted in real life) forces Howard to confront the reality of the blacklist. (Hecky's suicide is loosely based on the actual suicide of Philip Loeb, an actor in the popular television series "The Goldbergs" who was unable to find work after being blacklisted.) In this he is reinforced by the loss of Florence, to whom he confesses he is not really a writer, and who withdraws when Howard expresses no desire to fight the blacklist. ("What's the Fifth Amendment?" Howard asks the writers during a strategy session.) Called before a congressional investigating committee, Howard first tries fencing verbally with the committee, responding to questions without really answering them, thus echoing one of the unsuccessful tactics used by the Hollywood Ten. He is offered the chance to emerge unharmed simply by naming names; indeed, all he needs to do, an executive (played by Herschel Bernardi, another real-life blacklist victim) tells him, is to name the dead Hecky Green and the committee will be satisfied. In the climactic scene, Howard finally tells the committee they have no right to ask him such questons and concludes, "And furthermore, you can all go fuck yourselves."

In the film's final scene, a triumphant Howard is led off to prison, surrounded by well-wishers and Florence, to the strains of Frank Sinatra singing "Young at Heart": "Fairy tales can come true/It can happen to you." Thus, Howard Prince does the right thing, politically and personally.

The Front is part history (the blacklist was real: many people in the film lived it), part wish-fulfillment ("go fuck yourselves"), and part sugarcoating (many "political" activities" are in fact engaged in for personal reasons). The apolitical Howard Prince becomes a front to help a friend and to make some money, reinforced by his desire to impress a woman. His actions are not political but personal, as are Hecky Green's, who tells Howard that he joined the Communist party not for political reasons but to meet women. Still, Howard is also surrounded by politically serious people, who tell him that they are committed Communists and that Howard's actions place him in real danger. Finally, however, what galvanizes Howard is his inability to betray the dead Hecky and the belief that he will lose Florence. His political motives are not sharply drawn, save that he comes slowly to realize more clearly what he believes intuitively at the beginning of the film: that the blacklist is silly and destructive. Common sense, love, and friendship drive Howard to defy the committee—not ideology. What Howard sees, finally, are the personal costs of the blacklist. His words to the committee essentially say, "If only someone had done this at the beginning, none of it would have happened." In *The Front*, Hollywood did what it had done before the Depression and World War II and what it was to do for Vietnam: it made a movie about the way many wished things had been, not how they were. Fairy tales can come true.

High Noon, On the Waterfront, and *The Front* all deal with the politics of the blacklist by confronting the necessity for choice: Terry Malloy and Howard Prince must decide whether to inform; Gary Cooper must choose between fighting and running. In all these films, the tension between the majority and the minority is central. In all these films, the majority is wrong, and the hero, finally, chooses correctly, but only, of course, after a struggle (a Christ-like one in *On the Waterfront*, which is filled with Christian allusions). In all these films, the central character's essential heroism is manifested precisely when he elects to oppose the majority. But the films differ with respect to the inferences we might draw about the film's politics.

In *High Noon* the decision is easy: we know who the bad guys are, we know the townspeople are cowards, and the resolution is simple and straightforward. To view the film as a political allegory on the cowardice of the film industry, as many in Hollywood did, was doubtless not something done by most members of its audience. *On the Waterfront* had a more overtly political subtext and, certainly, a more overtly political background. By shifting its emphasis from communism to labor racketeering, however, the film does something not unlike *High Noon*: create a surrogate evil antagonist. The same is true for *The Front*: the forces representing the blacklist are portrayed as uniformly ignorant, and those in the industry who give in to them are thus necessarily cowardly. In all these films, finally, the necessity to choose—and choose rightly—is driven largely by personal reasons: love or kinship or friendship. While such personalization may be seen as wringing the politics out of political events, it also involves something at which movies are especially effective: making personal the consequences of those events.

The blacklist left a deep imprint on Hollywood, one felt to this day. In late 1989, a building named after Robert Taylor on what was the MGM lot in Culver City, California, had its name changed to honor director George Cukor. Taylor's name was removed in response to a petition circulated by writer Stanley Zimmerman. The objection to Taylor was that he had "named names" during the 1947 HUAC hearings. With regularity, conferences are held in Hollywood to remind those in the industry of those days (see Michaelson, 1987; Mathews, 1989). In 1987, the Public Broadcasting Service noted the fortieth anniversary of the HUAC hearing by airing "Legacy of the Hollywood Blacklist," a sympathetic program in which friends and family members reminisced about the period.

In 1970, Dalton Trumbo, one of the Hollywood Ten, upon receiving the Writers Guild of America Laurel Award, given for the body of a writer's work, gave what has come to be called the "Only Victims" speech. In it, Trumbo said the period of the blacklist was one of such evil that the circumstances of those called upon to testify "had passed beyond the control of mere individuals." Both sides, Trumbo said, displayed "bad faith and good, honesty and dishonesty, courage and cowardice, seflessness and opportunism, wisdom and stupidity." Searching for villains or heros, Trumbo went on, was fruitless: "Some suffered less than others, some grew and some diminished, but in the final tally we were *all* victims because almost without exception each of us felt compelled to say things he did not want to say, to do things he did not want to do, to deliver and receive wounds he truly did not want to exchange" (quoted in Schickel, 1989, 95). Trumbo, as it happened, figured in one of the most dramatic moments in the history of the blacklist when he won, under the front name "Robert Rich," the Academy Award for his screenplay for *The Brave One* (1956). When "Rich's" name was announced on Oscar night, no one came forward.

The rise of other forms of mass entertainment—television and recordings especially—has had the effect of deflecting some of the attention once paid to movies. The nature of the concern has also changed. In the blacklist period, as much if not more attention was paid to the personal politics of those in the industry, quite apart from the content of films themselves. In recent years, much more attention has been directed to such things as the content of television programming and the lyrics of popular songs. While the focus of concern has changed, the pressures applied are no less political.

In recent years, much of the overt political activity of film industry people has emphasized relatively safe subjects, most prominently the environment. And politicians have come to realize that the entertainment industry can be a rich source of funds. Election years—especially presidential election years— regularly see candidates arriving in Los Angeles to speak before various show-business groups seeking endorsements and money. And in much of this, contemporary politically active entertainment people echo complaints made by generations of California political activists: they come here for our money, then take it somewhere else to spend.

While the primal fear of a renewed blacklist is always present in Hollywood, there is one central fact that is likely to assure that, if a blacklist mentality is ever to arise again, it may not be as wide and deep as it was in the 1950s: the death of the studio system. In the studio days, a handful of executives could be persuaded to blacklist writers, performers, and directors and to have their will become industry policy. Contemporary film production is less fertile ground for a blacklist, if only because power is less centralized.

NOTES

1. The *Burstyn* case involved a 1948 film, *The Miracle*, directed by Roberto Rossellini in which a demented woman is seduced by a stranger she thinks is St. Joseph. The film was allowed to open in New York by that state's censors, then was closed several days later by New York City's censor, who found the film "officially and personally blasphemous." The film's distributor sued and lost in the New York Supreme Court and won on appeal in the United States Supreme Court. In overturning the *Mutual Film* case of 1915, the court in 1952 affirmed that film was a "significant medium for the communication of ideas" and warranted First Amendment protection.

2. See Trevelyan (1973) for an interesting example of the British experience with film censorship. Trevelyan's book is part history, part memoir.

3. For a critical response to Forman, see Moley (1938).

4. The Catholic Legion of Decency also rated films under its own system:

Class A: Approved.

Section I. Morally unobjectionable for general patronage.

Section II. Morally unobjectionable for adults.

Class B: Morally Objectionable, in part, for all.

Class C: Condemned.

Legion of Decency ratings were printed in church newspapers, and churchgoers were warned from the pulpit about films, especially those rated Condemned.

5. The list of writers who went (with varying degrees of misgiving) to work in Hollywood (with varying degrees of success) is long: Robert Benchley, F. Scott Fitzgerald, Bertolt Brecht, Raymond Chandler, James M. Cain, Dorothy Parker, George S. Kaufman, Moss Hart, Dashiell Hammett, Aldous Huxley, Raymond Chandler, Sinclair Lewis, William Faulkner, Ben Hecht, Ring Lardner, Jr., Clifford Odets, Paddy Chayefsky, Nunnally Johnson, Gene Fowler, among many others.

6. One of the Nineteen, Bertolt Brecht, denied in his testimony before HUAC of ever having been a CP member and shortly thereafter returned to his native Germany. Fearful that the investigation would jeopardize his chances of returning there, Brecht's actions were supported by the others.

7. There was organized Hollywood opposition to the HUAC hearings, most visibly from the Committee for the First Amendment spearheaded by writer Philip Dunne and directors William Wyler and John Huston. The Committee sent a delegation to Washington to dramatize opposition to HUAC's hearings, its most prominent members being Danny Kaye, Lauren Bacall, and Humphrey Bogart, though Bogart later recanted his participation.

4

APPROACH, AVOIDANCE, AND ACCOMMODATION: MOVIES AND THE GREAT DEPRESSION

In 1932, three years after the stock market crash of October 1929, the Great Depression reached its political climax with the election to the presidency of Franklin D. Roosevelt. Just prior to the election, the head of President Hoover's Organization on Unemployment Relief urged giving free movie tickets to the poor. They were, he said, a necessity that ranked just behind food and clothing (Bergman, 1971, xii). Necessity or not, the Great Depression was recorded in film with an combination of approach and avoidance, culminating with the reactionary pseudo-populism of Frank Capra.

For the first few years after the stock market plunge the movie industry continued to do well; roughly half the population still took its weekly trip to theaters. By 1932, however, battered by an unemployment rate between one-quarter and one-third of a labor force that was without unemployment insurance, the largely working-class movie audience declined and the industry worried. Bank failures reduced capital and the industry found itself the victim of overexpansion and the challenge of radio. The New Deal's efforts to insure bank deposits and to regulate the stock market returned some stability to the studios' access to credit, and theater operators introduced gimmicks like Bank Night, featuring drawings for prizes, and giveaways of dishes to lure patrons back. This, along with a modest recovery by the mid-1930s, improved studios' fortunes. And films, taking note of the Depression, changed too.

GANGSTERS

"Mother of Mercy, is this the end of Rico?" The astonished words of Caesar Enrico Bandello (Edward G. Robinson) in *Little Caesar* (1930) are indeed his last, though they were not the last to be heard from Depression-era movie gangsters. *Little Caesar* created the gangster genre, as Robinson's performance created the gangster. Gangster films are second only to westerns in their durability, and, like the western, their survival speaks volumes about the society in which they took root and flourished. The society in which the classic gangster films took hold was one of massive economic dislocation, class-consciousness, and a pervasive lack of faith in political and economic institutions. Roosevelt's reference to fear in his inaugural address was no exaggeration. *Little Caesar,* along with the two other gangster classics of the period, *Scarface* (1932) and the 1931 *The Public Enemy* (which did for James Cagney what *Little Caesar* did for Edward G. Robinson), placed the immigrant-stock working-class gangster firmly in the context of a country fearful about its future.

Little Caesar introduces us to its title character as a small time hoodlum who, with his friend Joe Masara (Douglas Fairbanks, Jr.), robs a gas station. At an all-night diner afterwards, we learn of Rico's huge ambition. "Money's all right but it ain't everything," Rico says to Joe. "No, be somebody, know that a bunch of guys will do everything you tell 'em, have your own way or nothing." Rico does not have the usual Depression-era problem of making money; he can get that knocking off gas stations. Rico wants power and status.

Rico and Joe go to Chicago to join the gang of Sam Vettori, who introduces the new recruits to "the boys," including Killer and Kid. "The boys," in classic movie gangster parlance, are not yellow; they don't squeal. The headstrong Rico is warned by Vettori to be careful with the gunplay and to do things Vettori's way. But Joe, unlike Rico, has doubts about gangster life. He tells Rico what he really wants to do is make a little money and retire to pursue his real interest—dancing—and to settle down with a woman. Dancing and women: Rico regards both with contempt.

Joe gets a job in a dance act partnered with Olga Strassoff (Glenda Farrell) at the Palermo Club; Joe now has his dancing and his woman. Vettori plans to rob the Palermo Club. Joe wants out of the crime life, but Rico won't let him—once you're in, you're in, Rico tells Joe, and Joe is assigned to be lookout. Rico finds a flaw in Vettori's plan and challenges his boss's judgment. Demonstrating his ruthlessness, Rico kills McClure, the newly arrived head of the city Crime Commission, during the robbery. No less ruthlessly, Rico orders the young Tony Passa (William Collier), the getaway driver, killed when Tony, after a tearful scene with his distraught mother, refuses his cut of the proceeds and decides to go straight. Tony is gunned down on the steps of his parish church on the way to visit his old priest, Father MacNeill. The nightclub robbery distills much of the film—Rico's ambition, his ruthlessness, his intelligence, and the code that does not permit his friend Joe to leave gangster life. The robbery is shot in rapid montage: the rich patrons celebrating New Year's inside the elegant club, the working class gangsters on the outside taking their money.

After the robbery Rico rejects Vettori's condemnation for killing McClure ("You're slipping, Sam") and challenges Vettori for leadership by proposing his own division of the loot. "You're through," Rico tells him; Vettori yields and Rico's ascent continues. Rico's ambition now turns to Little Arnie Lorch

(Maurice Black), a gangster upset at Rico's pretensions and jealous of the publicity Rico receives. Lorch orders Rico killed; Joe overhears the order and warns Rico, who escapes an assassination attempt with an arm wound. Rico confronts Lorch and, as he did with Vettori, tells him he is through. Lorch responds that his boss, Pete Montana (Ralph Ince), will protect him. Rico is not impressed: "There's no use being scared of these big guys. The bigger they come the harder they fall." Rico gets his way and we learn of Lorch's departure from town thorough a notice in the society pages, confirmation that Lorch has indeed gone soft.

Rico receives the ultimate accolade; an invitation to the home the Big Boy (Sidney Blackman), the top gangster in town, who tells him that Pete Montana is through and Rico will replace him. Rico prospers: his apartment becomes a scaled down version of the Big Boy's huge home, his attire becomes nattier (including a tie clasp like that worn by the recently deposed Lorch), and he buys paintings just slightly less expensive that those owned by the Big Boy. He acquires his own flunky, Otero (George Stone), who does what he is told.

Rico asks Joe to help him run the expanded territory given him by the Big Boy. But Joe still wants out, and for this Rico blames Olga. "Love—soft stuff," Rico snarls, telling Joe that if he goes back to "that dame," it's "suicide— suicide—for both of you." Joe plans to run away with Olga, but she convinces him that would be futile—Rico would find them. Instead she call Sergeant. Flaherty (Thomas Jackson), a laconic cop devoted to getting Rico. Rico and Otero burst in, and Otero urges a suddenly reluctant Rico to kill Joe (does the pliant flunky now think Rico is getting soft?) but Rico cannot. In one of the few close-ups in the film used by director Mervyn LeRoy, we see Rico's stricken expression as he backs away from Joe, unable to fire. Otero tries to shoot Joe but Rico pulls his arm away. Joe is wounded and Rico and Otero flee. Olga suggests telling the police that Rico shot Joe and Joe wordlessly assents. It is in this scene that Rico's downfall begins, and it begins because Rico takes action based on emotion. As Robert Warshow noted in his essay on gangster films:

No convention of the gangster film is more strongly established than this: it is dangerous to be alone. And yet the very conditions of success make it impossible not to be alone, for success is always the establishment of *individual* preeminence that must be imposed on others, in whom it automatically arouses hatred. The gangster's whole life is an effort to assert himself as an individual . . . and he always dies *because* he is an individual.

(Warshow, 1964, 88)

Virtually every shot in *Little Caesar* is a medium or long shot; only when Rico has his moment of doubt about killing Joe do we get a close-up of his stricken face. All Rico's successes are visually associated with groups of men working together to plan their crimes; his downfall begins with Rico shown alone in close-up and filled with doubt. Rico—alone—runs for months, ends up broke in a flophouse, and is finally gunned down by Flaherty. Rico dies on a dark street beneath a sign announcing a new revue starring Joe Masara and Olga Strassoff.

The durability of the gangster genre—it is remarkably unchanged, as the

Godfather films (1972, 1974, 1990), *Bonnie and Clyde* (1967), and the 1983 remake of *Scarface* show—lies in its establishment of an alternative and parallel system of mobility, power, and wealth for the socially and economically dispossessed, a system apart from the legitimate system to which the dispossessed are denied access. Unlike the cowboy hero, who often lives in ambivalent relationship to the law, the gangster is outside it. For a Depression audience there was the added element of revenge: the little guy got money, got power, got even—at least for a while— before he got killed.

The classic career of the gangster—from working class nobody to somebody to death—is a mirror-image of the classic American success story: Rico is smart, tough, ambitious, and ruthless—all the virtues of the classic captain of industry—succeeding in an alternative social system that exists in the shadows of and parallel with the legitimate economy and society.   Only in his preordained death is the gangster different. Like the heroes of the classic American success story, Rico has a code of loyalty, discipline, and self-denial: he warns his comrades at a banquet in his honor, "I wish you guys wouldn't get drunk and raise Cain. That's the way a lot of birds get bumped off," and he himself refuses to drink.

Nor is Rico distracted by women; they only get in the way. Rico's success comes entirely in groups of men: it is a conflicted man (Joe), influenced by a woman (Olga), who is the catalyst for Rico's downfall. And Rico is directly victimized by a female character: when he is fleeing the law he hides out in the ironically named Ma Magdalena's Fruit Store. Broke, he asks Ma for the money he has hidden there—ten thousand dollars. But only Ma knows where the money is hidden and she offers Rico only a tiny part of the money in return for hiding him in her store a few days. The gangster world is a world of men, alone or in groups.

The system against which all the Ricos operated but whose basic structure their activities nevertheless ironically mirrored pitted working-class immigrants or their children against an established order, and in *Little Caesar* even pitted one element of the working class against another. Rico is Italian; so are most of his comrades. The priest to whom Tony is going when he is killed, the head of the Crime Commission who is killed, and the cop who kills Rico all have Irish names: MacNeill, McClure, Flaherty. Even they, not long in the United States, are the establishment. Even they speak standard English, while Rico and his friends speak in the classic gangster argot of "deses" and "dems," where women are "dames" and men aren't "yellow." In their fashion, the Ricos of the gangster films played by the rules and, however temporarily, succeeded. The gangster films were at once a radical challenge to established economic authority but also a confirmation of it, a revenge fantasy for the dispossessed in which justice nonetheless prevailed. As Bergman observes:

The classic gangster film was less a barometer of despair than an act of faith. Despite all the gunplay, mayhem, and omnipresence of death, the gangster film of the thirties served primarily as a success story....The outlaw cycle represented not so much a mass desertion of the law as a clinging to past forms of achievement. That only gangsters could make upward mobility believable tells much about how legitimate institutions had failed—but that mobility was still the core of what Americans held to be the American dream. (Bergman, 1971, 6-7)

The background of the gangster film was one of economic collapse in which the gangster triumphs by applying all the virtues of the American ethos. At its deepest level, it is the revenge and triumph of the least of American society—the poor, uneducated, urban male of immigrant stock. He triumphs despite the collapse of economic and political institutions—indeed, he triumphs *because* these institutions collapse.

Foremost of the failed institutions that formed the social setting of gangster films was law enforcement, the chief representation in film of the institutions of government, of the state. In gangster films, law is often nonexistent—rules are enforced by the gangsters themselves, not unlike the western hero with whom gangsters have so much in common. And when the law is present, it is either something to be overcome, dispensed by incompetents (Mack Sennett's Keystone Cops were the prototype), represented by the amiable but none-too-industrious cop on the beat, or it is corrupt. Movie gangsters flourished because the political environment of the films in which they operated permitted it. The message was clear: city and state governments were at best indifferent or at worst corrupt, and their law enforcement agencies reflected it. It is no accident that the advent of comic book (and later serial and feature film) superheroes occurred during the Depression, or that these heroes were private citizens (vigilantes, really), or that they are so closely associated with cities—Superman with Metropolis and Batman with Gotham City. The local cop was often comic relief compared to the gangster and the superhero when it came to movies' portrayal of urban America early in the Depression.

It would not be until the mid-1930s that such films as *G-Men* (1935) and *Bullets or Ballots* (1936) would celebrate the lawman as the central character, often with the hero played by the same actors who had played gangsters only a few years earlier: thus Edward G. Robinson starred as the lawman in *Bullets or Ballots* and James Cagney in a similar role in *G-Men*. But now the hero was a federal officer, not the city cop or state trooper. In lionizing Treasury agents and G-men, filmmakers did J. Edgar Hoover's FBI and Franklin D. Roosevelt's New Deal a considerable favor. The hidden hero was the federal government in general and the New Deal in particular. These films bolstered the role and legitimacy of the federal government relative to the states and cities in 1930s America at a time when the expansion of federal authority was deeply controversial; they also helped establish in the mind of many the durable idea that crime policy was a national issue.

DISPOSSESSED

Little Caesar and *The Public Enemy* were both produced by Warner Brothers, a studio that had a reputation, alone among the major studios, of making films aimed at the urban working-class audience. The house style at Warners was marked, by "the cynicism of the sociopolitically disinherited.

Whether gangster or secretary, entertainer or reporter, detective or killer's girlfriend, Warner's people are heroes of the city, always aware that *Little Caesar*'s 'be somebody' implies that most of the population is nobody" (Mordden, 1988, 217).

Warners produced scores of "social problem" films, movies which would in later years appear as television movies-of-the-week, or as they were derisively called, "disease-of-the-week" movies, which focused on some sort of social or personal pathology. The Warners production style encouraged the use of such topical movies. Warners movies were produced fast and in quantity—very much like television—and stories were likely to come from the headlines. These films are less interesting for the problems with which they dealt—they were the familiar problems of urban America in a time of economic dislocation—than the manner in which they explained their existence.

Gangster films paid scant attention to their protagonists' motivation. When we meet Rico he is a criminal; there is no backstory for Rico in Francis Faragoh's screenplay to tell us how he got that way. In *The Public Enemy*, we meet James Cagney's character, Tommy Powers, when he is six and already in trouble with the police, but we also meet his older brother, a model youth, who stays that way into adulthood. So much for heredity versus environment; after this interesting beginning there is no further attempt in *The Public Enemy* to address Tommy's motivation for a life of crime.[1] A major exception, however, to what Bergman (1971, 92) calls the "total inability to give any coherent reasons for social difficulties" in Warners social problem films is the 1932 Warners release *I Am a Fugitive from a Chain Gang* directed, like *Little Caesar*, by Mervyn LeRoy.

I Am a Fugitive from a Chain Gang is the story of a man's journey through Depression America, but unlike the entirely urban world of the gangster film, James Allen's (Paul Muni, who played the Al Capone-like lead in *Scarface*) travels take him through rural and city settings and cover a substantial portion of the United States. Allen's very name and backstory are straight from mainstream America. Ostensibly a social problem film aimed at the chain-gang system widely used in prisons of the American South, *I Am a Fugitive from a Chain Gang* emerges as a depiction of political and economic hopelessness that destroys an ordinary man.

James Allen has returned home from World War I intent on avoiding his old factory job. His service in the war has broadened his horizons and provided him with skills as an engineer, a career he wants now to pursue. Pressured by his family to return, instead, to his old shoe factory job, he chafes at the routine and sets out on the road traveling through the Midwest, the South, and New England looking for work. He finds none. In St. Louis, broke and disheveled, he tries to pawn his war medals; the pawnbroker shows him a case filled with other such medals. In a dismal roadhouse a newly acquired hobo companion forces Allen to help him in a robbery by emptying the till. The police arrive and Allen is sentenced to ten years at hard labor—the chain gang.

The routine Allen so wanted to escape now becomes his life: LeRoy's camera lingers on walls, gates, chains. We see the prisoners—including segregated black prisoners—in close-up, individualizing them.[2] The prisoners must ask permission to do everything. Sadistic guards beat prisoners for infractions—real, imagined, or trivial. The desperate Allen escapes and becomes the fugitive of the film's title. Allen manages slowly to reintegrate himself into the outside world. For the five years leading up to 1929 he rebuilds his life, working as an engineer and becoming a respected and legitimate member of society. A 1920s-style flapper learns of his past and blackmails Allen into marriage. On the eve of the stock market crash, his wife, in an alcoholic fit, informs on him. A deal is made by which the now-respectable Allen will return to prison for a symbolic ninety-day term. But when the term is up, another sadistic minion of the law, the prison commissioner, refuses to release him. Desperate again, Allen escapes again, this time straight into the depths of the Depression. Now a permanent fugitive, Allen can only run and hide; he is an outlaw in a society in economic collapse. His own situation and that of his society are equally desperate. His society imprisons him as much as did prison itself.

The conclusion of *I Am a Fugitive from a Chain Gang* is powerful and deeply pessimistic: Allen sneaks back home to say goodbye to his second wife, his face emerging from the shadows in which he now must live. "How do you live, Jim?" his wife asks. "I steal," he replies, then disappears. No happy ending here.

James Allen is almost entirely a victim of circumstances. The gangster elects to be a gangster and enjoys, for a while, the fruits of crime. Every social, economic, and political institution that can fail James Allen does so: family, friends, the law, the economy. Wherever he goes, geographically or socially, he is betrayed. His five brief years of success before 1929 were on borrowed time, an empty promise: the economy would collapse and his wife would betray him. The contrast between *I Am a Fugitive from a Chain Gang* and the 1946 William Wyler film *The Best Years of Our Lives* is instructive: while both deal with the circumstances of the returning soldier, *I Am a Fugitive from a Chain Gang* is vastly more bleak and hopeless in tone. One comes away from *I Am a Fugitive from a Chain Gang* with a picture of a society in disarray, conspiring to destroy a man. James Allen—unlike Rico—has not gone wrong: his society has. The parallel system of rewards and power available to Rico in his world is denied to James Allen in his.

The great majority of Depression-era movies were concerned with the Depression's consequences, not its causes; nor did many films attempt a statement about how to deal with it. *The Grapes of Wrath* (1940) did a little of both. Directed by John Ford, the film was largely spearheaded by producer Darryl F. Zanuck, who bought the rights to the John Steinbeck novel and signed Nunnally Johnson to write the screenplay. As with many of his projects, Zanuck was extensively involved in the film's production (Zanuck was notorious for his frequent and detailed memos to writers, directors, and the wardrobe department, among others). Zanuck's participation extended even to the point of, according to some, restructuring the conclusion of the film to change it from Steinbeck's more downbeat novel and make it more positive and audience-pleasing and writing the film's final speech, though Steinbeck himself had final say over any changes.[3]

The opening of *The Grapes of Wrath* (photographed by Gregg Toland) is classic John Ford: the open Midwest landscape against a huge sky along which walks a lone figure. Young Tom Joad (Henry Fonda) is coming home after serving four years in prison for murder (a drunken dance-hall fight, Tom says). Approaching home, Tom meet Casey (John Carradine), a man Tom used to know as a preacher. But Casey tells Tom that now he has "lost the call." The certainty that Casey once possessed about things—including religion—is gone.

Tom arrives at the Joad home in a gathering dust storm to find it deserted except for Muley (John Qualen), a half-crazed sharecropper who tells Tom that everyone has left. It's the "dusters," Muley says, the dust storms that devastated Midwestern farmers and provided the rural element of the Great Depression. Everyone is going to California except Muley. True to his name, Muley tells Tom that being born on the land, working on the land, and dying on the land has made it theirs; no piece of paper can make it any different. Thus enunciating the movie version of Marx's labor theory of value, Muley will stay.

In a series of flashbacks, we learn that the Joad family has sharecropped their forty acres for a half century. But now a combination of things—the dusters, mechanization (the Cats, or Caterpillar tractors) and corporations and banks—"orders from the East," Muley says—have conspired to drive the Joads and the others from what they think of as their land. The villain in all this is not clear: "Then who do we shoot?" a neighbor wants to know. The news of eviction is delivered by men in convertibles smoking cigars; they are not mean, just matter-of-fact. But when a Cat bulldozes Muley's house it is not driven by a banker but by a young sharecropper who needs the money to feed his family.

At Uncle John's house where the Joads are temporarily living, they talk of the promised land of California: jobs, oranges, sunshine, a new life. The Joads and others like them head for California not just because they have been driven from their Oklahoma home but because flyers have appeared announcing jobs out west, jobs for 800 pickers. The Joads sell their possessions, yielding two hundred dollars, seventy-five of which goes to buy the truck in which they head west. Creaking, overheating, and overloaded with Joads, the truck is a twentieth-century Conestoga wagon of the sort John Ford and others filmed for so many westerns. The night before they leave, Ma Joad (Jane Darwell, who won an Oscar for her performance) looks over mementos of earlier and better times—a postcard, knickknacks, and earrings, which she wears one last time—then tosses her possessions into a fire. Twelve people—three generations of Joads and their son-in-law—head west, to the strains of "Red River Valley," music director Alfred Newman's musical motif of *The Grapes of Wrath*. The defiant ("this is my dirt!") Grampa Joad (Charley Grapewin) has to be gotten drunk before he can be hauled aboard the truck. At the last minute, Casey is invited along and accepts. Scarcely has the journey begun than Grampa dies, clutching a handful of his beloved dirt. He is buried along the road and Casey, though no longer a preacher, improvises an eloquent eulogy:

This here old man just lived a life an' just died out of it. I don't know whether it was good or bad. An' it don't matter much. Heard a fella say a poem once. An' he says, "All that lives is holy." But I wouldn't pray just for an old man that's dead. Cause he's all right. If I was to pray, I'd pray for folks that's alive, an' don't know which way to turn. Grampa here, he ain't got no more trouble like that. He's got his job all cut out for him. So cover him up an' let him get to it.

On the road, the Joads learn from a man on his way back from California that the flyer promising jobs is a sham, designed to lure more job-seekers than there are jobs so wages can be driven down. The Joads' only help on the road comes from other working-class people. In a nicely crafted scene a kind of poor people's economy is created in a cafe: Pa Joad (Russell Simpson) tries to buy a loaf of bread for Grandma Joad (Zeffie Tilbury), who must eat water-softened bread because she has no teeth. A waitress says the bread costs more than Pa has to spend. The cafe proprietor tells her to sell Pa the bread for a dime—he lies and says it's day-old bread. Pa buys the bread, then is tempted by candy the children want. The waitress in turn lies about the price of the candy so that Pa can buy enough for both children. After Pa gives the candy to the children and leaves, two truck drivers in the cafe who have observed this leave the waitress more money than they are charged on their bill. The tiny economy of the cafe is complete: Grandma has her bread, the children have their candy, the cafe has its money.

The Joads enter the West. After crossing the Arizona border and being told by a trooper that they had better keep moving on through the state, we see the ironic counterpoint of a Route 66 sign and below it another sign reading "Will Rogers Highway"—named after the man who never met someone he didn't like. The Joads enter California at the desert town of Needles: the promised land is the bleak Mojave Desert. As they enter the state, Grandma dies.

In California the film's political focus sharpens through the contrasting experiences in two different migrant camps. The most important of these is the first, Keene Ranch, into which the Joads and others are directed by men along the road. We see Keene Ranch largely from the Joads' point of view—the camera tracks through the camp as if on the truck, past family after family just like the Joads: worn-down adults, dirty, ragged children, all looking for work. The ranch, we learn, is run by the growers, who pit worker against worker in an effort to keep wages down and the labor force passive. Once again the economically powerful appear as men in convertibles smoking cigars and, as was the case back in Oklahoma, sheriff's deputies are in the car with them; wealth and the law are allies. The Keene Ranch is an enclave of fascism: it exists to harness the institutions of the state in the service of private profit by exploiting those who have no apparent alternative.

It is at Keene Ranch that Tom again encounters Casey, who tells Tom of the growers' plans to pit worker against worker to keep wages down. But Tom now can see no alternative; he is resigned. Casey is a union organizer—the peaches are ripe and the workers therefore have a bargaining tool, he tells Tom. But Casey is killed by the growers' goons for his organizing work, and Tom, drawn into the fray, accidentally kills one of the goons. His cheek broken in the fight, Tom is now readily identifiable. The Joads, with Tom hidden, leave. Their next stop is the antithesis of Keene Ranch.

The sign reads "Farmworkers Wheat Patch Camp," and below it a smaller sign—the camera tracks toward it—reads "Department of Agriculture." If Keene Ranch is fascism, Wheat Patch Camp is socialism. The Joads are greeted by the pleasant and gentle manager, casually and nicely dressed—mostly in white—who looks not unlike Franklin Roosevelt. (This is reinforced in later scenes when we see him in profile, a cigarette jutting from his mouth, though without Roosevelt's trademark cigarette holder.) The camp is a paradise: the living quarters ("sanitary units" they are called) are clean; they have running water—showers and toilets (which the children, unaccustomed to such luxuries, think they have broken when they flush them). Work is available. There are schools. The workers in each of the five units of the camp elect their own representatives. And they have dancing every Saturday night. Perhaps best of all, the local authorities, who are the growers' allies, can't enter the camp without proper cause. "Who runs it?" Tom asks. "The government," he is told. "Why aren't there more like it?" Tom wants to know. Told that the local growers don't like the organization of the camp—it is the New Deal antithesis of Keene Ranch—Tom edges as close as he ever comes to a political discussion when he asks why the growers are so concerned about "reds." "What is these reds, anyway?" For Tom, "these reds" may not be too bad if they help people to work together to help each other: "If all our people got together and yelled."

The residents of Wheat Patch Camp manage to avoid a trumped-up fight engineered by the growers in order to justify the entrance into the camp by the local authorities, but Tom knows it is only a matter of time before he is found out for the murder at Keene Ranch. He decides to leave, though not simply to flee. He has been inspired by Casey's example and Casey's death and must now choose between two alternatives: to stay and become the head of the household (Pa is, by his own admission, weak and tired, and Tom's brother-in-law deserted the family on the road) or go off on his own and follow the example presented by the martyred Casey. Casey, the lapsed preacher, recommitted himself to championing the downtrodden ("If I was to pray I'd pray for folks that's alive, an' don't know which way to turn"). Tom chooses Casey's way rather than Ma Joad's way. Recalling Casey, Tom tells Ma he remembers, "What he said, what he done, how he died. I remember all of it." As Tom prepares to leave he gives his famous "I'll be there" speech:

Maybe it's like Casey said—a fella ain't got a soul of his own, just a little piece of a big soul, a soul that belongs to everybody....I'll be all around in the dark. I'll be everywhere, wherever you can look. When there's a fight so hungry people can eat, I'll be there. When there's a cop beating up a guy, I'll be there....And when the people are eating the stuff they raise and living in the houses they build, I'll be there too.

Ford cuts twice to Ma during this speech; she is fearful and uncomprehending. But so is Tom uncomprehending: he tells Ma he doesn't understand what he is doing either, that he'll "maybe scrounge around and find out what it is that's wrong." But Tom does go, and, in an almost perfect repeat of the opening of the film, we see Tom walking off alone.

Had *The Grapes of Wrath* ended there, we would have been left with the image of Tom, the lone hero, leaving his family—essentially a female world, for Ma is the heart of the family—to fight for the little guy. But in a decision to shift the focus back to Ma and the family and to provide an upbeat ending, we return to the truck and Ma's—and the film's—final speech. She tells Pa, "Rich fellas come up and they die an' their kids ain't no good and they die out, but we keep acomin'. We're the people that live. Can't wipe us out, can't lick us. We'll go on forever, Pa, 'cause we're the people."

The ostensible center of the film is the family. The film was structured to emphasize the family by ending it with Ma's speech celebrating the resiliency of the people rather than ending it with Tom's speech, which emphasizes justice. Ma represents apolitical resignation and perseverance; Tom, commitment and justice. While the central characters in many Depression films were men, often single men, in *The Grapes of Wrath* the emphasis is on keeping the family together—it is, especially, Ma's driving motivation. John Ford's own analysis was that "Before all else, it is the story of a family, the way it reacts, how it is shaken by a serious problem which overwhelms it. It is not a social film on this problem, it's a study of a family" (Quoted in Gallagher, 1986, 177).

But at precisely the time when the Joads find their best opportunity to remain together—the government camp is by far the best situation they encounter—Tom elects to leave and pursue (we suppose) the life of a labor organizer, leaving his family behind. While this is motivated in the context of the film by the second murder, it remains the case that at the end of *The Grapes of Wrath* the family goes one way, represented by Ma's simple belief in the people, and Tom goes another, driven by his own hunger for justice and the memory of the Christ-like Casey's particular version of faith. The choice Tom makes between Ma and Casey is anticipated earlier by Ford's shot of Tom greeting his mother on his return from prison. Tom turns slowly (reluctantly?) from Casey toward his mother while we see Casey in the background, turned partially away from Tom and Ma's reunion, alone and removed from mother and son. The alternatives for Tom represented by Ma and Casey are subtly suggested, and in the end Tom chooses the world of political action and leaves his family behind. They will persevere; he will fight.

ESCAPE

As the Depression abated, films turned—rather rapidly—from approach to avoidance. Sometimes the avoidance was sugar-coated—films in which problems were acknowledged but, in the tradition of the happy ending, overcome. One of the best examples of this is *Sullivan's Travels* (1941), a film whose release date provides a clue to its tone: by 1941 the worst of the Depression was gone, and *Sullivan's Travels* could safely make fun of social problem films. *Sullivan's Travels* is the work of Preston Sturges (1898-1959) who, after an apprenticeship as a playwright and screenwriter made a series of hugely successful films in which he happily seized all the major production roles—producer, writer, director—as he did in *Sullivan's Travels*.

Sullivan's Travels opens at night with a desperate fight between two men atop a rushing train; they both fall into a river from which emerge the words "The End." We are in a studio screening room watching the end of a social problem film and we hear John L. Sullivan (Joel McCrea), movie director:

Sullivan: You see? You see the symbolism of it? Capital and labor destroy each other. It teaches a lesson, a moral lesson. It has social significance.
Producer: Who wants to see that kind of stuff? It gives me the creeps.
Sullivan [to an executive]: Tell him how long it played at the Music Hall.
Executive: It was held over a fifth week.
Producer: Who goes to the Music Hall? Communists!
Sullivan: Communists? This picture's an answer to communism. It means we're awake and not dunking our heads in the sand like a bunch of ostriches. I want this picture to be a commentary on modern conditions—stark realism—the problems that confront the average man.
Producer: But with a little sex.
Sullivan: A little—but I don't want to stress it. I want this picture to be a document. I want to hold a mirror up to life, a true canvas of the suffering of humanity.
Producer: But with a little sex.
Producer: Something like Capra.
Sullivan: What's the matter with Capra?

All this is said in classic screwball comedy style—rapid-fire delivery with the characters rushing about. The entire sequence is very long, all in one shot, and from it we learn that the successful Sullivan is feeling guilty about his movies, that he wants to do something serious, to be taken as an artist—and artists do work on serious subjects. He wants to use film as an artistic, "sociological" medium (in contrast to his recent hits *Ants in Your Pants of 1939* and *Hey Hey in the Hayloft*). Sullivan's profitable films lead the executives to humor him in his wish to make a study of suffering to be called *O Brother, Where Art Thou?* But before he makes it, Sullivan wants to go on the road incognito to live as a hobo, to learn the life he wants to film.

In his beautiful home, Sullivan tells his butler (William Demarest) his plans. The butler is not impressed:

I have never been sympathetic to the caricaturing of the poor and the needy, sir....The poor know all about poverty and only the morbidly rich would find the topic glamorous....Rich people and theorists, who are usually rich people, think of poverty in the negative, as a lack of riches....But it isn't, sir. Poverty is not a lack of anything, but a positive plague, virulent in itself, contagious as cholera, with filth, criminality, vice and despair. It is to be stayed away from....It is to be shunned.

Despite being chastised by his servant, Sullivan is not dissuaded. The studio decides to capitalize on Sullivan's plans to go on the road by assigning a publicity team to follow him. After a slapstick car chase in which Sullivan hitches a ride in a racing car and outruns the studio van following, he is at last alone on the road. He briefly finds work with two sexually frustrated spinster sisters, who, anticipating the film's finale, take him to a triple-bill of romantic melodramas. Sullivan escapes the sisters and hitchhikes back to Hollywood where in a cafe he meets The Girl (the character has no name and is identified this way in the credits), played by Veronica Lake—she of the famous long-blonde-hair-over-the-eye hair style (which Lake cut for symbolic purposes during World War II). The Girl is an aspiring actress and after Sullivan reveals his true identity, he offers to buy her a ticket home: the movie business is tough, he tells her. Sullivan takes The Girl to his home—he needs to get the cash for her ticket—and while there she persuades him to take her along on his travels. He agrees, disguising her as a boy, and they set off.

Their travels are grim—they ride the rails, live in a shantytown, and meet the desperately poor people of whom the butler spoke. So grim are their experiences that Sullivan successfully persuades The Girl to return to Hollywood to seek work: however tough Hollywood might be for a struggling actress, the prospects are better there than on the road.

On his own again, Sullivan gives money to some hobos and is seen by another hobo who follows him, robs him, beats him unconscious, and throws him on a passing train. The robber is killed by another train as he scrambles after the stolen money. On the robber's body is found Sullivan's identification, hidden by Sullivan in his shoe unbeknownst to the robber. The mixup leads to the announcement that famed movie director John L. Sullivan has been killed.

Suffering from amnesia as a result of the beating, Sullivan fights with a railroad guard and is arrested. He is found guilty and sentenced to six years at hard labor, where he is beaten and confined to solitary confinement for trivial infractions—James Allen's fate. His only solace is an evening at a local church where the prisoners are treated to cartoons. Sturges shoots the scene as a series of loving close-ups of the prisoners laughing, briefly escaping from prison life. Sullivan initially resists joining in the laughter, looking with wonderment at the others, perhaps too sophisticated to be seduced by such simple fare, but finally abandons himself to laughter. This is Sullivan's epiphany: he sees what pleasure frivolous movies like his bring.

Sullivan eventually finally conceives a way out of prison: he confesses to the murder of the mis-identified John L. Sullivan, and his celebrity clears up the mistaken identity and frees him. Back in Hollywood—and reunited with The Girl—he finds that the studio executives are now anxious that he make *O Brother Where Art Thou?* But instead Sullivan now wants to make a comedy: "There's a lot to be said for making people laugh. Did you know that's all some people have? It isn't much but it's better than nothing in this cockeyed caravan."

Sullivan's Travels, besides its self-referential qualities—it is a Preston Sturges film about the redemptive qualities of Preston Sturges films—shows the great distance between the America of James Allen in *I Am a Fugitive from a Chain Gang,* the Joad family in *The Grapes of Wrath*, and that of John L. Sullivan in *Sullivan's Travels.* All take journeys through America, but there the similarities end: Allen is a working-class war veteran whose dream is to get a better job; the Joads' situation is even more desperate; Sullivan is a wealthy director who wants to make a movie about people like James Allen and the Joads. Allen's journey is one of rejection and failure, as is the Joads'; Sullivan's is largely a romp, and when it is not—for he does meet with the dispossessed—we know he can always get out. Allen and the Joads cannot. Allen and the Joads are devastated by the Depression; Sullivan gets rich helping people escape from it. Allen escapes from prison by becoming a fugitive; Tom Joad flees Keene Ranch a fugitive too, and his relatives are economic fugitives; Sullivan escapes prison by being a celebrity. Allen's first wife betrays him; the Joads see Grampa and Grandma die, their son-in-law desert them, and Tom's lonely departure; Sullivan gets Veronica Lake.

Sullivan's Travels may be read as a film whose analysis of economic deprivation and imprisonment amounts to this: they may be dealt with by laughing at a movie cartoon. But it may also be read as a modest acknowledgment of what movies can and cannot do in such times: entertain people and not much more. And that is why, while the film begins with the dramatic "labor versus capital" fight scene from an imaginary social problem film, it ends with a reprise of the faces of the prisoners laughing at cartoons. The first shot of *Sullivan's Travels* shows a movie. The last shows the audience.

What these films have in common is the use of the journey as their basic narrative device. The journey is a powerful metaphor, most often a metaphor for life. In the context of the Depression, however, the journey is more properly a metaphor for the discovery or rediscovery of a country in disarray. James Allen's journey is unimaginably bleak: there is no optimism, no happy ending. The Joads' journey is more complex: Ma ends up with her simple, strong optimism, and the family ends up in the bosom of the New Deal. Tom is lured by neither and goes his own way. And John L. Sullivan, a dozen years after the Great Crash of 1929, will make more comedies so that people can laugh.

SCREWBALL

One step away from the world of the gangster films, the odd mix of realism and escape of *Sullivan's Travels* and the dismal worlds of *I Am a Fugitive from a Chain Gang* and *The Grapes of Wrath* were the screwball comedies, whose heyday beginning in the early 1930s almost exactly paralleled that of the gangster and social problem films. That the Great Depression could simultaneously generate and sustain what were essentially three quite different types of movies demonstrates not just the extent of the social disruption of the Depression but the schizoid nature with which the country responded to it. The reformist liberalism of the New Deal, while hugely popular politically, was by no means unchallenged. The wealthiest Americans hated Roosevelt and all he stood for (though the film industry, despite many of its own being among those very wealthy, could overlook that: its core audience was anything but wealthy). Beyond its natural adversaries among Republicans and the wealthy, the Depression era supported an unusually large number of challenges to the New Deal: Norman Thomas's Socialist party and Gus Hall's Communist party U.S.A. had the greatest electoral support they ever had or ever would have during this era. Father James Coughlin, a Detroit Roman Catholic priest with a large national radio following; Huey ("Every Man a King!") Long in Louisiana, a renegade Democrat who was a potential challenger to Roosevelt until he was assassinated; Upton ("End Poverty in California") Sinclair; and Charles Townsend, with his plan for a national pension for all of America's elderly—all led movements based on discontent both with the Depression and with New Deal programs. Inevitably, this ferment was reflected in popular culture.

Of the film genres born during this time, screwball comedy was the most durable during the Depression. *Little Caesar* spawned fifty similar movies in a few years, after which the genre temporarily died out, though it reappeared in later years, taking root in a cynical post-Vietnam and post-Watergate America. Social problem films peaked in the 1930s, reappeared in a different guise in the 1950s—this time centered around juvenile delinquency—and subsequently left movie theaters for television. Screwball was the most durable of Depression-era genres: from the seminal *It Happened One Night* (1934) through revisionist screwball films like *Sullivan's Travels* and other similar Preston Sturges films like *The Lady Eve* (1941), *The Palm Beach Story* (1942), and *Hail the Conquering Hero* (1944), Depression-era audiences could see comedic readings of their problems.

A memorable, though short-lived, approach to film comedy in the Depression years came from the anarchic and absurdist vision of the Marx Brothers. No analysis of social problems or reformist liberal solutions for them: placing themselves always in opposition to custom and convention, the Brothers' job was to wreck whatever they encountered. This they did in a series of films in the early Depression years: *The Cocoanuts* (1929), *Animal Crackers* (1930), *Monkey Business* (1931), *Horsefeathers* (1932), and *Duck Soup* (1933)—in all of which, whatever the circumstance, their job was to create chaos. The damage was done principally by Groucho, and his targets were order and structure. The Marx Brothers, in a time when the political world of movies ranged from acknowledgment of problems to avoidance of them, responded with anarchy.

The anarchy was often verbal. In *Animal Crackers*, Groucho and Chico discuss a search for a stolen painting:

Groucho: Suppose nobody in the house took the painting?
Chico: Go to the house next door.
Groucho: Suppose there isn't any house next door?
Chico: Then we gotta build one.

The absurdist language and word-play of the Marx Brothers films collapsed the rational into the irrational, the significant into the trivial, and demolished cause and effect. The absurdist world of the Marxes found political focus in *Duck Soup,* in which Groucho plays Prime Minister Rufus T. Firefly of Freedonia, who has been placed in power by the rich dowager Mrs. Teasedale (played by Margaret Dumont, a frequent target for gags in Marx Brothers films). Having achieved power via a wealthy patron, Firefly now commences to destroy everything. He arrives at his own inauguration by sliding down a fire pole, then performs card tricks. He presides over the Chamber of Deputies while playing jacks, refuses to conduct business, and admits he cannot comprehend a treasurer's report. Having demolished and mocked Freedonia internally, Firefly now drives himself into a rage over an imaginary insult—the anticipated refusal of a handshake—from the ambassador of the state of Sylvania. "So you refuse to shake hands with me!" cries Firefly, and slaps the ambassador.

Thus, in a parody of diplomatic protocol, Firefly starts a war. The Freedonian people obediently comply, joyously singing songs celebrating the battle ("We're Going to War!"). Firefly does a handstand; the Freedonian people do the same. Freedonians and Sylvanians switch sides, then switch back. Firefly mocks obedience and sacrifice in war: "While you're out there risking life and limb...we'll be in here thinking what a sucker you are." The Marxes appear in a series of costumes—as World War I soldiers, British Redcoats, frontier pioneers. War has become comic opera. When Firefly is informed he is firing on his own men he responds, "Here's five dollars, keep it under your hat. Never mind—I'll keep it under my hat." When Freedonia wins the war, Mrs. Teasedale bursts into "Hail, Hail Freedonia," and the brothers, who started it all, pelt her with fruit.

Despite the Marx Brothers' box-office history, *Duck Soup* was not the hit its predecessors were. Perhaps the trashing of politics and politicians was too intense in light of the optimism that characterized the early New Deal era in which the film was released. Perhaps the audience was not prepared to see citizens—not just leaders—portrayed as fools. Perhaps the satire of war, which takes up most of the film, was too close to home for those who had lost friends or family in World War I. Subsequent Marx Brothers films *A Night at the Opera* (1935) and *A Day at the Races* (1937) were much more successful though no less anarchic than *Duck Soup*. Their targets, however, were no longer political. The Marx Brothers' audience apparently was prepared to enjoy their "hymn to anarchy and whole-hearted revolt" (Bergman, 1971, 32, quoting Antonin Artaud), but only outside the sphere of politics.

The more durable comedic genre of screwball was the American version of the classic comedy of manners—comedies based on the premise that the social and sexual antics of the rich and wellborn are entertaining, especially for those who are not rich and wellborn. Screwball was typically based in a specific place and time, unlike the timeless and fictional Freedonia of *Duck Soup*. Stylistically, screwball is characterized by rapid-fire editing, a fast narrative pace, and equally rapid exchanges between characters. Screwball comedy characters are fast-talking, witty, and acerbic. If one's only knowledge of 1930s America is from movies, the temptation is to conclude that Americans were either the unfortunates typified by the Joads or James Allen or the frivolous and witty wealthy in such early screwball comedies as *Twentieth Century* (1934), *Trouble in Paradise* (1932), *Dinner at Eight* (1933), and *Design for Living* (1933)—that is, a society of stark class conflict. With the release in 1934 of *It Happened One Night*, however, screwball took its standard subjects—the social and sexual foibles of the idle rich—and added to them a distinctly Depression-driven ingredient: class conflict mediated by screwball.

The screenplay of *It Happened One Night* was a collaboration between director Frank Capra (1897-1991) and writer Robert Riskin (1897-1955), a frequent collaborator on Capra films. The film was a huge hit, the first to sweep all the major Academy Awards categories, wining Oscars for picture, director, writer, actor (Clark Gable), and actress (Claudette Colbert). As with many other films of the era, *It Happened One Night* is the story of a journey, this time from Miami to New York City. The principal travelers are Peter Warne (Clark Gable) and Ellie Andrews (Claudette Colbert). Colbert was not especially anxious to make the film. Only after being assured that production would be rapid did she agree to appear. Gable was a relative unknown at the time; *It Happened One Night* made him a star.

Newspaperman Peter Warne, with a history of being fired, has been fired again. He is in a bar commiserating with other victims of the Depression when he learns he is out of work, and as he slams down the phone he is applauded by the bar's patrons for his courage in standing up to authority. Warne is the classic movie reporter: tough, cynical, streetwise. But, with a typical Capra-Riskin emphasis, he is also a little old-fashioned. He believes in traditional values, he wants to find the right woman, he believes in marriage, family, hard work. At that moment in the bar, as his journey begins, he has none of these. But his circumstances are decidedly less grim, and they are portrayed more comedically, than those that faced the Joads and James Allen. Peter Warne's circumstances are somewhere between those of John L. Sullivan and Tom Joad.

Ellie Andrews (Claudette Colbert) also begins her journey by standing up to authority, in the person of her wealthy father (Walter Connolly). Ellie flees her father's yacht, determined not to marry the man her father has chosen for her. She wants instead to marry an even more insensitive and superficial son of privilege, King Westley (Jameson Thomas). Superficially, Ellie's revolt is less significant than Peter's, at least economically: Peter is out of a job; Ellie has only run from her wealthy father's choice of a wealthy husband to her own choice of a wealthy husband. But Peter has been fired many times; we expect he will land on his feet and he has, after all, only had a dispute with an editor. Ellie, though shielded economically, has broken with her own father. Thus, each of the main characters, though with different emphasis and likely consequence, has broken as a matter of principle with an authority figure. The relationship between a younger character and an older one—regardless of whether the older character is a parent or a boss—is typical of Frank Capra's work. Capra's films are among the preeminent examples of ancestor worship in film.

Peter and Ellie meet accidentally; had each not made their break from authority they never would have met at all. And in their meeting a series of dichotomies—a social scientist would call them reinforcing cleavages—are established: not just male/female but working-class/leisure-class. Initially, Peter and Ellie's relationship is one of convenience. She needs his street smarts and cash (she has none with her) to avoid being found by her father's detectives. He needs her story to revive his journalistic fortunes. Of course they fall in love, and the story of their falling in love becomes also the story of the reconciliation of disparate social classes.

The basic structure of *It Happened One Night* became the prototype for countless similar films: Having been thrown together as a matter of chance and choice, the principals form an uneasy alliance based on necessity and punctuated by conflict, sexual and social. In so doing each character discovers things about the other that are admirable and each helps the other discard things that are not. The characters complement and complete each other (as also happens, for instance, among the more numerous characters in *The Wizard of Oz*, who acquire characteristics from one another). At the personal level in *It Happened One Night*, this leads to Ellie and Peter falling in love; at the social level it leads to a reconciling of social classes. For Peter and Ellie to fall in love is to banish class conflict by rejecting the social and economic in favor of the personal.

Peter and Ellie travel toward New York from Miami, meeting mainstream America along the way, but it is a happier group than those we see as we travel with the Joads, James Allen, or even John L. Sullivan. Two scenes distill the growing class accommodation and personal affection between Peter and Ellie: Peter teaches Ellie the pleasures of playing piggyback ("I've never met a rich man yet who could give piggybacks"), and Ellie, in the most famous scene in the film and one of the best-remembered in any film, succeeds where Peter has failed by hitching a ride for them both by flashing a little leg. Their distance as well as their attraction are embodied in the "Walls of Jericho," a sheet Peter places between their beds as the two travel, pretending to be married. When the "Walls" come tumbling down (off screen) at the end, all is reconciled. The humor with which all these scenes are directed is typical of Capra. A former gag writer for silent short comedies, Capra rarely lost his light comic touch, which is usually as much visual as verbal. And his frequent use of medium and close-up shots—often with fairly long takes—individualized his characters.

Also typical of Capra is the manner in which Peter and Ellie finally get together: intervention from benevolent elders. Peter's former editor, realizing that his former employee has fallen in love, is transformed from an angry boss to a supportive father. Ellie's father is likewise chastised by his daughter's love of Peter into realizing that the very qualities that made him successful (hard work, honesty, a sense of perspective on the role of wealth) are present both in Ellie and Peter. Peter gets a surrogate father and Ellie gets her own father back. The only character who does not change is the superficial and insensitive rich twit King Westley, and Ellie nearly marries him. Now, as Ellie and Westley are about to marry, it is Mr. Andrews who urges his daughter to flee to Peter, a precise reversal of Ellie's situation at the beginning of the film.[4] Mr. Andrews, who is a self-made man, rediscovers in Peter those values that made him successful. Westley inherited his money and has learned nothing. (One recalls Ma Joad saying of this, "Rich folks come up and they die and their kids ain't no good and they die out.")

Within the world of many Capra films, crises are resolved in one of two ways: the benevolent intervention of elders, as in *It Happened One Night*, or through the threat of suicide, as in *Mr. Smith Goes to Washington* (1939), *Meet John Doe* (1941), and *It's A Wonderful Life* (1946). Some Capra films offer their characters either suicide or salvation by ancestors as the only alternatives: *Smith, Doe,* and *Wonderful Life*, for example. For a director whose films are regularly viewed as celebrations of optimism, Capra often presents stark alternatives: heed the wisdom of your elders or die. Ellie does heed her father, of course, and escapes her planned marriage with Westley by fleeing to Peter, to whom she has been symbolically married throughout the film. Thus are individuals and social classes reconciled—all at the urging and with the blessings of the benevolent, wealthy father. Ellie and Peter's rejection of authority at the beginning of *It Happened One Night* is transformed into an acceptance of it by the end: Mr. Andrews effectively orders Peter and Ellie to follow their hearts and marry—and presumably, to be rich as well. Thus seen, *It Happened One Night* does not so much reconcile social classes as it makes everyone wealthy or in love, or, for its central characters, both.

CAPRA

The mix of muted social realism and generational, sexual, and economic conflict resolved in terms confirming conventional authority in *It Happened One Night* would come into fuller development in Frank Capra's "Depression trilogy" of *Mr. Deeds Goes to Town* (1936), *Mr. Smith Goes to Washington* (1939), and *Meet John Doe* (1941), the last two a darker version of their predecessors. That these three films maintain their structural similarity is in no small part due to the huge success of *It Happened One Night*. Success breeds power, and Capra used his newly acquired leverage to negotiate a deal with Harry Cohn of Columbia Pictures, at the time one of the "poverty row" studios, a status from which Capra's successes lifted Columbia. His deal with Cohn gave Capra complete control over his films, an unprecedented arrangement at the time when directors were hired hands. Capra would title his autobiography *The Name Above the Title* (Capra, 1971) in recognition of his films' title credits, which read "Frank Capra's *Meet John Doe*"—a first—and he would repeat throughout the book his belief in "one man, one film." Those who believed in the *auteur* theory had an enthusiastic ally in Capra.

Capra's own story, as so many observed, was like a Capra movie. Arriving in the United States from Sicily as a child of six with his large family, young Capra got up early, worked hard, did well in school, and succeeded. Like many immigrants, he did not just gratefully take advantage of his economic opportunities: he enthusiastically accepted the American Dream. If it is possible for a person to overassimilate into a new society, Capra did: not only did he accept the American credo, he ignored or rejected his own family's origins (see McBride, 1992, chap. 1). He begins the preface of his autobiography thus: "I hated being poor. Hated being a peasant. Hated being a scrounging newskid trapped in the sleazy Sicilian ghetto of Los Angeles. My family couldn't read or write. I wanted out. A quick out" (Capra, 1971, xi).

After graduating from what later became the California Institute of Technology, Capra, uncertain of his future, bluffed his way into gag writing for Hal Roach and directed some Harry Langdon silent comedies, developing a verbal and visual comedic touch that would stay with him and characterize and humanize his best work. With the eventual success of *It Happened One Night*, Frank Capra became the most powerful director in Hollywood.

Capra's Depression trilogy films progressively diminish the romantic and comedic elements of *It Happened One Night* and other screwball comedies and emphasize instead—film by film—a deepening and grimmer involvement in economic and political matters. With each film the mood is more desperate and the problems harder to resolve, for they now go well beyond whether love can conquer all. All the trilogy films are broadly similar in structure: a decent but naive country boy is thrust by events into a journey to the city where he meets a worldly and street-wise woman who first uses him but is finally won over. In the city the hero finds his beliefs outmoded and his actions ridiculed. By force of his own decency and the values he represents, he triumphs.

Mr. Deeds Goes to Town, the most conventional of the trilogy films, is the story of Longfellow Deeds (Gary Cooper), a small-town businessman, volunteer firefighter, and amateur tuba player entirely content with his life. His life changes radically for the worse when an unknown relative dies and leaves him a fortune. Curious about city life, he leaves the Eden of small-town America and goes to New York, where he is victimized by a series of city shysters—a common villain in Depression-era films, as evil could be attributed to bad individuals rather than economic or political conditions. In New York, Deeds meets Babe Bennett (Jean Arthur, she of the wonderful voice that combined the huskiness of a woman with the innocence of a girl). Babe is a reporter for whom Deeds is a great story; she strings him along by convincing Deeds that she is a weak woman in need. Appalled at the corruption and decadence of the big city and not needing all that money anyway, Deeds decides to give his fortune to the Depression poor. A sanity hearing is scheduled: Deeds must be mad to want to give away a fortune. At the hearing, Deeds routs the experts who testify against him with his common sense and good heart. Deeds wins over the judge, who pronounces him the sanest man around, the cheering spectators, and finally Babe, who, from the witness, stand admits her manipulation of Deeds and then proclaims her love.

Mr. Smith Goes to Washington ups the ante over *Deeds* in every respect. Somewhere out West lives Jefferson Smith (James Stewart), head of the Boy Rangers, son of a legendary and fearless editor of a crusading small newspaper slain while working at his desk. Jeff lives with his gentle and saintly mother ("Ma," played by Beulah Bondi) and devotes himself to teaching the Boy Rangers sturdy, traditional values, including the love of the land implied by Jeff's first name.

One of the two U.S. senators from Jeff's state dies unexpectedly in office, and Governor Hopper (Guy Kibbee) must name a replacement. The governor's initial choices are hooted down, and in a dinner table scene at the governor's mansion, Hopper's children unanimously recommend Jeff Smith. All the state's children love Jeff Smith, they tell their father, and his son reminds the governor that children have parents who vote. Hopper clears Jeff Smith's name with James Taylor (Edward Arnold), the state's political boss, and with the state's other senator, Joseph Paine (Claude Raines), the "Silver Fox."[5] Thus, Sidney Buchman's screenplay establishes the political circumstances of the film: that politicians are dim bulbs, who, like Hopper, hop to the wishes of private wealth in the person of Jim Taylor, and that children are wise and good, as are child-like adults like Jeff Smith.

On the train to Washington, Paine and Smith talk of Jeff's father. We learn that Jeff's father and Senator Paine were youthful comrades in the service of the little guy—Smith the crusading editor and Paine the idealistic lawyer. Buchman's dialogue (Buchman was for a time a member of the Communist party of the U.S.) establishes Paine's lost idealism by contrasting it not only with his and Jeff's father's past—they are recalled as crusaders for lost causes—but with Jeff himself, and a visual association between Jeff and his father is also established by linking the two through the motif of hats. The circle between Jeff's martyred father, Senator Paine, and Jefferson Smith is completed when Paine alludes to Jeff as a son. Jeff recalls his father's own admiration for Paine and tells the senator of his respect for him. But now, Senator Paine gently suggests to Jeff, he has given up on fighting for lost causes, and Jeff Smith as gently quotes his father to the senator: "Sometimes lost causes are the only ones worth fighting for." The scene establishes the common bond between Joseph Paine and Jeff Smith; it also suggests future conflict between them.

In Washington, the newly arrived-from-the-boondocks Jeff Smith is good newspaper copy. He is met by the usual worldly-wise reporters and a group of pretty young Washington women, including Senator Paine's daughter, Susan. Like the simple country boy he is, Smith happily tells reporters about his homing pigeons and his skill at birdcalls; the reporters laugh and the photographers take their pictures. Awed to be in Washington, Smith rushes off to visit every available national monument (he knows all the great patriotic utterances by heart, and the film is full of allusions to national heroes), leaving his welcoming party fearing he is lost.

His tour of the monuments over, Smith wanders to his own office and meekly identifies himself to his chief aide, Clarissa Saunders (Jean Arthur), and her friend, Diz (Thomas Mitchell), the film's resident cynical, boozing reporter. Both regard Smith with amused contempt. They know his role is that of prop, placed in the Senate by Governor Hopper at the behest of Jim Taylor, to be kept in line by Senator Paine. Smith learns this—but only in very general terms—from the chorus of reporters after he chases after them for publishing embarrassing newspaper photographs of him doing a birdcall and stories deriding him as an overgrown child come to Washington. One after another, Smith confronts the reporters, punches them (a common action for a Capra hero), then verbally berates them. The reporters give as good as they get and tell Smith he is a stooge, appointed to the Senate so as not to upset things back home or in the Senate.

Smith has other plans. He wants to make his mark with a boys' camp back home so that boys from everywhere can enjoy the advantages—physical and spiritual—of rural life. No big government spender, Smith figures this will be paid for by the government but repaid by voluntary contributions from the children themselves. But Smith's planned location for the camp, unbeknownst to him, runs afoul of the Taylor machine's own plans for the land, a good old-fashioned political land deal. To build the boys' camp would wreck the Taylor machine's profits. As Smith and Saunders work on plans for the camp—she knows about Taylor's plans but does not tell the enthusiastic Smith—Smith and Saunders begin to fall in love, Smith becoming associated in Saunders' mind with her own sainted father and with the rural life about which Smith rhapsodizes but about which Saunders, being a city girl, knows nothing. Saunders, for her part, imparts to Smith her knowledge of Congressional procedure and executive-legislative relations. She becomes the head, he the heart, of their collaboration.

Senator Paine, informed of Smith's plans, tries to divert Jeff with his own daughter—that is, he symbolically prostitutes her. In a scene in the Paine home, Susan Paine so flusters Smith that Capra shows us—repeatedly—Jeff fumbling with his hat (that is, his father's hat) in confusion. Smith eventually learns of the Taylor machine's plans and Senator Paine's role in it. Smith confronts Paine, who gives one of the film's most interesting political speeches, telling young Jeff that politics is compromise and that, despite his complicity in the workings of the Taylor organization, he has served the people in "a thousand honest ways." Smith rejects Paine's explanation.

The Taylor machine now goes to work, trumping up the charge that Jeff Smith owns the very land on which the boys' camp is to be built and has proposed the camp only to profit personally from it. Senator Paine is persuaded to become Jim Taylor's Senate point man—to betray Jeff Smith, his symbolic son—and spreads the phony story about Smith's ownership of the land. He demands that Smith resign. Dismayed and bewildered, Smith is ready to quit. At the Lincoln Memorial (it appears several times in the film), Saunders, who herself was briefly tempted to run from it all by accepting Diz's standing invitation of marriage, persuades Smith to stay and fight. In the Memorial, with Lincoln looking on, Capra shoots Saunders in sharp, strong profile, wearing a hat, while Smith himself is formless, his head bowed. Smith decides to make a stand.

His reputation and his Senate seat at stake, Smith wins recognition to speak from the president of the Senate, the vice president of the United States (Harry Carey). This ruling by the presiding officer and the filibuster scene that follows, are key references in *Mr. Smith Goes to Washington* to formal rules and procedures. The climactic filibuster scene of the film could not happen without the vice president's initial recognition of Smith or without the Senate's rules on debate: politics in *Smith* may be Jim Taylor directing Senator Paine, but it is also procedure. In *Mr. Smith Goes to Washington*, the hero finally wins not just because he is good but because of rules.

Guided by Saunders with Diz at her side, Smith begins a twenty-three-hour filibuster, words replacing punches as his weapons. Capra shows actual news commentators of the day observing the "exercise in democracy" taking place below, adding visual and verbal references to representatives of other countries (referring to Fascist Germany and Italy) where such debate cannot occur.

As Smith talks—he jokes, reads the Constitution, and watches Saunders carefully so he won't be fooled by a parliamentary maneuver—the Taylor machine goes into action to sway public opinion back home. Jeff says he will resign if the folks back home tell him to do so and the Taylor machine means to get the public to do just that. Paine, though deeply conflicted ("Jim, they're crucifying that boy"), does Taylor's bidding, in part because the vice presidential nomination is dangled in front of him. Taylor is prepared to do anything to win: in a phone call overheard by Senator Paine, Taylor tells one of his men back home to be sure to go after small local newspaper editors. A very quick cut to Senator Paine tells us that he suspects it may have been Taylor himself who was responsible for the death years ago of Jeff Smith's father and Paine's old comrade.

In a series of quick cuts, Capra shows Taylor's men back home orchestrating radio and newspaper coverage, unfurling banners, and operating blaring sound trucks, all with the same message: Jeff Smith is a liar and should resign. Saunders learns of this disinformation campaign (Saunders to Diz, sarcastically: "Freedom of the press!") and calls Ma Smith, who galvanizes the Boy Rangers to respond with their own defense of Smith in the Boy Rangers newspaper. Exhausted boys labor to get out the truth about Smith, only to have their presses destroyed and their wagons run off the road by Taylor's men.

The filibuster continues; the exhausted Smith is barely able to talk or stand. Senator Paine dramatically displays telegrams from home—the result of the Taylor machine's efficient work—demanding that Smith heed the people as he said he would and resign. Smith, having demanded to hear the people speak, now refuses to listen to them because he knows their message is the result of manipulation. All the messages are lies, he says, he will not quit. Alluding to his sainted father, Smith vows to fight for lost causes. Exhausted, Smith collapses. As he does, a shot is heard, and Senator Paine, having tried unsuccessfully to kill himself, rushes to the Senate floor and confesses all, telling his colleagues that "this boy" has been telling the truth and that he, Senator Paine, is not fit to be a senator. Saunders, a recent recipient of some of Ma Smith's preserves and having acknowledged during the filibuster her love for Jeff, yips for joy.

Meet John Doe takes *Smith* further; if *Smith* is an extension of *Deeds* then *Doe* is a radical mutation of *Smith*. Reporter Ann Mitchell (Barbara Stanwyck) is about to lose her job when the newspaper she works for is bought by wealthy industrialist D.B. Norton (Edward Arnold, who played boss Jim Taylor in *Smith*). The opening shot shows the legend "A Free Press for a Free People" being jackhammered into dust and replaced by "A Streamlined Paper for a Streamlined Age," and Ann Mitchell is one of many victims of the streamlining. Desperate and angry, she writes a column based on a faked letter from "John Doe," a little guy so disgusted at the state of the world that he threateners to jump off city hall on Christmas Eve. The column is a sensation: letters flood into the newspaper and the harried Mayor Lovett (Gene Lockhart, in a typical film portrayal of a politician as a middle-aged, overweight, bumbling male) is besieged by phone calls to stop Doe from killing himself.

Ann Mitchell's colleagues suspect the letter is a fake and so does the opposition newspaper; she finally admits the letter is a phony. But rather than admit the lie publicly, Mitchell and her editors strike a deal: she will continue to write columns based on John Doe's ruminations on greed and hypocrisy and the paper will publish them. John Doe is good for circulation, and Ann Mitchell keeps her job and blackmails her editors into giving her a raise to boot. As part of the charade, Mitchell and her editor, Connell (James Gleason), decide to find someone to play the role of Doe, an easy task as many men have come forward claiming to be the fictional potential suicide.

In a montage of close-ups we see one face after another—some sad, some funny—of men claiming to be John Doe. The last face we see is that of Long John Willoughby (Gary Cooper), who is at least honest enough to admit that he is not John Doe but only hopes that there might be some work available. Long John is a down-on-his-luck baseball pitcher with a bad arm. He and his friend the Colonel (Walter Brennan) have been on the road for some time. Long John—without much reflection and the promise of food and some money to get his pitching arm repaired—agrees to play the role of Doe despite the protests of the Colonel, who delivers a warning to Long John about the evils of money. Better to be poor and free than have money—even a little money—and be owned by it, the Colonel says.[6] The Colonel's speech takes place in a hotel room to which he and Long John have been sent by the newspaper. In the luxury of the room they eat—Long John ravenously, the Colonel less so—and Long John tests the comfort of a real bed. Long John—now known as John Doe to the reporters invited to meet him—goes through his baseball windup for the photographers and mimics an argument with an umpire, an echo of Jeff Smith and his birdcalls. Long John Willoughby, once a baseball pitcher and a poor but free man is now the fictional John Doe, an amiable accomplice to a rich man's newspaper and a conniving reporter; he has lost his name and plays pantomime baseball in a hotel room.

Adapting to his new persona, Doe agrees to deliver a radio speech celebrating the virtues of the little guys of the world. The speech, written by Ann, is a nationwide hit. John Doe Clubs are spontaneously formed in response. D.B. Norton, politically ambitious as well as wealthy, sees his chance in the John Doe phenomenon and organizes the clubs into a national movement. Ann's speech reflects the values of her honest and idealistic father, even as she is well paid by Norton for the words that are placed in the mouth of an impostor. Ann's confusion between her real father and Doe/Willoughby are further complicated (or confused) when Doe tells Ann of a dream in which he imagines himself to be her father, and when Doe tells Ann's mother (Spring Byington) of his love for her and effectively proposes to Ann's mother rather than to Ann herself. The usually clear path of ancestor worship between generations in Capra films is blurred and warped in *Meet John Doe*.

Ann and Doe come to believe, or least not entirely to disbelieve, the John Doe myth. Finally, persuaded by the Colonel and by the realization that even if he gets his arm fixed he will be unable to play ball because he will have been exposed as a fake, Doe is about to give up the ruse when he is convinced not to do so by a group of John Doe Club members. One after another the club members, led by a soda jerk named Bert (Regis Toomey), tell Doe how the John Doe movement has inspired them to be more cooperative and understanding. The Colonel observes all this Capraesque sentiment with a roll of his eyes. Doe decides to persevere.

Doe is scheduled to speak at a huge rally to be broadcast nationally. His speech, which Doe has not yet seen (and which again has been written by Ann), is to announce the formation of a third political party, based on the thousands of John Doe Clubs nationwide. The party's nominee for president will be D.B. Norton. But prior to the speech, Doe has a long talk with a drunken Connell, who explains to Doe just what Norton's intentions are. Doe goes to Norton's mansion where he sees Ann draped in a new fur and a new diamond bracelet, gifts from Norton. It is here, as Norton presides over a huge table surrounded by his associates, that we learn (if we have not already figured it out) that Norton is a Fascist: he talks of "discipline," of an "iron hand," of a "New Order." Before a now-contrite Ann can renounce her role in Norton's plans and her use of Doe in their furtherance, Doe enters and concludes that he has been betrayed by both Ann and Norton. He threatens to tell the truth at the rally. Norton responds that he (Norton) created the movement and he can kill it. Doe goes to the rally, but arrives to find the newspapers that Norton controls have branded him a fraud. Norton denounces Doe, the crowd turns on their hero, and when Doe tries to speak, he is literally cut off when Norton's henchmen sever a cable. Doe is scorned by the very people who previously professed their love of him. Doe and the Colonel escape to their old lives on the road.

Some months later, on Christmas Eve, Doe/Willoughby appears at city hall, contemplating suicide. Ann, Connell, and the Colonel all are there and try to dissuade him, to no avail, despite Ann's tearful pledge of love. Norton and his henchmen arrive and tell him if he does jumps he will be buried in a pauper's grave and will have died for nothing, but Doe responds that the whole story is in a letter to be opened after his death. Only the arrival of Bert, the soda jerk from the John Doe Club, and others from the club finally persuades Doe not to jump; and to the strains of the "Ode to Joy" from Beethoven's Ninth Symphony, Connell turns to Norton and says, "The people—try and lick that."

The resolution of *Meet John Doe* is confusing and dramatically unsatisfying: John Doe doesn't jump, but how have "the people" triumphed, how have they licked D.B. Norton? At best, Doe and Ann Mitchell have both conspired to lie to the public about the fictional John Doe's threat. What "the people" have done is to prevent a suicide based on a fiction—no more. Certainly the villain, D.B. Norton, will emerge unscathed from all this. Capra himself acknowledged the unsatisfying nature of the conclusion. In his memoirs (Capra, 1971, 305), he tells of shooting five different endings to the film, the first four of which were unsatisfying. After the film was in limited release, as Capra tells it, he received a letter signed "John Doe" suggesting that the only way for John Doe to be saved was by other John Does—the version finally used and the fifth and final conclusion to the film. It was, said Capra (1971, 305), "the best of a sorry lot" of conclusions.

The inconclusive resolution of *Meet John Doe* stands in stark contrast to the upbeat and dramatically tidy conclusions to *Deeds* and *Smith*. To compare Capra's Depression trilogy of films with one another is to see an increasingly complex and pessimistic view of American society and politics from this allegedly most optimistic and populist of filmmakers. The contrast between

Deeds and *Smith* on the one hand and *Doe* on the other is especially telling.

The Male Lead. Deeds, Smith, and Willoughby/Doe are all country boys, but in quite different ways. The former two are associated positively with rural life: they live in the country and are entirely at home there. Deeds is appalled by New York City and yearns to return to the simple life and pleasures of home, and Mr. Smith goes *to* Washington from the country, where he lives with his gentle mother, the warm memory of his sainted country newspaper editor father, and his Boy Rangers. Jeff Smith knows and reveres the land: he, like Deeds, is a simple man whose strength comes from the land and from his family and friends. Willoughby/Doe is also from the land, but from a much harsher version of it: he and the Colonel are hobos who sleep under bridges. They do not live in the land by choice, they live off it by necessity. Deeds and Smith are pillars of their communities; Willoughby/Doe is the damaged representative of the all-American game of baseball—a pitcher with a bad arm and without a family. Most importantly, however, Deeds and Smith know who they are and what they believe; it is these beliefs and their commitment to them that save both. Willoughby/Doe—who makes no speeches about the land, who never celebrates his ancestors, who is never inspired by patriotic heroes—is prepared to be the front-man for a phony newspaper campaign in return for food and money. As Capra himself noted:

We had thus abandoned our usual formula—a sane, honest "man of the people," thrust into a confrontation with the forces of evil, wins out with his innate goodness. This time our hero was a bindle stiff, a drifting piece of human flotsam as devoid of ideals as he was of change in his pocket. (Capra, 1971, 303).

And the characters' names are also telling: Longfellow Deeds and Jefferson Smith evoke good acts, culture, national heroes, and the common man. Willoughby's alias, John Doe (he is called John throughout the film and answers to it as though it is his own name), suggests the common man to be sure, but a particularly generic and empty version of it; more importantly, it suggests the money that motivates him to assume the Doe identity in the first place as well as his dough-like pliability, and the film title is just a little chilling: *Meet John Doe* invites us to meet ourselves.

The Female Lead. Babe, Clarissa Saunders, and Ann Mitchell all initially use the hero: Babe and Mitchell for a good newspaper story, while Saunders is more gentle with Jeff Smith, though she too considers him a naive chump. All the female leads fall for the hero, convinced finally by both his goodness and her own disloyalty to him that the hero deserves respect and love. Mitchell, however, holds out the longest. Months after Willoughby/Doe disappears she still has not told the truth about her hoax, and she profits greatly from the success of the Doe phenomenon. (She loves her fur and jewels and is quick to blackmail her boss for her job and a raise when the Doe hoax is created.) While Saunders supportively coaches Smith in his climactic Senate filibuster and Babe supports Deeds in his sanity hearing, Mitchell writes speeches for

Willoughby/Doe long after she knows of Norton's political ambitions. And in a dark twist on the Capra theme of revered parents, Mitchell tells Doe she thinks of her own father when she writes his speeches, prostituting his memory in the service of D.B. Norton's ambitions.

The Villain. Deeds faces not so much a villain as he does opponents—people who believe him crazy for wanting to give away a fortune. This opposition manifests itself in his sanity hearing, but there his own goodness and common sense win out, and his apparent opponent, the judge, becomes Deeds' ally and vindicator. Smith and Willoughby/Doe face more conventional villains: wealthy and powerful men who enlist politicians, the media, and, ultimately, the public in their cause. The Capra version of power in America is a common one: private wealth directing public institutions. But the scope of that power is quite different. In *Smith*, Boss Jim Taylor is surely ruthless, but his primary motivation is to keep intact his statewide political organization and the profit that flows from it. In D.B. Norton, the villain of *Doe*, we have a Fascist whose ambitions are national: we see Norton happily contemplating a map of the U.S. with pins indicating the locations of hundreds of John Doe Clubs. Norton's associations with fascism are also clear. In addition to his references to a New Order and iron will, when we first see Norton he is astride a horse as he reviews his private army of motorcycle-mounted troops; and later in his office we see on Norton's desk a statue of Napoleon on a horse. Norton's ambitions and his resources vastly outstrip those of the Taylor machine.

The Capra hero in the Depression trilogy films successively faces adversaries ranging from a local judge to a state political boss to a Fascist industrialist with national aspirations. And these adversaries are increasingly unfettered: the judge in Deeds is bound by the law and his interpretation of it; in Jeff Smith's filibuster, the rules of the Senate, however annoying to Smith's accusers, must be followed. But when Willoughby/Doe attempts to make his dramatic speech to the crowded nighttime political rally (visually very reminiscent of the Nazi rally filmed by Leni Riefenstahl for *Triumph of the Will*) of the John Doe Clubs, there are no rules or officials to which he may appeal: Norton, his private police at his disposal, quite literally has the power to have the cable cut, silencing Doe. Doe, unlike Deeds and Smith, has no appeal, no procedure, no authorities, to help him.

"The People." The most distinctive political characteristic of Capra's films was that they depicted the mass public, "the people." The portrayal of politics in most U.S. films is usually a portrayal of political elites and their economic allies, not their mass political base, and Capra's version of that mass public is an unattractive one indeed. In the Depression trilogy, the public comes into sharpest relief in the scenes in which the hero confronts his adversaries with "the people" in the background yet playing a major role.

In *Deeds* the public is thinly sketched: it is represented primarily by the audience in Deeds's sanity hearing. But in *Deeds* both the audience and the judge are won over by the hero; mass and elite agree, largely because they have direct contact in the courtroom with the hero. In *Smith* and *Doe*, however, that contact is mediated in the climactic Senate and political rally scenes. In *Smith* the Taylor machine destroys the Boy Rangers' newspaper campaign and Taylor actives his own newspapers to discredit Smith; in *Doe*, Norton destroys Willoughby/Doe in similar ways but with greater brutality. In both these instances, the public, which is the target of all this media manipulation, is entirely responsive: whatever they read or hear they believe. Jeff Smith goes from hero to villain, as the mail that pours into the Senate from back home attests. Willoughby/Doe is vilified at the rally when Norton destroys, through the media, what he has earlier created by the same means.

When the chief representative of "the people" in *Doe*, Bert the soda jerk, convinces Willoughby/Doe not to kill himself, he tells him that he never really believed all the bad publicity, but this is impossible to believe: we have already seen thousands of other Berts pulled back and forth by Norton's manipulations and seen Bert himself turn on Doe at the rally.   Whether the public is represented indirectly by the letters to the Senate, by the jeers of the John Doe Club members at the rally, or by the child-like credulity of Bert, "the people" in these films emerge as decent, credulous sheep. If by populist filmmaker, as Capra has been so often called, one means a celebration of the basic decency and wisdom of the average person, Capra was no populist. That the little guy is decent in Capra's films is clear; that he is anything but wise is no less clear. The decency of the mass public is the very cause of its downfall: it will decently believe anything. In Capra's films, "the people" when activated are a mob—what political philosophers have long called a tyrannical majority.

If Capra was no populist, what was he? He was a hero-worshipper, whether his characters' heroes were personal ones—a revered parent—or national, as in Jeff Smith's association with Lincoln. Capra's heroes were populist only in the sense of being ordinary men with extraordinary qualities—that is, not ordinary at all. The least heroic of all the male leads of the Depression trilogy, interestingly, is also the most common: Willoughby/Doe at the beginning of *Doe* is simply one of a succession of anxious male faces shown in close-up, each claiming to be the fictional John Doe. He is chosen because, ironically, he looks honest. Smith and Deeds, in contrast, are uncommon men.

A less attractive view of Capra's film politics is that, while his villains were authoritarians, so were his heroes.[7] This is especially so of Jeff Smith, who continues his filibuster even as the folks back home demand that he resign. Smith knows, of course, that he is in the right, as does the audience; but the fact remains that, having promised to heed the will of the people, he refuses to, and does so self-righteously in the name of every conceivable symbol of the American nation. David Thomson writes:

Compromise is that wicked ploy loathed and condemned by Jefferson Smith—and thus his horrendous, hysterical reduction of the Senate to grotesque melodrama, game show and a Ross Perot rally....Democracy in America is a noble hope that needs to be guarded against corruption, but compromise is the essential American way—without it we risk dictatorship. Jefferson Smith is a tyrant, a wicked folksy idiot, who commandeers James Stewart's alarming sweetness. He is the real threat in that film. (Thomson, 1994, 108)

The Capra view of U.S. society and politics is deeply pessimistic, a world filled with good people gone collectively wrong, manipulated by men of wealth, to be saved only by equally committed—but good—men. The political world of Capra's films is the antithesis of populism; it is instead a system comprised of good and bad elites with "the people" simply ratifying the result, pulled this way and that by whoever controls the means of communication, a point made clear in both *Smith* and *Doe* when media manipulation leads the public first to praise and then to condemn the male lead. Capra's heroes resonated with their time: the political setting that drove, and sustained for a time, populist politicians and activists like Huey Long and Father Coughlin—men who professed to speak for the little guy whose world had collapsed—also sustained the audience for the uncommon Everyman who stood at the center of Frank Capra's films.

It is tempting to take the increasingly pessimistic nature of the Depression trilogy films as indicative of a corresponding pessimism in Capra and his collaborators; it is probably more correct to say, however, that these films represented the stretching of a formula to the point of exhaustion, as Capra himself noted of *Doe*. The elements of *Smith*, and even of *It Happened One Night*, came to some sort of twisted conclusion in *Meet John Doe*, as questions of social class, of politics, of the relationship between wealth and power, and finally of the relationship between political elites and the mass public found themselves played out and finally exhausted on the screen.

The thread which binds Depression-era films most tightly is social class conflict. For the gangster, class conflict manifested itself in the creation of an alternative system of mobility and power outside the existing legitimate social structure, providing not just power but revenge for the disadvantaged. The social problem film explored the effects, if not usually the causes, of economic and social dislocation. Even Tom Joad, when he leaves his family, does not quite know what to make of things, only that he cannot follow Ma's ways. Screwball comedy taught that the rich could be just as foolish as the poor, and films like *It Happened One Night* added to that the lesson that love and humanity could overcome (at least for the right two lovers) economic differences. By the time Frank Capra made the last of his trilogy films, however, these considerations of the relationship between social class and power had reached a dead end. The gangster might have been able to create a separate social word for himself, apart from the rest of society, but John Doe could not.

NOTES

1. An interesting example on the heredity/environment question in film is the 1951 *Bedtime for Bonzo* starring Ronald Reagan. Reagan plays a psychology professor who hires a nurse to pretend to be his wife in order to provide a home for a chimpanzee. The professor's goal is to demonstrate that environment will triumph over heredity.

2. Samples of positively portraying and humanizing prisoners can also be seen in *Birdman of Alcatraz* (1962), *Cool Hand Luke* (1967) and *The Shawshank Redemption* (1994).

3. For a discussion of several different versions of Zanuck's role in *The Grapes of Wrath*, see Gallagher, 1986, 179-80.

4. This scene provides an interesting contrast with the similar scene in *The Graduate*. In that film, Elaine also rushes off to be with her real love, Benjamin, but does it at Benjamin's behest and in the face of the enraged opposition of her parents. In *It Happened One Night*, it is Ellie's father who urges her to flee, not Peter.

5. None of the politicians in *Mr. Smith Goes to Washington* are identified by party, though, based on their locations in the Senate chamber, both Senator Joe Paine and Senator Jefferson Smith are Democrats, the majority party in the Senate at the time the film was made.

6. In Riskin and Capra's script, the motif of the Colonel's speech is the evils of money which, says the Colonel, makes people "a lotta heels," what he calls "heelots." In ancient Greece, helots were the serf or slave class of the city-state of Sparta.

7. Capra's own politics are interesting in this respect. He was a conservative Republican, anti-Semitic, a cold-war era anti-Communist, and an admirer of Benito Mussolini, as was Harry Cohn of Columbia Pictures, for whom Capra made many of his most successful films. (See McBride, 1992, 252-63.)

5

THE MOVIES AND WORLD
WAR II

Two world wars have occurred since movies were invented. It is a remarkable fact of film history that the first of these wars, while the subject of fewer films, gave us proportionately more great ones.

The primary reason is political. The approach of the Second World War was watched closely by the U.S. film industry. Many in that industry were refugees from Nazi Germany, and the industry watched the coming war closely because it was concerned about the loss of European markets. And hindsight to World War I helped, as did the ease with which World War II enemies could be identified and stereotyped: Was there ever a better enemy, in fact or in film, than Adolf Hitler?

None of this was true for World War I. Its outbreak was a surprise, and its approach, clear in retrospect, was not the subject of years of mass public discussion as was the case with World War II. That is why such a high percentage of World War I films were so good and why so many were pacifist in tone: they treated the war as a war, as a hideous, generic phenomenon, not as a confrontation between good on one side and evil on another. In film terms, World War II was a specific historical contest between clearly identified sides; World War I was simply a war, any war, and that is why most of the great World War I movies—*All Quiet on the Western Front* (1930), *The Big Parade* (1925), *Sergeant York* (1941), and *Paths of Glory* (1957)—regardless of when they were produced, are classic antiwar films or films which treat war with the ambivalence and complexity that time and distance make easier. None of this should be taken to mean, however, that filmmakers were characteristically pacifist in nature. Business is business: Lewis Milestone, who directed the anti-war classic *All Quiet on the Western Front* would in the next world war direct such combat films as *Edge of Darkness* (1943) and *The Purple Heart* (1944).

ISOLATIONISM

"If it's December 1941 in Casablanca, what time is it in New York?" asks Rick Blaine (Humphrey Bogart) in *Casablanca* (1942). "I bet they're asleep in New York. I bet they're asleep all over America." In *Casablanca*, U.S. movies addressed World War II. But before movies addressed the war, they addressed the wisdom of even fighting it.

Isolationist sentiments were strong in the prewar United States. College students opposed to U.S. intervention formed the Veterans of Future Wars; the American First Committee, whose chief spokesman was Charles A. Lindbergh—the Lone Eagle, the national hero of the 1927 New York-to-Paris flight—mounted a national campaign to keep the United States out of what they saw as simply an "age-old squabble among our own family of nations." A country emerging from the First World War and the Great Depression was not especially anxious to take on new challenges, especially foreign ones. Nor was the movie industry notably anxious. Politics aside, the U.S. film industry was increasingly wedded to foreign, especially European, markets—markets on both sides of the emerging European conflict.

As was to happen with the arrival of videocassettes a half-century later, filmmakers discovered that profits could be increased—or the costs of a failed film salvaged—by expanding the markets in which films were exhibited. A domestic box-office failure might do sufficient business in overseas markets at least to break even, and in 1930s Hollywood that market was Europe. For some studios, over half the profits from a film came from international markets. To the caution with which filmmakers approached political topics was now added concern about how such topics would be greeted by Europeans. Joseph P. Kennedy, U.S. ambassador to the Court of St. James's (Great Britain), was expressing a common concern when he cabled Harry Cohn of Columbia Pictures about his belief that *Mr. Smith Goes to Washington* ridiculed democracy and might be seen as propaganda favoring the Axis powers. Kennedy unsuccessfully urged that the film be withdrawn from European distribution (Capra, 1971, 289).[1]

Hollywood was concerned that films might offend Italian and German—especially German—audiences. For filmmakers interested in exploring the dramatic possibilities of the growing political schisms in Europe, especially the treatment of Jews in Nazi Germany, Joseph Breen, head of the Production Code Administration, had an answer: such efforts constituted an attempt to "capture the screens of the United States for Communistic propaganda purposes" (quoted in Koppes and Black, 1987, 22). All this Breen attributed to the Hollywood Anti-Nazi League, which was, Breen said, financed and led almost entirely by Jews.

Casablanca, produced in 1942, and *Foreign Correspondent,* produced only two years earlier, nicely illustrate the caution with which the industry approached the war at a time when isolationist sympathies were strong. *Casablanca* is a political love story at whose center is Rick Blaine, an expatriate American with a vague and apparently unsavory past. Now in Casablanca, Rick tells us he will stick out his neck for nobody, but his past and his present tell otherwise: we learn that he fought the Fascists in Spain and Ethiopia and we see that in his bar he employs and serves a microcosm of the victims of fascism: a Russian bartender, a French waitress, and a headwaiter from Leipzig, a former professor of mathematics and astronomy. (The crew of the film, too, was unusually international in character.) Rick's piano player and old friend Sam (Dooley Wilson) is a black American, and a number of minor characters round out the multinational habitués of Rick's Café Americain. Ferrari (Sidney Greenstreet), one of the many shady characters who populate Casablanca, offers to buy from Rick not only the Cafe Americain but Sam as well. Rick declines the offer: fascism, in the form of symbolic slavery, threatens even Rick's cafe itself.

Into Rick's Cafe Americain walks Ilsa Lund (Ingrid Bergman), whose presence Rick first learns of when he hears Sam playing his and Ilsa's song, "As Time Goes By," in a scene that is one of the most evocative of love lost in all of film. "Of all the gin joints in all the towns in all the world, she walks into mine," Rick says, in one of the many memorable lines given the characters by writers Howard Koch and Julius and Philip Epstein. When Ilsa walks into the insulated world Rick has fashioned for himself in Casablanca, the outside world, despite Rick's wish to ignore it, enters too.

Casablanca, as we are told at the beginning of the film via a map and a scrolled introduction, is a crossroads for those fleeing Nazi Europe and a staging area for the activities of the Free French forces seeking to overthrow the Nazi-dominated Vichy government of France. Rick's Cafe provides an escape from all this, at least on the surface. But through it pass refugees arranging passage to or from the political realities of Europe, or locals who have made a comfortable accommodation with these realities, most notably Captain Louis Renault (Claude Raines), the archetypal war profiteer. Whatever needs to be arranged, Renault will arrange it, enforcing the law or breaking it as the situation requires. Renault is entirely happy to accept money or sex in return for whatever favors his position permits him to dispense. As the film's prime symbol of the law, Renault is eminently flexible and self-serving. (He is "shocked, shocked" to learn that gambling occurs at Rick's even as he pockets his winnings.) Rick presides over all this confidently in command of the little world that is the Cafe Americain—until Ilsa arrives.

Ilsa and Rick were lovers once, before the war. Now Rick learns that Ilsa is married to a legendary member of the Czechoslovakian resistance, Victor Laszlo (played by Paul Henreid, in a role which had been considered for Ronald Reagan). Ilsa asks Rick's help in getting herself and Victor out of Casablanca in order to permit Victor to continue his work against the Vichy government. Rick is in a position to do this: he has two letters of transit, stolen when Ugarte (Peter Lorre) kills two couriers carrying the letters. Just before Ugarte's own arrest, he gives the letters to Rick.

The letters of transit are priceless, and the Nazi fear of Laszlo, great. Major Strasser (Conrad Veidt), in Casablanca to capture Laszlo, tells Renault that he is not to turn the letters over to Laszlo no matter how big a price Renault is offered. Strasser similarly warns Rick, who coldly responds, "Your business is politics. Mine is running a saloon."

Now, when Ilsa and Victor enter Rick's Cafe, we learn that Rick and Ilsa had planned to marry, to run from Paris before the Nazis arrived. But Ilsa had left Rick waiting at the train station. We learn later, via flashback, that Ilsa, married to Victor at the time, believed her husband had been killed in a concentration camp; she leaves Rick when she learns that Victor is alive. Thus we learn that Rick's cynicism and his retreat to Casablanca are the result of a failed love affair as much as they are of a failure of political commitment. In running from the failed affair, he runs also from politics. Both find him in Casablanca.

Strasser offers Renault an exit visa if the captain will provide the names of leaders of the underground movement in several cities. Renault refuses, even declining to arrest Laszlo in Casablanca on the quaint grounds (for Renault) that he has no legal basis for doing so. Renault's flexibility is here in the service of the hero and the good cause. He does, it seems, have some principles after all.

The next evening at Rick's a dispute erupts between the German and French patrons. Rick breaks this up: he wants no trouble in his place. A Frenchman mutters (in French), "Dirty German, some day we'll have our revenge!" Renault tells Strasser, both of whom have heard the exchange, "My dear major, we are trying to cooperate with your government, but we cannot regulate the feelings of our people." The scene culminates in a duel of songs. The German soldiers sing *The Watch on the Rhine*, and Laszlo tells Sam to play *Le Marseillaise*. Uncertain, Sam looks to Rick, who almost imperceptibly nods assent. The entire bar, it seems, joins in the song, isolating the German soldiers. As the French national anthem overwhelms the soundtrack, director Michael Curtiz cuts from one close-up to another, lingering longest on the tear-stained face of the French waitress (Joy Page), who represents the French victims of the Vichy regime.

Finally, of course, Rick gives the letters to Ilsa and Victor in the final famous airport scene, but only after leading Ilsa to believe that they are intended for Ilsa and Rick. In giving up love for principle and politics, Rick tells Ilsa that the problems of two people "don't amount to a hill of beans in this crazy world." Now it is Ilsa who is reluctant to go without Rick; he must push her toward the waiting plane. (Earlier, a confused Ilsa tells Rick that he "must think for both of us" and now he does.) Strasser, having detected the escape, arrives and is shot by Rick, who is prepared to be turned in by Renault. But, instead, Renault covers for Rick and diverts his men by telling them to "round up the usual suspects." After Rick suggests they both might become involved in Resistance activities, the two walk off into the fog, arm in arm, and Rick tells Renault, "Louis, this could be the beginning of a beautiful friendship." But Rick's participation in the war is only as an individual. He is returning to the fray in his earlier role—the lone, idealistic adventurer. His actions, while surely intended as a call to arms to isolationist America, are still those of one person alone.

With Rick and Renault's arm-in-arm walk in the fog is formed not only an alliance between the United States and France but also an alliance between two men, an alliance possible now that the central female character, who, unlike Rick, was prepared to give up principle for love, is no longer involved. The overt bond now formed between the two reinforces a male bonding—vaguely gay—subtext between Rick and Renault. Renault calls Rick "Ricky" several times in the film, and he playfully expresses jealously toward Ilsa because of Rick's solicitude toward her when she first enters the cafe.

In giving up his great personal love for a greater political purpose, Rick's transformation is complete. His personal and political isolationism are replaced by an acknowledgment of the wider world in which he really lives. That world initially invades Rick's through Ilsa's unwelcome entrance into the Cafe Americain, though we know that Rick has not rejected it so much as he has run from it. In all this the fate of the cafe itself is instructive. Initially, it is the center of Casablanca (the screenplay was based on an unproduced play titled *Everybody Goes to Rick's*), its interior lively and inviting but also insulated. As the film progresses, less of the action takes place in Rick's, until finally the cafe is closed by Renault and we see it dark and empty. The climactic scene is at an airport, as open to the outside world as Rick's Cafe Americain was closed to it, though the outside world is as uncertain as the fog and darkness into which the characters depart. By the end of the film, two marriages are created: Ilsa and Victor and Rick and Renault. Both are political marriages, marriages of principle. Both couples are rejoining the war effort. One member of each marriage has forsaken romantic love for a greater good. It is possible to sense that Victor and Ilsa's relationship is something less than a real marriage. When Victor earlier tells Ilsa that he loves her very much, her only reply is, "I know." The principled and steadfast Victor has given up nothing; Ilsa and Rick have given up much.

In *Casablanca* love and politics do not flow together. In *The Front* and *High Noon*, for instance, the politically and morally correct actions of the chief male character are consistent with the wishes of his love interest; the same is true in *Mr. Smith Goes to Washington*: Howard Prince, Will Kane, and Jefferson Smith do the right thing and get the girl; Rick Blaine does the right thing and loses her.

A final political point about *Casablanca* is made by Ebert:

There came a time in my history with *Casablanca* when I decided I did not like Victor Laszlo, the Paul Henreid character, very much. He is a heroic leader of the resistance, but he has no humor and no resilience. If in peacetime he finds himself in political office, I believe he will be most comfortable in a totalitarian regime. When at the end of the film Rick tells a lie to preserve Ilsa's image in Lazlo's eyes, Lazlo hardly seems to care. In fact, I think he hardly deserves Ilsa. Rick tells her that her place is at Victor's side, but does Victor notice her there, or need her there? In the long run he is married to his career and his heroism, and there will be more nights when she hears "As Time Goes By" and realizes she made a mistake when she got on that airplane.

The Henreid character is a pig because he wants to have his cake and eat it too. What kind of a serious resistance fighter wants to drag a woman around with him, placing her and his work in unnecessary danger, unless his ego required her adoration? (Ebert, 1994, 824)

This reading of Laszlo—and of Henreid's playing of him—illuminates the essentially noble and democratic nature of the Rick character. Rick is uncertain, conflicted, ambivalent; but he is also democratic in his politics and his relationships with people. Laszlo is something of a plaster saint—utterly committed to his cause but also cold, aloof, and, one suspects, rigid. One suspects also that he is the sort who could become deeply committed to almost any cause. Laszlo agonizes about nothing, Rick about everything. And in his agonizing, Rick's sacrifice—and he sacrifices both himself and Ilsa—becomes that much more noble and tragic. *Casablanca* is less an allegory on isolationism than it is a study of nobility.

Casablanca is a perfect merging of the personal and the political, all the more remarkable because its visible political elements are never allowed to cloak the love story in which audiences were more interested. *Casablanca* also illustrates a recurring aspect of film production: the role of serendipity and luck. Production of the film was an on-again, off-again proposition: assembling the cast was difficult, costs were greater than expected, and the screenplay was written during shooting.[2] The timing of the film's release was fortunate as well: by the time it was shown the United States had entered the war and the subtexts of the untenability of isolationism and the necessity personal sacrifice (many in the audience were themselves giving up loved ones for the war) were as current as the day's news. While it was expected that director Curtiz, a capable and prolific craftsman but not a man thought of by himself or others as a serious filmmaker, would turn in a competent and commercial film, no one expected the classic that *Casablanca* would become.

Though *Foreign Correspondent* preceded *Casablanca* by only two years—it was released in 1940—and dealt with the same themes of isolationism and responsibility, it was a considerably more cautious film. Producer Walter Wanger had in 1936 purchased the memoirs of foreign correspondent Vincent Sheean. Writer John Howard Lawson, later to become one of the Hollywood Ten, worked unsuccessfully on the screenplay. The project was set aside, then revived in 1938 when Sheean's memoirs were again refashioned by several more writers, setting the story in Nazi Germany and adding material about the Spanish Civil War and the growing threat of war in Europe. The film seemed ready for production when the Bank of America, concerned about upsetting the then-current U.S. stance of cautious neutrality, declined to finance the project. By the time the film was ready for production in 1940, Wanger had secured Alfred Hitchcock to direct,[3] and what had been planned as a strongly prointervention, anti-Nazi film had become, instead, a romantic melodrama with considerable comic overtones, its politics present but diluted.

Johnny Jones (Joel McCrea, playing a character whose name simultaneously suggests Everyman and a child) is an amiable but breathtakingly unaware reporter sent to 1939 Europe to replace Stebbins (played by humorist Robert Benchley, who also contributed to the screenplay), a considerably more aware man but one who is on the verge of alcoholism. In this, Stebbins is a classic stereotype: the knowledgeable, cynical, alcoholic journalist, who is the film realization of the axiom *in vino veritas*—in wine there is truth. In London, Jones meets Van Meer (Albert Basserman), a Dutch diplomat who has knowledge of a secret clause in a treaty that could mean continued peace in Europe. Jones follows Van Meer to Amsterdam accompanied by Carol Fisher

(Laraine Day), whose British father, Stephen (Herbert Marshall), passes himself off as the head of a pacifist organization when, in fact, he works secretly for the enemy. (Stephen Fisher is reminiscent of such real-life British Fascists and Nazi sympathizers of the time as Sir Oswald Mosley.) Carol Fisher and Jones, with the help of a British reporter (George Sanders), pursue Van Meer and Carol's father's secret until even the initially disbelieving Carol is convinced of her father's complicity. The action returns to London, where Jones avoids assassination by Stephen Fisher's men, then boards a plane for the United States. The plane is shot down by the enemy, but Jones survives, and the film ends with his radio broadcast home.

As in so many of his other films, Hitchcock in *Foreign Correspondent* addressed what he called "my old theme of the innocent bystander who becomes involved in an intrigue" (Truffaut, 1968, 134). In this case, the innocent bystander is the United States and the intrigue is the war in Europe. (In one scene Jones, escaping from the enemy, disables two letters in his hotel's sign: the "Hotel Europe" becomes "Hot Europe.")

The basic structure of the film is Jones's journey from New York to London to Amsterdam, and, finally, via his radio broadcast, back to New York. From America to Europe back to America, the circle is closed. Jones leaves home an amiable dunce; he returns a voice of warning. Not unlike Howard Prince in *The Front*, Johnny Jones is an apolitical Everyman, a representative of the indifferent and ignorant political center without any real political values facing events about which he initially knows or cares little. The naive American joins the idealistic British woman, Carol, and the worldly British journalist in combating the Nazis: thus is forged an alliance of the type interventionists were then advocating. They educate him; he animates them.

In his film-ending radio broadcast to the United States, the now aware Jones tell his listeners:

I can't read the rest of this speech because the lights have gone out. So I'll have to talk off the cuff. All that noise you hear isn't static, it's death coming to London. Yes, they're coming here now. You can hear the bombs falling on the streets and homes. Don't tune me out—hang on—this is a big story, and you're part of it. It's too late now to do anything but stand in the dark and let them come as if the lights are out everywhere except but in America. [The song "America" begins playing softly.] Keep those lights burning, cover them with steel, build them in with guns, build a canopy of battleships and bombing planes around them and, hello America, hang on to your lights. They're the only lights in the world!

Rick Blaine and Johnny Jones provide interesting contrasts: Rick is a cynical adult, Johnny an innocent child; Rick is an American who has seen too much of the world, Johnny an American who knows the world not at all. The world Rick seeks to escape comes to him; the world Johnny knows nothing about is one he must leave America to find. Yet both end up interventionists: Rick's idealism is rekindled, Johnny's created. And both end up in relationships that are surrogate political alliances: Rick with the Frenchman Renault, Johnny with his British lover, Carol, and his Dutch friend and political tutor, Van Meer.

Alliances also plays a central role in another wartime Hitchcock film, *Lifeboat*, which was released well into the war in 1943.[4] The film is set entirely in a lifeboat filled with survivors of a German submarine attack on an Allied ship. The opening montage shows debris floating by, all representative of comfort and civility now denied the passengers: magazines, playing cards, a checkerboard. One after another, the passengers board, each representative of the British-U.S. anti-Nazi alliance.

From the United States are Constance Porter (Tallulah Bankhead), a journalist; Charles Rittenhouse (Henry Hull), a wealthy industrialist; Gus (William Bendix), a seaman; John Kovac (John Hodiak), an engineman from the sunken ship; and George Spencer (Canada Lee), known as "Joe," a steward on the ship and the only black person among the passengers in the lifeboat. From Britain are Mary Anderson (Alice MacKenzie), a nurse; Mrs. Higgins (Heather Angel), a young mother with her very ill child; and Stanley Garett (Hume Cronyn). As each of these characters boards the lifeboat, Connie Porter, ever the journalist, films the action with her movie camera, detached and perhaps a little amused, concerned that she not lose any possessions; she is certain they will be rescued soon.

As the characters become acquainted, we learn more about them, including some things about them politically: that Rittenhouse is indeed very wealthy but that he seems a little embarrassed about it; that Kovac resents Rittenhouse's wealth and that Kovac himself has fairly explicitly left-wing political views; that Gus is amiable, not terribly bright, and not at all political; and that Joe, sometimes called "Charcoal" by his white boat-mates, says little and stands away from the others. Connie, in the best tradition of journalist characters, is caustic and cavalier. None of the British characters, significantly, has sharply drawn political characteristics: they are a gentle and sorry lot, especially Mrs. Higgins, whose grief over her child (who eventually dies) leads to her going quietly mad.

The boat, of course, is a social and political microcosm of the British and their U.S. allies during the war, and the first task of the survivors is to establish a political structure by which to decide what to do. Here the first clash occurs between Rittenhouse, the capitalist, and Kovac, the anti-capitalist, when they disagree over who ought to assume command of the lifeboat. Rittenhouse, the oldest, richest, U.S. male character automatically assumes command, but he is uncertain about what course to pursue. His automatic assumption of command is challenged by Kovac, and Rittenhouse readily agrees to share power. The political structure of the vessel settles into a loose form of consensual decision making. This decision-making structure, however, is led entirely by the American characters Rittenhouse, Kovac, and Porter—that is, capital, labor, and the middle class. The British characters play very much of a secondary role in governing the boat. And invited to have his say, Joe, the only black aboard, asks, "You mean I get a vote too?" but declines the offer. Later, with the overt political struggle in the boat over, labor and capital still compete, but this time for money rather than power when Rittenhouse and Kovac play poker. A gust of wind blows away the cards before the crucial hand is complete.

The basic flow of political events in the film involves the creation, dissolution, and re-creation of unity among the allies, a dynamic upset when German-speaking Willy (Walter Slezak) is hauled aboard the lifeboat. The working-class character played by Hodiak is for immediate retribution, but cooler heads, including Rittenhouse, prevail. Rittenhouse, though a capitalist to the core (we learn of his enthusiasm for making big money in the postwar environment), emerges nonetheless as something of a stickler for procedure and process compared to the more hot-headed Kovac. Willy, we and the others learn later, is the captain of the U-boat that sank the freighter on which the others sailed. He is also, we learn, a surgeon (he amputates Gus's gangrenous foot), multilingual, and bent on duping the others by steering the lifeboat toward German ships. All this takes time for the others to learn. Only Willy knows where he wants to go and how to get there. The others are disorganized and caught up in their own concerns, principally the class-based tension between Rittenhouse and Kovac and Connie and Kovac's growing mutual attraction.

The folly of all this comes to a head when a storm hits the vessel. Willy, speaking English for the first time to the surprise of the others, yells, "Stop thinking about yourselves, you fools, think about the boat!" and overtly assumes the command he has previously only covertly exercised. The storm safely passed, the camera slowly pulls back, and we see Willy contentedly at the bow rowing the boat by himself, singing in German, while the others—exhausted—flirt, relax, and talk about food and peacetime pleasures. The others are all slouched and lounging, while Willy presides above them. Their demeanor is postcoital. Willie continues rowing. He is prepared, he tells the others. He has a plan. Willie now controls the ship; the others have let him. Rittenhouse, accompanying Willy's singing, is told by Willy, "You're a born accompanist," and Kovac listlessly adds, "We're all born accompanists."

When Gus discovers that Willy is hoarding water, Willy persuades the delusional Gus to jump into the water and death. The others, discovering what Willy has done, attack Willy as a group and kill him, beating him to death with Gus's shoe, thus avenging Gus. Only Joe plays no role in the killing. But, in a repetition of the group's underlying disarray, the passengers once again fall into lethargy and bickering—only this time there is no Willy. An angry Connie tells the others that Willy not only did their rowing for them but did their thinking as well, and it is she who finally assumes the moral leadership of the passengers that allows them to survive until the inevitable rescue ship arrives, finally giving up her treasured bracelet so that it may be used as bait. The bracelet is the last of her possessions, which she has spent the entire film losing or giving up.

Connie, the character, and Tallulah Bankhead, the actress, are perfectly suited for this, for Connie's behavior and Bankhead's speaking style combine for the synthesizing role Connie finally plays: Bankhead plays an American but her style is much more British than American; thus, Connie comes across as suggesting both countries. Similarly, Connie was born poor but has become successful as a journalist on her own merit; thus, she crosses class lines. It is this Anglo-American/working-class and upper-middle-class amalgam that finally saves the day for the passengers. Politically, the Anglo-American center triumphs.

At its center, *Lifeboat* took the dynamic of the combat film—a diverse group overcomes external and internal conflict and wins—and transferred it to a civilian setting. For director Hitchcock, the film was an allegory on the necessity for Allied cooperation in the war. Many critics, however, were outraged at the depiction of the Nazi Willy as the most powerful and knowledgeable character in the film and at the disarray and weakness of the allies.

Other films of this era were more bold, if less interesting politically. The 1939 Warner Brothers release *Confessions of a Nazi Spy,* a rather ordinary melodrama, was based on an trial involving allegations of German espionage in the United States. When Warners considered developing the trial into a film, the German consul in Los Angeles attempted first to persuade Warners to drop the project (Jack Warner declined), then to persuade the Breen Office to do the same. The Breen Office itself was divided on the idea. One faction believed that there was, in fact, no proof of German espionage in the United States and argued that the proposed film failed to acknowledge Hitler's "unchallenged political and social achievements." Such an argument was consistent with Production Code rules prohibiting films that ridiculed or criticized other countries. Another faction in the Breen Office supported the project, and Breen himself, finally concluding that the script was not in violation of the Code, could do little more than try to persuade the studio not to produce the film.

The film, when released, was hailed for its courage by most critics and did respectably at the box office. As with most films dealing with the European political situation, however, it entirely avoided Nazi anti-Semitism, and instead, simply placed the Nazi spy apparatus in the same villain role that would be played in a later generation by Communist spies or was played in earlier films by gangsters. In its emphasis on the internal threat, the film was in its way as isolationist as it was interventionist in tone.

A much better and more important film was Charles Chaplin's first entirely talking picture, *The Great Dictator* (1940), in which Chaplin plays the dual role of a barber in a Jewish ghetto and the dictator Adenoid Hynkel of Tomania. In addition to the rare appearance of an explicitly Jewish character in such a context, the film also features Jack Oakie as Benzino Napaloni of the rival country of Bacteria. The overt and mocking references to Hitler and Mussolini were, for the time, courageous, and the film was a critical and financial success.

Despite its direct attack on Nazism, however, *Confessions of a Nazi Spy* essentially portrayed the Nazi threat as one of internal security. The German American Bund—the villain of the film—was an arm of Nazi Germany; to take care of the former was to take care of the latter. *The Great Dictator*, by making fools of Hitler and Mussolini, placed them in a rather common popular cultural mold: the foolish, megalomaniac politician, a characterization brought to something of an apotheosis by the Marx Brothers in *Duck Soup* (1937). *Confessions of a Nazi Spy* portrayed German fascism as a phenomenon whose main threat was one of internal U.S. subversion; in *The Great Dictator* the threat was wholly external to the United States. Both films, in their way, were isolationist in tone if not intent as neither linked the Nazi threat both to Europe and the United States.

Without exception, all the films of this period and for some time later avoided anything more than indirect references to Nazi anti-Semitism or, later, to the Holocaust. It would be left to later films to address these events directly, first through documentaries (*The Sorrow and the Pity*, 1970; *Shoah*, 1985; *The Hotel Terminus: The Life and Times of Klaus Barbie*, 1987) and later in fiction films (*The Pawnbroker*, 1965; *Sophie's Choice*, 1982; *Schindler's List*, 1994).

The Depression-era screwball comedies and celebrations of romance and plucky individualism gave way to the oblique interventionism of *Casablanca* and *Foreign Correspondent* or to the more overtly political themes of *Confessions of a Nazi Spy* or *The Great Dictator*. By the time these films were released, however, the war was either a foregone conclusion or an accomplished fact, and Hollywood soon shifted to the production of films that were shorn of political ambivalence or caution and, instead, unabashedly supported the war. In this, art, patriotism, and commerce were congruent: the country was at war, its enemies were clear, and several of Hollywood's most lucrative former international markets were gone. All commercial impediments to ambivalence were removed.

The nature of studio production and the durability of established film genres guaranteed that the initial response of Hollywood to the war was to take well-entrenched formulas and adapt them to war themes. Musicals, variations on the gangster genre (like *Confessions of a Nazi Spy*), and other durable subjects became staples of Hollywood production during the war. Thus, the film portrayal of Sherlock Holmes simply moved Holmes and Dr. Watson from Victorian England into the center of the fight against the Nazis (*Sherlock Holmes and the Secret Weapon*, 1942), and even Tarzan was enlisted in the 1942 *Tarzan Triumphs* in which an all-white group of natives is led by Tarzan against Nazi agents who parachute into the hero's jungle home. For the film industry, the war pumped new life into established story lines.

COMBAT

Hollywood films that dealt with the wisdom of fighting World War II were characterized with at least some ambivalence that reflected both the real politics of the time but also the commercial concerns of studios wishing to maximize the number of markets in which their films were exhibited. Once the war began, however, the focus changed largely to outright combat films. While wars are more than simply combat, the films we call "war movies" are almost exclusively films about combat.

The basic structure of these films was simple: a diverse group of U.S. soldiers overcomes adversity, both external and internal, and wins. The diversity was usually represented in terms of race, ethnicity, religion, geography, social class, and age, with one character typically representing several of these characteristics. There was some irony in this as well as considerable historical inaccuracy: the U.S. armed forces were not racially desegregated until after the war in 1948 by Harry Truman's executive order, though countless films portrayed racially mixed military units during the war.

The portrayal of the small diverse group as the basic unit of the combat film is central to understanding the movies' treatment of the war. Prior to the war, much isolationist sentiment was centered on the argument that political and economic elites were behind the pressure for war and that the price of war would be paid by millions of "little guys," a view that was argued by both the political Left and Right in the United States. The depiction of just these "little guys" as fighting the war—honestly, bravely, and surrounded by others who, though socially different, were united against the enemy—was a continuing and powerful statement that World War II was a people's war, not a war of one set of national political and economic elites versus another.

This theme would almost certainly have arisen on its own, consistent as it was with broad patterns of political culture, national self-image, and commercial imperatives. But the "people's war" theme was also reinforced—and to a large extent, enforced—by the Office of War Information (OWI) and its Bureau of Motion Pictures (BMP), a federal agency created in 1942. The Roosevelt administration was acutely aware of the persuasive effect of films, particularly in this pretelevision time, and mindful also of the use to which Hitler had put such films as Leni Riefenstahl's documentary *Triumph of the Will* (1935). For most citizens, the most dramatic sources of images about the war came in weekly visits to the movie theater in feature films, cartoons (which had war-related themes with caricatures of Hitler, Mussolini, and Japanese soldiers playing prominent roles), and newsreels. It was the job of the OWI to help win the war through movies.

The guiding principle of the OWI was that every film, regardless of its subject, was of potential relevance as far as the war was concerned. Filmmakers were asked to consider the following (quoted in Koppes and Black, 1987, 66-67):

1. Will this picture help win the war?
2. What war information problem does it seek to clarify?
3. If it is an "escape" picture, will it harm the war effort by creating a false picture of America, her allies, or the world we live in?
4. Does it merely use the war as the basis of a profitable picture?
5. Does it contribute something new to our understanding of the world conflict?
6. When the picture reaches its maximum circulation on the screen...will it be outdated?
7. Does the picture tell the truth or will the young people of today have reason to say they were misled by propaganda?

The OWI criteria coexisted uneasily with the already established Production Code, for their goals were quite different. The Production Code, emphasizing "Shalt Nots," was designed to exclude material from films; the OWI criteria effectively redefined film content in terms of what should be included—"Will this picture help win the war?"

Placing a film, however superficially or artlessly, in the context of the war by making the villain a Nazi or Japanese officer not only tapped into the events of the time, it gave new life to old film formulas while meeting the concerns of the

OWI, which reviewed all plot synopses of proposed films in addition to completed scripts. To the extent that the OWI's criteria were generally consistent with the Roosevelt administration's domestic and foreign policy goals—particularly its opposition to isolationism and its support for a dilute form of social and economic equality—it existed in some tension with the more traditionalist conservatism that underlay the Production Code. The Code implicitly and explicitly avoided controversy, violence and political questions; the OWI guidelines essentially demanded that these things, though sanitized, become part of film content.

As hackneyed as were most combat films, a small handful stand out as relatively subtle readings of the reality of war, despite their being set within the standard platoon-as-social-microcosm structure. *The Story of G.I. Joe* (1945), based on the experiences of journalist Ernie Pyle, and *They Were Expendable* (1945) are perhaps the best. Both avoided the empty heroics of most of their predecessors. It is perhaps not accidental that both were released relatively late in the war, when Allied prospects were brighter and the reality of the war had been impressed upon civilians. Even more impressive were documentaries made by Hollywood directors during their own wartime service. John Ford's *The Battle of Midway* (1942), William Wyler's *The Memphis Belle* (1942), and John Huston's *The Battle of San Pietro* (1945), all shot on 16-mm film largely by the directors themselves, are easily the best of the World War II combat films. In 1945, Huston also made *Let There Be Light*, a film so powerful it was banned by the War Department and not released until 1982. These films were heartbreaking in the directness with which they looked at the lives and deaths of young, frightened combat troops. No fiction film representations of war come close to them.

ENEMIES

The dynamics of narrative film require an antagonist to provide the tension and conflict whose resolution is temporarily uncertain. Wars provide the ultimate antagonist in an enemy that is defined, simplified, and demonized. Of the U.S. enemies in World War II, it was easiest to demonize the Japanese.

Both the OWI and the Production Code criteria were at some pains in urging filmmakers to avoid national and racial stereotyping, and, in the context of World War II, the OWI staff—liberals, serving a liberal administration—emphasized that the enemy was fascism as ideology and practice, not a particular nation or people or race, though the OWI was never especially precise as to what it meant by fascism (Koppes and Black, 1987, 249). Despite this, throughout the war and with very few and very weak exceptions, the Japanese monarchy, government, military, and people were treated as an undifferentiated and wholly evil phenomenon.

Three things made this treatment easy: outrage at the Pearl Harbor attack, which instantly crystallized U.S. public opinion against Japan; the simple fact that Japan and the Japanese were for most Americans almost entirely unknown; and the setting of the Pacific theater of the war, which, in the popular mind, was associated not with the familiar countries and cities of the European theater of war but with exotic locales—most particularly the jungle and all its primeval associations. All these elements worked to create a film portrait of the Japanese that, even given wartime conditions and passions, was uniquely stereotyped. If Willy the German was superhuman in his range of skills, the Japanese were subhuman beasts associated with a primitive world.

Portrayals of the Japanese were remarkably consistent throughout the war. As late as 1945, in one of a series of films he made for the War Department, the Frank Capra-directed *Know Your Enemy—Japan* referred to the Japanese as "photographic prints off the same negative" (Koppes and Black, 1987, 250).[5] Films portrayed the Japanese enemy in almost exclusively racial terms, not in terms of the OWI-preferred characterization of the enemy as fascism. As two students of the period discussing OWI analysis of scripts note (Koppes and Black, 1987, 254):

In *A Prisoner of Japan* the enemy kills "for no apparent reason other than to satisfy their blood-lust," said OWI. *Menace of the Rising Sun* described Tokyo's diplomacy as "a filthy game of treachery" and the Japanese as "murderers." *Remember Pearl Harbor* and *Danger in the Pacific* repeated the theme of the "fiendish, diabolical" enemy. *Pacific Rendezvous* and *Manila Calling* embroidered the espionage theme. It was a rare film that did not employ such terms as "Japs," "beasts," "yellow monkeys," "nips," "or slant-eyed rats."

Throughout the war the OWI found itself, as an agency charged with furthering the war effort, in the position of struggling with the studios to tone down racist characterizations of the Japanese enemy. There was a further irony, for in the early U.S. combat films featuring the Pacific theater and the Japanese adversary the story line often dealt with a U.S. defeat, as in the 1942 *Wake Island* and the 1943 *Bataan*, both of which portrayed overmatched U.S. forces fighting selflessly to the last man—actions ironically like those engaged in by the Japanese kamikaze pilots later in the war, when the strategic positions of the contending forces were precisely reversed. Almost uniformly, the Japanese forces were portrayed as displaying behavior that, rather than being driven by political decisions or military commands, was rooted in the brutal, sadistic, and unfathomable character of a race of people.

The fate of the Italian component of the Axis powers was, in its way, just as simply told in film: Italians, either as individuals or as representatives of the Mussolini regime, were hardly ever seriously observed. Both as junior partners in the Berlin-Rome Axis and as a nationality whose popular stereotype has always involved attributions of gaiety, style, and culture but not, in modern times, the military, Italian characters, when they appeared at all, appeared as comic relief. Note, for instance, the opening sequence in *Casablanca*, when Major Strasser arrives in Casablanca and is met by, among others, Tonelli (Charles la Torre), a representative of Fascist Italy. Strasser snubs Tonelli, who runs along after Strasser attempting to draw the German's attention and win his approbation. Later, when Tonelli is arguing with a subordinate of Renault, Renault notes that if Tonelli "gets a word in edgewise it will be a major Italian victory." Even in *The Great Dictator*, in which both Hitler and Mussolini are made fools of, the Mussolini stand-in, Benzino Napaloni, is the weaker of the two. For the wartime audience it perhaps provided some comfort to be told that at least one of one's enemies was not to be taken too seriously.

An Italian character plays a less comedic role, however, in *Sahara* (1943), which may be seen as a combat version of *Casablanca*, in which Humphrey Bogart plays a U.S. Army sergeant in command of a tank in North Africa in search of Allied lines. Along the way he and his comrades acquire a group of four Britishers, each representative of a different social stratum, and later a South African, a Frenchman, a Sudanese (one of the few black non-Americans to be seen in films of this type), and an Italian. The Italian character has relatives in the United States, talks often about his family, and has no interest in politics. The essential difference between him and a captured German pilot emerges when the Italian tries to prevent the German's escape and is killed by him. Thus are the two Axis powers distinguished from each other.

The film characterization of German Nazis, however, was more complex, as can be seen, among many other films, in *Lifeboat*. The U-boat captain, Willy, is the embodiment of Nazi evil but also of German competence and skill, and the chief victim of both these characteristics is the simple and trusting American of German descent, Gus, whose last name is Smith but whom Willy calls "Herr Schmidt," and whom he urges not to forget that he is German. Willie dupes Gus, then persuades him into the water and death. Thus was highlighted the frequently portrayed contrast between the evil German Nazi and the good German citizen. The "good German" stereotype was comprised of equal parts duty, affability, and competence. In the context of the war these characteristics, as in the case of the doomed Gus, were traits that led to the betrayal of Germans by nazism even at the price of the betrayal of one German (Gus) by another (Willy).

Crude as this stereotype was in the context of World War II filmmaking, it nevertheless provided a sort of cultural-political analysis of Nazi behavior, rooted in a "national character" that allowed the same characteristics to explain both the evils of nazism and the willingness of its subjects to obey. The attribution to Germans of competence and discipline served nicely to differentiate the German people from the Nazi leadership. In all cases, however, whether films dealt with the Italian, Japanese, or German enemy, the implicit political analysis was that some sort of national or racial or cultural characteristics led not only to the war itself but to the manner in which the war was prosecuted.

The Japanese were presented as monolithically evil, with little differentiation between one individual and another or between leaders and followers. The Italians, as in *Sahara*, were portrayed in such as way that the audience could conclude that "one man, Mussolini, and not the Italian people wanted war" (Suid, 1978, 50). The representation of Germany, while hardly a model of subtlety, was nonetheless the most differentiated and complex that films would provide. Much of this naturally followed from market considerations. There were many more U.S. citizens with ties to Germany and Italy than there were with ties to Japan; and Japan, unlike Italy and especially Germany, had never been a major market for U.S. films.

ALLIES

The great majority of the characters in *Lifeboat, Casablanca,* and countless combat films were all on the Allied side; yet much of the dramatic tension in these films followed from uncertainty about whether the protagonists could hold together long enough to get the job done. For filmmakers as well as politicians, enemies are easy, allies are hard. As the government agency that dealt most directly with such questions, the OWI was acutely aware of this problem.

Despite political and cultural ties of the sort that made Great Britain seem to be the easiest of allies to portray, the OWI had two problems with Hollywood's portrayal of British life—the rigid class system at home and British imperialism abroad (Koppes and Black, 1987, 224). Films like *Clive of India* (1935) and *Gunga Din* (1939) romanticized British imperialism at a time when that might have been good at the box office, but with the circumstances of approaching war such characterizations became troublesome. It was not until later, as with the 1950 *Kim,* that U.S. movie audiences could be again reminded that Britain was an imperial power.

Neither the British class system nor British imperial policy was an image calculated to further the OWI's goals of presenting a democracy and its allies fighting a people's war against imperialist enemies. The OWI, a creature of the Roosevelt administration and sensitive to Democratic party politics, was also aware of anti-British sentiment among Irish-Catholic Democratic voters in urban America, a constituency that was one of the foundations of Roosevelt's Democratic party. And there were the lingering charges that U.S. and British munitions manufacturers had colluded to insure U.S. entry into World War I to their mutual profit. For many U.S. isolationists, Great Britain was not a potential ally so much as it was an alien power attempting once again to lure the United States into its war.

For filmmakers and the OWI the biggest problem was somehow to democratize British society and humanize, if not eliminate, its class structure. The film that best epitomized this—winning the enthusiastic approval of the newly-established OWI, the hearts of the public, and Oscars for best picture, actress, and director—was the 1942 production *Mrs. Miniver,* a conventional family melodrama pressed into wartime duty.[6]

Directed by William Wyler, the film is centered on the upper-middle-class household of the Miniver family in 1939, on the eve of the war. *Mrs. Miniver* opens in a busy London street where the title character, played by Greer Garson, asks a bus driver to stop so she can buy an expensive hat she has coveted. Mrs. Miniver is an impulsive, affluent, and perhaps just slightly selfish consumer. On her way home, Mrs. Miniver encounters the film's representation of the British upper class, Lady Beldon (Dame May Whitty), who complains about middle-class women who buy things they simply cannot afford. "I don't know what the country's coming to, everyone trying to be better than their betters," she says.

"No wonder Germany's arming." Lady Beldon's complaint is that the British middle class does not know its place, and her reference to Germany suggests that Lady Beldon somehow concludes that there is a relationship between Germany arming and socially inappropriate consumer spending by the British middle class.

When she arrives home, Mrs. Miniver is asked by her local railroad stationmaster, Mr. Ballard (Henry Travers), if he can name after her a rose he has spent years developing and plans to enter in a local flower competition. Pleasantly surprised and flattered, she agrees. Ballard explains to Mrs. Miniver that he wants to name the rose after her because she has always over the years been so kind to him; these kindnesses include Mrs. Miniver talking to him. Through these brief, personal interchanges the film's version of the British class system emerges: the older aristocracy resistant to change (Lady Beldon), the economically ascendant and more democratic middle class (Mrs. Miniver), and the obedient, respectful lower class (Mr. Ballard). In a later scene we met Clem Miniver (Walter Pidgeon), an architect, and learn that he has just purchased a sports car, thus trumping his wife's hat purchase, and that the Miniver household supports two full-time servants whom the Minivers treat with respect and near-equality with themselves. The class alliances established to this point in the film highlight the central role of the middle class, which has some of the economic pretensions and wealth of the aristocracy but which is nonetheless able and willing to be civil (democratic) to the lower classes. We learn also that the lower classes appreciate this treatment.

Vin, the eldest son of the family, returns home from his first year at Oxford where he has evidently learned to be socially conscious, for he berates his father for the car purchase and, in a lecture to his family, equates the British class system with feudalism. We next meet Lady Beldon's granddaughter Carol (Teresa Wright), who hesitantly asks Mrs. Miniver to persuade Mr. Ballard to withdraw his "Mrs. Miniver" rose because her grandmother, Lady Beldon, has up until now won the flower contest uncontested. Before an uncomfortable Mrs. Miniver can respond, Vin demands to know whether the lower-class Ballard must withdraw his rose simply because he is not a member of the British ruling class. Carol demands to know what Vin has done to change a system with which he is so evidently unhappy. At least, she tells him, she spends some of her time helping the poor. The implication is clear: Vin's reformist philosophy is an affectation acquired at the university and not much more, and the protofeminist Carol is happy to tell him so. Despite this budding political conflict the two young characters are, of course, attracted to each other, and the audience is thereby introduced to the final element of the British social structure as presented in the film—the next generation of British citizens, better educated and less wedded to traditional social and economic differences either by virtue of education (Vin) or temperament (Carol).

In a scene set in the parish church we see the entire British social structure in microcosm: at the front, the aristocracy (Lady Beldon and Carol), in the middle the Minivers, and at the back the stationmaster surrounded by other members of the working class—each stratum larger than the one above it. It is here that this model of the British system is told by the minister that the war has begun with the German invasion of Poland. Having introduced us to the characters and the divisions they represent, the film now places them all together in the symbolic embrace of the Church of England and asks whether, like the habitués of Rick's or the passengers in the lifeboat or the soldiers in the foxholes, they can overcome their differences.

They do, of course, and in so doing classes reconcile. All pull together in the service of the war effort, led, significantly, by the working class, with the rest following. The working classes join the military or shore up the home front, but the middle classes do as well: Vin joins the Royal Air Force, Mr. Miniver does civilian defense work, and Mrs. Miniver captures an injured German pilot. Even Lady Beldon signs on to the war effort, obeying orders to cooperate in a blackout in anticipation of a German bombing run, and establishing an air raid shelter. In all of this traditional class patterns are destroyed, with the old aristocracy taking orders from the newly energized working classes who, we learn, have skills and abilities essential to the war effort.

Love is not ignored. Vin and Carol decide to marry, and when Lady Beldon objects, we learn that her opposition does not come from the class discrimination we suspect of her but because she was herself in World War I a young bride whose husband was killed in the war. She is concerned about her granddaughter, not class privilege, in opposing the marriage. The young couple marries, though inevitably we fear for the life of the young soldier. Instead, during a German air raid, Carol and Mrs. Miniver pull their car off the road to escape and Carol is killed.

The flower show is not ignored either, as it has earlier been established as a symbol for social class conflict. It now becomes a vehicle for reconciliation when, despite the argument of some working-class people that Lady Beldon as a matter of right should be allowed to win the prize yet again (for these are working class people who know their proper place) and despite the decision of the judges to award her the prize (for these are judges who know what the proper outcome ought to be), Lady Beldon, announcing the winner, changes the judges' decision and declares Mr. Ballard's rose—the "Mrs. Miniver"—to be the winner. The working class and middles class win, though only with the sanction of the aristocracy.

The film returns to the parish church for the final scene, the place where we earlier saw all of British society represented in microcosm. The congregation is now less segregated than when we first saw it, and the minister delivers a sermon that obliterates social class divisions and reinterprets British society as a unified whole:

"This is not only a war of soldiers in uniform. It is a war of the people, of all of the people, and it must be fought not only in the battlefields but in the cities and in the villages, in the factories and on the farms, in the homes and in the hearts of every man, woman and child who loves freedom. This is a people's war! It is our war!"

This was language with which U.S. film audiences were familiar, for it described their own conception of the war and their own country's role in it. The basic social and political point of *Mrs. Miniver* was that a rigidly socially stratified imperial Great Britain could become, in the running time of a movie, something very much like the United States.

In addition to reinventing Great Britain for U.S. audiences, the OWI and the studios faced another, related task: reinventing the Soviet Union for the same market. In some respects this was easier, as the collective knowledge and memory of the public was sparse when it came to the U.S.S.R. But there were two problems: most of what the public believed was negative, and the Soviet Union in its brief history, so far as the U.S. public was concerned, had gone from being an enigma to an adversary to an ally. What the OWI and the industry wanted was a *Mrs. Miniver* set in the U.S.S.R.

The biggest prewar U.S. film dealing with the Soviet Union had been *Ninotchka* (1939), a film now remembered as the one in which Greta Garbo laughs on screen for the first time. *Ninotchka* was directed by Ernst Lubitsch, a master of light comedy, with a screenplay by Billy Wilder, who was just beginning his career in Hollywood. Its portrayal of the U.S.S.R. is reflected in the behavior of the title character, played by Garbo. The epitome of Russian socialism, she is humorless and dour and holds Western capitalist societies in complete contempt—until she is assigned to Paris and meets her love interest, Count Leon, a White Russian émigré played by Melvyn Douglas.

In Paris, Ninotchka falls in love, discovers she likes to shop, drinks champagne, dances, wears makeup, and laughs; and, after the usual complications involving separation and reunion, Ninotchka and the count defect. Love conquers indifference, capitalism conquers socialism, Paris defeats Moscow, humanity defeats rigid ideology. The image left with the audience is the U.S.S.R. as a drab, soulless, and doctrinaire place indeed. When the U.S.S.R. signed a non-aggression pact with Hitler, then was invaded by Hitler's troops, then allied itself with the United States against Hitler, the reputation of the Soviet Union among the U.S. mass public required immediate clarification and rehabilitation. Enter Joseph E. Davies.

Davies was the second U.S. ambassador to the U.S.S.R., serving between 1936 and 1938. A corporate attorney by profession, he was something of an internationalist, a Republican in his politics, and a friend of Franklin Roosevelt. His time in Moscow was not distinguished, in large part because he had absolutely no training or experience in diplomacy. He served an additional two years in Belgium after his time in U.S.S.R. and returned to the United States in 1940 as an official in the State Department. The Nazi invasion of Russia in the summer of 1941 heightened interest in the Soviet Union and in Davies's own experiences, and he quickly began work on a book that became the basis of *Mission to Moscow* (1943), a film fairly described as "a notorious example of pro-Soviet special pleading" (Culbert, 1980, 11).

Mission to Moscow also illustrated other aspects of film and politics in this period: the extreme interest displayed by Franklin Roosevelt in getting the film made; the enthusiastic cooperation of Warner Brothers, the studio which produced it; and the abrupt about-face required when *Mission to Moscow* became a major political and corporate liability a few years later at the height of the Cold War, when suddenly the U.S.S.R. was again an adversary.

Franklin Roosevelt was interested that *Mission to Moscow* be brought to the screen and in Warner Brothers he had enthusiastic allies (Koppes and Black, 1987, 190-91). Warners as a studio had long had a corporate style that emphasized gritty, working-class-based films and was generally sympathetic to the aims of the Roosevelt administration in both domestic and foreign policy. A student of the Warner brothers notes:

Their studio was as powerful as a major newspaper, dealing vigorously with crooked politics, with the Mafia, with the prohibition gangs, with the lack of privileges of women in a male-dominated society, with the ugliness of theatrical life. Even their musicals were unlike any others: bitter and acrid portraits of the realities of show business. They exposed the evils of newspaper reporting. By their pioneering efforts they attacked racial prejudice in the Deep South and had the chains struck from the ankles of the prison gangs in Georgia. (Higham, 1975, 2)

Joseph Davies's book, also titled *Mission to Moscow,* was published in 1942 and became a best-seller. The book, along with additional material supplied by Davies, became the basis of the screenplay for the film written by Howard Koch. Koch, exhausted from his work on the just completed *Casablanca* and anxious to take some time off, was lobbied heavily to write the screenplay, and another workhorse filmmaker, Michael Curtiz, himself having just finished *Casablanca*, directed. Davies demanded and got script approval, unusual even for a veteran writer and unprecedented for a novice. Several other writers had a hand in the script before the final task was given to Koch, though Davies constantly intervened—even to the point of recasting a scene to give more emphasis to his wife's character. Davies's meddling in the script as well as his view of Soviet politics colored and damaged the entire film.

Mission to Moscow opens with the real Davies introducing his story, which is structured broadly as a sort of geopolitical *Mr. Smith Goes to Washington* in which an honest but naive man leaves his initial bucolic country home (where we first meet the fictional Davies) and travels to the old, urban, and intensely political environment of Europe and Russia, finally to learn the truth. Davies is cast in the film as the diplomatic equivalent of the Joel McCrea character in *Foreign Correspondent.*

The introductory portion mixes documentary footage, footage of the real Davies shot in the studio, and fictional representations of characters, lending verisimilitude to the narrative. This visual style is used throughout the film and is one its best executed production characteristics. (Owen Marks edited the film.) We read the opening paragraphs of the book:

In the fire of war and revolution was forged a new Russian government that promised to promote the welfare of its people and the cause of world peace. How well that promise was kept is of special import at this hour when Russia is an ally in the struggle against a common enemy who would destroy all we value in life. So without prejudice or partisanship I offer to my fellow Americans the facts as I saw them.

Then Davies himself appears on screen:

No leaders of a nation have been so misrepresented and misunderstood as those of the Soviet government during those crucial years between the world wars. I hope that my book will help to correct that misunderstanding in presenting Russia and its people in their gallant struggle.

Davies recounts his recruitment by Roosevelt (Roosevelt to Davies: "It's your job to get me the right answers. No, 'job' is too small a word, Joe. This is a mission."), his passage through Germany (where he encounters a catalog of anti-Nazi film clichés) into Russia, where his initial contacts with the Russian people are uniformly pleasant: the Russians are happy, friendly, industrious, committed, and well-fed. Ninotchka may have needed to go to Paris to laugh but the Russians of *Mission to Moscow* do it at home. The Russians are misunderstood, as Davies's opening comments indicate, and the film is of interest politically because of what it says about questions at issue in U.S.-Soviet relations of the time, questions whose settlement would presumably make the U.S. public more accepting of their new ally against Hitler.

Essentially, *Mission to Moscow* is a rebuttal to critics of the Soviet Union which does not justify the U.S.-Soviet alliance as a necessary evil (or completely ignore criticisms of the Soviet Union, as was the case in the Frank Capra-directed *Battle of Russia*, one of the *Why We Fight* series) but instead asserts that the critics were factually wrong and that Davies's own experiences, told in the film, prove it. And the film makes clear that we are to believe Davies: in one of many self-serving references in the film to Davies's basic honesty, Davies (played by Walter Huston) tells Soviet president Kalinin (Vladimir Sokoloff), "You see, I'm not a professional diplomat. The only language I know is to say what I think." Revisionist history as presented in the film centered on two primary areas: the Hitler-Stalin non-aggression agreement of 1939 and the Soviet purge trials of the 1930s.

These two threads come together in the film's political climax, the purge trials, which are compressed in the film into a single trial, though there were, in fact, many trials held over several years. The explanation offered in the film for the 1939 nonaggression treaty between the U.S.S.R. and Nazi Germany—essentially the rationalization offered by Stalin himself—is heard in an exchange between defendant Bukharin (Konstantin Shayne) and his prosecutor Vyshinsky (Victor Francen):

Vyshinsky: At any rate, you admit similar conversations? [About cooperating with Stalin's adversary Leon Trotsky in bettering relations between Nazi Germany and the Soviet Union.]
Bukharin: Yes.
Vyshinsky: With representatives of Germany?
Bukharin: Of Germany and Japan.
[The courtroom audience buzzes in excited conversation.]
Vyshinsky: What was the general purpose of these conversations?
Bukharin: To make arrangements by which our bloc [Trotsky, the Nazis, and the Japanese] would receive help from these two countries in our effort to rise to power.

Vyshinsky: So you were working out a deal?

Bukharin: Naturally. Germany and Japan were not going to back us for the sake of Trotsky's blue eyes.

Vyshinsky: What were their conditions?

Bukharin: The partition of our country. Japan was to get our maritime province and our guarantee of Siberian oil in the event of war with the United States.

Vyshinsky: And Germany?

Bukharin: We agreed to open the border for German expansion into the Ukraine.

[Indignant murmurs from the spectators.]

Bukharin eventually confesses, telling the courtroom the only pressure to do so "came from my own conscience."

Bukharin: For three months I refused to testify—then I decided to tell everything. Why? Because while in prison I made an entire revaluation of my past. For when you ask yourself, "If you must die, what are you dying for?" an absolutely black vacuity rises before you with startling vividness....One has only to weight the wise leadership of the present government against the sordid, persona; ambitions of those who would overthrow it to realize the monstrousness of our crimes.

In case the point of this two-for-one explanation was lost, Walter Huston, as Davies, tells us in a voice-over:

Consequently all of the trials, purges, and liquidations which at first seemed so violent and shocking to the rest of the world are now seen clearly as part of a vigorous and determined effort by the Stalin government to protect itself from not only revolution from within, but attack from without. They went to work thoroughly and ruthlessly to clean out all treasonable elements...within the country.

In fact, the purge trials had nothing to do with such matters; they were internal to the Soviet Communist party and involved a struggle between Stalin and his more moderate Communist party adversaries, chief among them Leon Trotsky, who was ultimately exiled and was assassinated in Mexico in 1940 on Stalin's orders. *Mission to Moscow* had essentially bought the party line and thus justified not only the purge trials (which resulted in many deaths and the decimation of a significant part of the leadership of the Red Army) but also the 1939 Hitler-Stalin nonaggression pact as a necessary tactic by Stalin to buy time in anticipation of what Stalin knew would be a Nazi invasion of Russia. Stalin himself is further lionized in a scene with Davies:

Stalin: I understand you have visited many other sections of the Soviet Union.

Davies: And I've been deeply impressed by what I've seen—your industrial plans, the development of your natural resources, and the work being done to improve living conditions everywhere in your country. I believe history will record you as a great builder for the benefit of the common man.

Stalin: It is not my achievement, Mr. Davies. Our five-year plan was conceived by Lenin and carried out by the people themselves.

Davies: Well, the results have been a revelation to me. I confess I wasn't prepared for all I've found here. [Smiling] You see, Mr. Stalin, I'm a capitalist, as you probably know.

Stalin (laughing): Yes, we know you are a capitalist—there can be no doubt about that.

Kalinin: We also know this about you, Mr. Davies—the worst things you've had to say, you have said to our faces, the best things you have said to our enemies.

Stalin: We want you to realize that we feel more friendly toward the government of the
  United States than any other nation.

Thus, in addition to explaining the purge trials and the 1939 nonaggression
pact, we now learn that the Soviet Union is strong internally (as Davies learned
first-hand anyway when he entered the country), that Stalin is a great leader, and
that Stalin is deeply fond of the United States. The picture of Stalinist Russia as
a desirable and worthy ally is complete. For the filmmakers, justifying alliance
with the Soviet Union as a wartime political necessity was insufficient: it was
necessary, as with Britain in *Mrs. Miniver*, to craft a film in which an ally was
transformed into a replica of the United States.

Rarely has a feature film so blatantly distorted history, particularly when that
history was only recently passed. Unlike *Mrs. Miniver,* however, audiences and
critics were much less kind in responding to *Mission to Moscow*'s efforts to
shore up support for a wartime ally despite the best-seller status of the book on
which it was based, an unusually vigorous advertising campaign by the studio,
and despite the film being shown widely on military bases. Critics focused on
Mission to Moscow's glorification of Stalin and on its essential dullness as a
work of entertainment. In an episode reminiscent of the later controversy over
the historical accuracy of Oliver Stone's *JFK* (1991), philosopher John Dewey
and Suzanne La Follette, respectively chairman and secretary to an international
commission on the Moscow purge trials, published in 1943 a lengthy letter in
The New York Times attacking the accuracy of *Mission to Moscow* in general
and its treatment of the trials in particular. (The letter is reproduced in its
entirely in Higham, 1975, 162-171, along with a reply by Howard Koch.)

Beyond the film's heavy-handed politics and its relentlessly preachy tone is
the self-serving picture Davies paints of himself: the Davies character impresses
Franklin Roosevelt, Josef Stalin, and Mr. and Mrs. Winston Churchill with his
honesty and insight as he moves easily across the world's stage, a one-man truth
squad, even, toward the end of the film, bravely taking on the forces of
European appeasement and American isolationism. With the passage of time
since its release, *Mission to Moscow*, like the similarly intentioned but less
heavy-handed *North Star* (1943) and *Song of Russia* (1943), becomes less
entertaining as a film but more interesting as an exercise in wartime filmmaking.
These films, made with the encouragement of the government and sometimes at
its behest, were later to become political problems for the same studios that
made them when political circumstances changed with the arrival of the cold
war.

HOME

It is easy—too easy—to look at the great bulk of nonwar-related films of the
era and read volumes into them, to interpret them in terms of their relationship
to the war. Certainly most films of this period were not war-related, and many
others used the war only as the flimsiest of backdrops for standard stories with
standard characters. But all this tells us is that the profitable business of making

films went on, adapting to new circumstances as it always had. And, indeed, the war years continued to be profitable for the studios, reinforcing the belief that bad times for the country were good ones for show business. But the war's effects on the United States were profound, and some of their clearest consequences were reflected in how the home front was represented in movies. Of these, the most interesting were film depictions of the worlds of work, the family, and the changing relationships between men and women.

The home front was what the war was about—the way of life for which soldiers fought. The OWI's and studios' interests were that movies show everyone, civilians included, pitching in to win the war. It was common to show people going about their daily lives complying with wartime rationing rules, doing volunteer work, and buying bonds—something they were also urged to do from the screen in public service announcements featuring movie stars.

Typical of these films was *Since You Went Away* (1944), directed by John Cromwell, which opens with a shot of a fiery hearth under a caption reading, "This is a story of the Unconquerable Fortress: the American Home . . . 1943." The camera pans slowly over the classic symbols of home, U.S. movie-style: family pictures, baby shoes, and an empty chair that obviously belongs to the man of the house (Tim, played by Joseph Cotten), who, we learn, has gone off to the war despite his wife's (Claudette Colbert) misgivings. She is afraid for him and for herself without him. "I have no courage and no vision," she tells him. David O. Selznik's screenplay crams in every possible convention of the home-front film: the family takes in boarders, scrimps, and adapts stoically to the war's demands. On a train trip to visit Tim, the family encounters wounded soldiers, European war refugees, and thoughtless, selfish American civilians who complain about wartime inconvenience. Later, however, as the necessity for sacrifice becomes clear, we see civilians—especially affluent ones (shades of Lady Beldon in *Mrs. Miniver*)—concluding that the sacrifice is justified. While Tim eventually returns home—on Christmas eve—there are nonetheless the inevitable combat deaths with their effects on those back home. Like many similar films, *Since You Went Away* takes the classic family melodrama and smoothly adapts it into a wartime tear-jerker. The role of most characters in such films—especially the women characters—was to wait, to hope, and to endure.

But many female characters also acted, and their actions changed their lives. Many went to work out of necessity, patriotism, or boredom, though often, if they were middle-class women, they did volunteer work rather than work for income, as does a daughter in *Since You Went Away*. In a very few films women fought, most prominently in *So Proudly We Hail* (1943), though the film is also shot through with stereotyping of its women characters. In most films, for a woman to enter the world of work was only a temporary thing: when the men came back the women went home, as in *Since You Went Away* and *Tender Comrade* (1943), a film in which a group of women working in aircraft production pool their resources and establish a communal household (thus obliquely addressing the question of the severe wartime housing shortage), but only do so until their men return. The longer-term consequences of the war on family structure and on male-female roles were more clearly seen in films produced at the very end of the war and immediately following it. As critic Molly Haskell notes, in the movies some women waited and some fought:

The waiting women were matched in fortitude only by the fighting women...The large number of women's films, war and otherwise, was a practical way of handling the shortage of men in Hollywood and the nation at large during the war. And they were given positions of authority, in the war and at home, in films and out, that they would be unwilling to relinquish. (Haskell, 1974, 192)

The Best Years of Our Lives (1946) stands as a transitional film between tradition-affirming films like *Since You Went Away* and the vastly darker representations of women in *film noir*. The idea behind *The Best Years of Our Lives* came when producer Sam Goldwyn read a magazine article about a group of returning U.S. soldiers suggesting that many were coming home with mixed emotions. The original script treatment was by MacKinlay Kantor with the final screenplay written by Robert Sherwood; the film was directed by William Wyler, who had also directed *Mrs. Miniver*. Like the earlier film, *The Best Years of Our Lives* resonated with the postwar audience. It was also a much better film and swept the Academy Awards in 1946, yielding Wyler two best director Oscars for the war years.

The basic structure rests on the return home to the small-town Midwest of three servicemen: an infantry sergeant and civilian bank vice-president (Fredric March), still in love with his wife but discontented with his return to his job; an Army Air Corps captain and prewar soda jerk (Dana Andrews), who returns to a wife who no longer loves him and whom he no longer loves; and a machinist's mate who had lost a hand in the war (played by Harold Russell, who actually did lose a hand in the war and who won an Oscar for his performance) but whose optimism is strong and who still has the love of his prewar girlfriend.

While the film is overlong and repetitive, it is remarkable for the extent to which it places the returning soldiers simultaneously into two social contexts, which they once understood but now do not: with women and with the postwar economy and job structure. The banker must balance the needs of his bank with the desire of his former comrades for loans, the former combat pilot must deal with the contempt of his customers as he now mans the soda fountain, the handicapped nice guy now worries about whether he will keep his girl. And the title is doubly ironic: the wife who claims to have given up the best years of her life waiting for her husband in fact has had a succession of lovers, and we wonder also if the best years were those of the war, not the aftermath that brings anxiety and uncertainty to the characters' lives. The prevailing mood of the film is one of discontent born of uncertainty as the characters refashion their lives.

The role of women in the family, in the society, and therefore in movies was forever changed by the war. Strong female characters had always been present in film. Sometimes this was attributed to personality (often the case in screwball comedy heroines), sometimes to necessity, as in the case of Clarissa Saunders in *Mr. Smith Goes to Washington* and Ann Mitchell in *Meet John Doe*, both of whom work because they have to. But the departure of many men from the home front and the emergence of women into new roles forever changed things;

and this was reflected in a number of films produced at the end of the war and beyond. As Haskell (1974, 189) observes: "In the dark melodramas of the forties, woman came down from her pedestal and she didn't stop when she reached the ground. She kept going—down, down, like Eurydice, to the depths of the criminal world, the *enfer* of the *film noir*—and then compelled her lover to glance back and betray himself."

These representations of women and men found their most pointed expression in *film noir* ("black film"), a genre that flourished during the forties. The city at night was the setting of classic *noir* films, whose dominant tone was treachery, betrayal, and death. The story usually centers on a cynical, hard-boiled detective long since accustomed to the dark side of human life—Humphrey Bogart as Dashiell Hammett's fictional detective, Sam Spade, in *The Maltese Falcon* (1941) being one of the most memorable. *Noir* visual conventions, many borrowed from German Expressionist films of the 1930s, are classic—darkness and shadow, cigarette smoke curling in the air, neon signs reflected in pools of water, light slanting through window blinds—but the most startling feature of *noir* was how often the villain was a woman—a strong, sexual, amoral woman—not driven to do wrong by love or necessity but by her own evil and selfish motives. *Noir* women did nothing for the love of a man: they used the love of a man to do something for themselves. The victim was always a man.

Noir's treatment of women is thus symptomatic of the way in which the genre transforms reality: women who in real life were strengthened by their wartime experience, while their husbands were away, appear in films as malevolent temptresses, their power confined almost entirely to the sexual realm, their strength achieved only at the expense of men. (Hirsch, 1983, 20)

Noir films portrayed their women as supremely powerful, supremely nonsentimental, and supremely sexual. Sexuality, power, death, and victimized men were at the heart of the social world of *noir*. And in many of these films, the victim was the returning soldier. In *The Blue Dahlia* (1946), *Crossfire* (1947), and *Criss-Cross* (1949), the victim of the predatory *noir* woman is a confused, sometimes shell-shocked soldier returned from war to a world that he no longer understands, in which he is a stranger in the country he has been away defending.

But it was not essential to *noir* that the male lead be an ex-soldier, for the deeper social point was that all *noir* men inhabited a world they did not understand and could not deal with, as in *Double Indemnity* (1944), whose male lead, played by Fred MacMurray, is an insurance salesman taken in by Barbara Stanwyck's Phyllis Dietrichson, or the apron-wearing, henpecked bank teller played by Edward G. Robinson in *Scarlet Street* (1945). The *noir* world was a particular kind of American self-portrait, a representation of urban working-class men whose world had come apart. It was an extraordinarily bleak portrait of the war and postwar years, telling the story of an alienating urban landscape where no one knew the rules of the sexual game anymore.

Noir films were nightmare versions of the war-related uncertainty and quiet desperation more gently observed in family melodramas. The war and postwar portrayals of social and family life—whether conventional melodrama or *noir* nightmares—were meditations on a world profoundly changed by a century of war.

NOTES

1. As it happened, *Mr. Smith Goes to Washington* was a hit in Europe and was widely celebrated for its portrayal of the United States. The film was chosen by Paris theater operators as the last U.S. or British film to be screened before the Nazis seized the city (Capra, 1971, 292-93).

2. Ingrid Bergman said later that uncertainty during production over how the story would end worked to her advantage as an actress as her character, Ilsa, didn't know how things would work out either. For a discussion of the background of the production of *Casablanca*, see Friedrich, 1986, 133-39.

3. Hitchcock joined the project through the then-common Hollywood practice of talent-swapping, in which an artist under contract to a studio would be "loaned" to another for other considerations, either financial or the "loan" of another artist. Thus were the studios able both to keep people under contract and also to obtain the services of others not under contract to them. In all this, the negotiations were between those holding the contract, not the artist.

4. Hitchcock made several other films with at least oblique references to political matters. These included a series of propaganda films produced for the British government during the war, as well as films dealing in varying degrees with the cold war (*North by Northwest,* 1959, and *Torn Curtain,* 1966) and with the consequences of Fascist ideologies (*Rope*, 1948).

5. While the *Why We Fight* series is the best known of government-produced films during the war, the range of official U.S. produced films made explicitly to further the war effort was considerable. (See MacCann, 1973, for a more complete discussion.)

6. While most involved in the film's production knew perfectly well what its political role was to be, Louis B. Mayer, for whose studio the film was made, apparently did not. In late 1941, Mayer called the director of *Mrs. Miniver*, William Wyler, and complained about the treatment of a German pilot, depicted in the film as a Nazi fanatic. "We're not at war with anybody," Mayer said. "This picture just shows these people [the British] having a hard time, and it's very sympathetic to them, but it's not directed against the Germans." "Mr. Mayer, you know what's going on, don't you?" Wyler responded. "This is a big corporation," Mayer said. "I'm responsible to my stockholders. We have theaters all over the world, including a couple in Berlin. We don't make hate pictures. We don't hate anybody. We're not at war" (Friedrich, 1986, 49).

6

THE COLD WAR AND
VIETNAM IN FILM

History, whether recorded by academics, journalists, or artists, does not divide as neatly into periods as we sometimes like to pretend: one era gives way to another and for a time eras may coexist. The era of the Great Depression was supplanted by World War II; and the war, as it wound down, yielded to the cold war, a period that produced some of the most subtly interesting of political films.

The quality of these films is in large part due to their indirection. In this respect, the cold war in film was like Vietnam in film: deeply divisive political questions were addressed obliquely at first and directly only much later, after the initial controversy had abated. The Depression and World War II, by contrast, were more directly addressed by moviemakers: the brute facts of the Depression were too wide, deep, and direct to ignore; and World War II, once it had begun, was a natural subject for movies. The indirection in mass-market film that political controversy brings also may bring artistic subtlety.

The term "cold war" was coined by speechwriter and publicist Herbert Bayard Swope in 1946. The cold war, like the shooting war that preceded it, colored everything in U.S. society: public policy on the military, transportation, education, science and technology, communications regulation, foreign policy, and domestic politics—all were structured and justified by the felt need to protect the United States from its new Soviet adversary (Sherry, 1995). But official U.S. policy was based on containing further expansion of the Soviet Union's sphere of political influence, not on vanquishing or shrinking it. With no shooting war, the domestic political goal was one of building a U.S. society that would be strong enough to sustain what, in John F. Kennedy's words, was seen as a "long twilight struggle" against the U.S.S.R. So far as mass culture was concerned, these unique circumstances diverted political anxieties from a sole focus on an external threat to a parallel focus on an internal threat—the threat of Communist subversion of U.S. society. The bipolar political stalemate that was at the heart of the cold war and the policy of containment that underlay it drove an essentially defensive cultural mindset: the point was as much to defend the United States from internal adversaries as from external ones.

A close cultural and intellectual companion to the cold war was the question of conformity versus individualism. Social critics such as David Riesman in *The Lonely Crowd* (1954), William H. Whyte in *The Organization Man* (1957) and scores of other writers and artists looked at postwar America and saw stultifying and frightening pressures toward uniformity.[1] Such critics—Whyte articulated the position most clearly—attributed these strains toward conformity to the organizational nature of postwar U.S. economic life—increasingly large and impersonal institutions whose demand for uniformity at work spilled beyond the office (for much of this discussion focused on white-collar jobs, not factory or farm work) into every aspect of life. The concern with conformity in the workplace expressed by social critics was reinforced by the politics of the cold war itself, for it was not uncommon for cold warriors as otherwise disparate as Senator Joseph McCarthy, Senator Hubert Humphrey and President Harry Truman to concern themselves with real or imagined transgression from what was usually termed Americanism. These two species of political, social, and economic creatures—anticommunism, manifested as both an internal and external threat, and conformity, rooted in the organizational structure of the American workplace—drove some artists, including filmmakers, to look at cold war American society as if examining an alien being.

ALIENS

The first—and least interesting—response by filmmakers to the onset of the cold war was the brief series of anti-Communist films rushed into release to respond both to the changing international political environment and to the first stirrings of domestic anti-Communism, animated especially by the House Committee on Un-American Activities hearings on the film industry. As noted above in chapter 3, these films were largely a mixture of family melodramas and crime films in which the villain was a Communist operative. By the time their brief lives were over, the industry had found a more interesting and profitable vessel for cold war-era stories by transforming them into allegories set in outer space. Space as a setting was a natural: cold-war-era events were driven by a frightening and other worldly technology; more importantly, space provided a literal and figurative distance from which to examine earthly matters: space was safer because it was distant.

The early years of the cold war as seen by U.S. filmmakers were characterized by awe at the power of nuclear weapons for either good or evil, a duality that lay at the center of *The Beginning or the End* (1947), which dealt with the development of the atomic bomb and the uncertain future associated with it.[2] By far the best of these awestruck early cold war films, however, was the Robert Wise-directed 1951 *The Day the Earth Stood Still*.

The film begins with the landing of a spacecraft in Washington, D.C., followed by a montage of excited international news commentary about the alien arrival, establishing the recurring motif of the community of all the nations of earth: earth in the movie is not just a single nation-state or its adversary, but a community uniting humans regardless of national boundaries. The craft is surrounded by a small army of curious and nervous military personnel, establishing another recurring motif: the primacy of military versus civilian authority. The stylized silver craft opens to reveal Gort, a huge robot, and the human-like Klaatu (Michael Rennie). Klaatu moves to offer a gift to the earthlings but instead is shot by a panicked young soldier, whose life and those of his comrades is spared when Klaatu orders Gort not to harm them. Instead, Gort simply fires a ray at the soldiers' weapons, disarming the soldiers without harm. Thus, a third motif: great power restrained. A fourth motif is implicit in all this: the earth as dystopic, for, at the conclusion of the opening scene, the audience finds itself identifying with the aliens.

Rennie plays Klaatu with great dignity and reserve: Klaatu's voice is deep, his manner polite, his attitude toward earthlings a combination of patience, hopefulness, and condescension. He has a message for earthlings, he says, but it must be delivered to all the people of earth. Taken to a hospital for observation, Klaatu is told by an official that his desire to speak to all the nations of earth is impossible to realize; there are too many political divisions to permit it. "I am not interested in your petty squabbles," Klaatu replies. Klaatu leaves the hospital, smiling to himself at the ease with which he overcomes the security designed to confine him. He eventually settles in a boardinghouse whose table conversation amuses him with its talk of the escaped spaceman and his craft, which several at the table suspect is from the Soviet Union. The only reasonable person at the table is Helen Benson (Patricia Neal), a widow with a young son, Bobby (Billy Gray). Klaatu tells them his name is Carpenter.

Klaatu and Bobby take a tour of Washington, where Klaatu learns that Bobby's father was killed in World War II. Looking across a sea of soldiers' tombstones, Klaatu/Carpenter tells Bobby that things don't have to be this way. Klaatu: "We don't have war." Bobby: "What a good idea!" Convinced that his efforts to communicate with political leaders will come to nothing, Klaatu asks Bobby the name the world's smartest man; Bobby responds that it is probably the great scientist Dr. Barnhardt (Sam Jaffe). They go to Barnhardt's home—on Harvard Street—where Klaatu goes to a blackboard and solves an equation by way of introducing himself. Barnhardt quickly surmises Klaatu's identity as the alien and asks for proof of Klaatu's power, which Klaatu provides by bringing almost everything on earth to a halt at noon the following day.

Convinced, Barnhardt arranges a meeting of all the world's scientists, a meeting that is thwarted by the treachery of Helen Benson's suitor, Tom Stevens (Hugh Marlow), whose jealously of Carpenter's relationship with Helen and Bobby and whose greed and desire for notoriety cause him to alert the military authorities, who ask Barnhardt to cancel the meeting. Barnhardt agrees, underlining again that the military governs the world of *The Day the Earth Stood Still*. Washington, D.C.'s monuments—the setting for Jefferson Smith's hero-worshipping awe of national heroes in *Mr. Smith Goes to Washington*—become in *The Day the Earth Stood Still* the stage for scores of police and military vehicles in pursuit of Klaatu.

The betrayed and misunderstood Klaatu is shot in the back by a soldier and killed, but then saved, by Gort, who takes him to the spacecraft where Klaatu is resurrected by the robot. Gort defends the spacecraft, but this time, in contrast to the earlier scene, he kills two soldiers rather than simply destroying their weapons. It is in this scene that the developing association between Klaatu and Christ is brought to a head: Klaatu's earth name is Carpenter; he is betrayed by Helen's boyfriend, Tom, for diamonds, the film's surrogate for silver; he is resurrected by the powerful Gort (though Edmund North's screenplay is quick to note that Gort is not God); and he comes from the skies with a message of peace, walks among the people, but is misunderstood and finally betrayed and killed before his resurrection. Dr. Barnhardt likewise is clearly associated with Albert Einstein, a man who in his political life expressed deep concern about nuclear weapons: not only is Barnhardt the world's greatest scientist but Sam Jaffe's physical appearance and manner cannot help but bring Einstein to mind. The film's heroes are thus creatures of cool intellect—Klaatu and Barnhardt— supported by a woman and a child, forming a family with the male characters dominant, the alien Christ-like Klaatu and the human Dr. Barnhardt the head, and Helen and Bobby Benson the heart.

Beyond the invocations of Christ and of science, the final scenes of *The Day the Earth Stood Still* invoke a third element: the social theory of Thomas Hobbes's *Leviathan* (1651). As Klaatu prepares to leave earth, he delivers a stern lecture to the earthlings: he and his interplanetary friends were prepared to overlook earthlings' trivial disputes, he says, but only until earthlings developed weapons of mass destruction. Ignoring earth is no longer possible now that its disputes have become a threat to other planets' safety. Klaatu tells his hushed audience that other planets learned to deal with this situation long ago by developing a race of robots—Gorts—who are empowered to enforce the peace by extracting a horrible price for transgressions. Klaatu offers earthlings a choice: live peacefully by your own designs or other planets will intervene to see that you do not threaten your neighbors. "The decision," he says, "rests with you."

Klaatu's political analysis of the world in the early cold war period is essentially that of Thomas Hobbes's (1588-1679) "war of all against all." The earth which Klaatu discovers exists on the verge of a Hobbesian state of nature, similar to that portrayed in many westerns, in which the survival of the community is threatened by the selfishness and violence of the very people who comprise it. Klaatu's answer is Hobbes's answer: leviathan, a state structure sufficiently powerful to compel compliance and thus guarantee survival and peace. For Hobbes, as for Klaatu, the dilemma is this: "During the time men live without a common power to keep them all in awe, they are in that condition which is called war; and such a war as is of every man against every man" (Hobbes; in Sommerville and Santoni, eds., 1963, 143), a state Hobbes memorably characterized as "poor, nasty, brutish and short." Klaatu's conclusion is also that of Hobbes: "The passions that incline men to peace are fear of death." (Hobbes; in Somerville and Santoni, 1963, 145); and in *The Day the Earth Stood Still*, the race of robots, of which Gort is only one of many, is the source of that death. As Hobbes celebrated human reason, so does Klaatu; as Hobbes celebrates the use of reason to achieve peace, so does Klaatu. As Hobbes wrote and as Klaatu might have said: "Now all the duties of the rulers are contained in this one sentence, the safety of the people is the supreme law." Gort provides that safety.

The Day the Earth Stood Still is very much a film of the head, of the intellect. Robert Wise's stately direction, the austere sets, Rennie's dignified portrayal of Klaatu, all contribute to the cool and thoughtful tone of the film, depicting the earth as dystopic and the alternative presented by Klaatu as utopic, or at least superior. We are encouraged to look at earth as Klaatu does: as a place of great danger in the nuclear age, which can nonetheless be mitigated by an unflinching self-examination and the application of sound judgment. From the outset, when Klaatu's craft lands and is surrounded by apprehensive soldiers, the audience is on Klaatu's side: how silly these soldiers are, how suspicious the people around the boardinghouse table are, how venal and selfish Tom is. Only the pure-of-heart Helen and her son—a woman and a child—and the man of science, Dr. Barnhard, really understand; the other scientists who might have understood Klaatu's message never hear it because the military cancels the meeting. Emotionally, the film encourages us to identify with the aliens and to look skeptically and even cynically at our own species.

The model of cold war-era governance in *The Day the Earth Stood Still* recurs in many films of this period: the virtual disappearance of civilian political authority and its legitimate—indeed, virtually unnoticed—replacement by the military. When civilian authority is referred to at all, as it is briefly in the beginning of the film, it is only to reinforce the futile and petty squabbling of political leaders. When action is to be taken, the military does it. In an early scene at the spacecraft a man selling newspapers yells the headline, "Army out in charge!" The national military establishment plays the same role in cold war era films that the FBI does in films of the gangster era: it effectively becomes the state, what was termed during the cold war era the "garrison state," in which the demands of the national security and military establishments become preeminent. The most remarkable political aspect of many cold war-era films is the extent to which their portrayals of governance involve either the complete disappearance of civilian authority or its subordination to the military.

Inevitably, this concern with the rise of the military—given its catch-phrase of the "military-industrial complex" in Dwight Eisenhower's presidential farewell address—led to film portrayals of the military gone mad, as in *Seven Days in May* (1964). Directed by John Frankenheimer with a screenplay by Rod Serling, the film is the story of an unsuccessful military coup led by an Air Force general (Burt Lancaster) appalled at the attempts of the president (Fredric March) to reduce the risk of nuclear war by negotiating an arms-reduction treaty with the Soviet Union.

To contemplate the ideas that animate *The Day the Earth Stood Still* is to find an extraordinary mix of science fiction, religion, and political philosophy: a Christ-like alien descending to earth in a spacecraft along with his god-like robot, bearing a message of warning, and a solution derived from seventeenth century British political philosophy. His allies are a war widow, her child, and a scientist. His temporary resurrection comes at the hands of the robot, and his ascension comes via the spacecraft that brought him. His final message is a warning and an ultimatum: live peacefully or die. Klaatu's final speech to the earthlings is as cold and austere as the film itself.

The sense of warning that underlay *The Day the Earth Stood Still*, its unremitting celebration of reason, and its dystopic view of the earth were all turned on their heads in another classic politically-charged science-fiction film of the era, Don Siegel's 1956 *Invasion of the Body Snatchers*, a story so robust that it was remade in 1978 and 1992. The contrast between *The Day the Earth Stood Still* and *Invasion of the Body Snatchers* is stark: the former begins in a national capital, moves immediately to an international focus with the excited comments of television reporters, to its ultimate focus on planets beyond earth. The latter film is set in the small town of Santa Mira (mira means "look!" in Spanish) and never leaves it: *The Day the Earth Stood Still* is as outward-looking as *Body Snatchers* is claustrophobic.

Invasion of the Body Snatchers begins with the uneasy feeling among some of the residents of Santa Mira that something is wrong: people just don't seem to be themselves any more, though it's hard to be certain why. They look the same, but something about their manner is different. This is noticed first by the women and children of Santa Mira. The men, including Dr. Miles Bennell (Kevin McCarthy), the town doctor, recently divorced, and a man of science, are skeptical. The town psychiatrist attributes the unease to some sort of "epidemic of mass hysteria," brought about by the tensions of the times. Whatever the reason, more and more people seem to be behaving this way. People's behavior is disquieting in an oddly negative way: it is not what they do that is odd, it is what they do not do, no longer displaying the small but telling characteristics that make people individuals.

Miles reacquaints himself with his former girlfriend, Becky Driscoll (Dana Wynter), herself recently divorced. The two form the film's primary couple, with their friends Jack (King Donovan) and Teddy (Carolyn Jones) playing secondary roles. Inevitably everyone, including Becky's father, Miles's nurse, and Jack and Teddy fall prey to the forces that are turning Santa Mirans into vacant-eyed, soulless creatures. Finally even Becky succumbs, as Miles discovers when he tries to kiss her and knows instantly by her coldness that she has been taken over.

Aliens are the culprit. Huge seed pods have landed throughout Santa Mira, each pod taking over one person at a time, each creature thereby created working to plant yet more pods to take over more people. The metaphor is quite chilling: soulless replicas of humans created in a way that leads the audience to be suspicious of everyone. Whatever else *Invasion of the Body Snatchers* is about, it is about suspicion and paranoia: it is impossible to watch the film without becoming suspicious of everyone in it. The wittiest line of dialogue in Daniel Mainwaring's screenplay refers to this fear and comes from a pre-pod Jack, who warns Miles and Becky, "Watch out for yourselves." In this film it is literally ourselves for whom we should watch out. Don Siegel's direction reinforces this: he uses many low close-ups, angular lighting with deep shadows, and hysterical, brass-driven music.

All this invites the audience to examine each character with suspicion: Will Becky become a pod-person? Has she become one already? Very much unlike *The Day the Earth Stood Still, Invasion of the Body Snatchers* asks the audience to consider each character as an individual exclusively in terms of whether that person has lost his or her humanity. Robert Wise, in contrast, frames his characters in *The Day the Earth Stood Still* in context, rarely using close-ups, and with stylized, eerie theramin-based music; *The Day the Earth Stood Still* in all its aspects is a cerebral, cool, detached film. *Invasion of the Body Snatchers* celebrates the heart, the emotions: people simply *feel* something is wrong in Santa Mira, and all the rationality and science in the world—the very things that Klaatu represents and advocates—will not change that ("Forget you're a doctor," Miles Bennett is told in an effort to get him to understand that all is not right in town). The human characteristics about which Klaatu is so dismissive in *The Day the Earth Stood Still* are the same things that are the saving graces of *Invasion of the Body Snatchers*. *The Day the Earth Stood Still* is a movie of the head; *Invasion of the Body Snatchers*, a movie of the heart. In *Invasion of the Body Snatchers* human emotions serve to alert the people of Santa Mira to the threat of takeover and to define humanity itself; in *The Day the Earth Stood Still* it is these same human qualities that threaten to destroy life on earth.

The political heart of *Invasion of the Body Snatchers* is the seductiveness of the state of pod-dom. Jack tells Miles that becoming a pod is quite pleasant: one needn't worry any more about such things as love or emotions; the life of a pod-person is free of all these distractions. Miles resists, of course, as does Becky, though Miles finally loses her just as she professes her love for him (the movie has much 1950s-style repressed sexual tension between Miles and Becky) and just after Miles and Becky watch the town square of Santa Mira become a staging area for distributing more pods to surrounding communities. Terrified at the possibility of more pods, late in the film we see Miles fleeing Santa Mira through a maze of pod-filled trucks and screaming into the camera, "You fools, you're in danger! They're after us! You're next!"[3]

The suspicion and paranoia at the heart of *Invasion of the Body Snatchers* are what make it in many respects the perfect cold war-era film, the perfect empty vessel for the concerns of the time. What are the pods? The present-day viewer is likely to see the pods as an allegory for communism. The pods display all the characteristics associated with communism in 1950s America. They are an alien threat. They take over their victims only when the humans sleep—that is, not vigilant. The pods promise freedom from worry, a kind of narcoticized equality based on the absence of messy human imperfections: urging them to join the ranks of the pod-people, Jack tells Miles and Becky, "Love, desire, ambition, faith—without them life is so simple," and assures them, "There's no pain; it's like being reborn into an untroubled world." And the podded humans are relentlessly and systematically imperialistic in their efforts to recruit more human fodder.

But one can as easily see *Invasion of the Body Snatchers* as an allegory on another cold war-era concern: the drive toward a dehumanizing conformity in behavior and orthodoxy of thought in the service of opposition to communism. It was this interpretation that director Don Siegel gave to his own film (Rogin, 1987, 266), arguing that the film was designed as a warning about the price in freedom to be paid by demanding political and social orthodoxy.

The continuing power of the story is its attractiveness both to those who see the film as an anti-Communist allegory and those who see it as a cautionary tale about conformity—an "anti-anti" Communist fable. Indeed, the film may be easily seen as reflecting both of these concerns simultaneously, as such concerns were felt simultaneously by many Americans of the time. The mutual suspicion so perfectly expressed by the metaphor of becoming a pod-creature nicely reflected the degree of projection by each side toward its adversaries that characterized much cold war rhetoric. Each side's view was a mirror image of the other. Hard-core cold warriors saw communism as monolithic, totalitarian, and implacable; the cold warriors' critics—many of them anti-Communist domestic liberals—viewed the cold warriors' insistence on demonstrations of loyalty and Americanism to be not much less authoritarian than those attributed to communism. The subtle implication of *Invasion of the Body Snatchers* was that there might be deep similarities as well as differences between the contending parties of the cold war. A few years later, as the science-fiction genre approached exhaustion and audiences tired of it, this motif of similarities between both sides in the cold war was to be examined in a new, absurdist style.

MADNESS

If *The Day the Earth Stood Still* was a warning about nuclear weapons in the hands of fallible humans and *Invasion of the Body Snatchers* a cautionary tale about the dangers of orthodoxy in the nuclear age, both films took the cold war and its politics seriously; and, in their fashion, both films took sides. As the cold war wore on, however, another trend appears in filmmakers' treatment of the nuclear era: films based on the premise that the cold war was institutionalized insanity, a natural setting for black comedy and satire. Some of these films were gentle satires. *The Russians Are Coming! The Russians Are Coming!* (1966) told the story of a Soviet submarine running aground on an island near Cape Cod, and *The Mouse That Roared* (1959) was a British comedy in which the microscopic Duchy of Grand Fenwick takes advantage of the cold war by declaring war on the United States, hoping to lose quickly and cash in on foreign aid.

Political venality and ambition played out against the backdrop of, say, the Taylor organization's machinations in *Mr. Smith Goes to Washington* is one thing. Seeing the same motivations played out against the backdrop of the thermonuclear destruction of the planet is something else, and it was this apocalyptic possibility—unimaginable only a few years earlier—that led to several memorable film portrayals of political lunacy.

One such film, *Dr. Strangelove, or: How I Learned to Stop Worrying and*

Love the Bomb (1964), essentially held that everyone involved in cold war politics was quite mad; another, *The Manchurian Candidate* (1962), essentially held that both sides, though allegedly adversaries, were essentially the same and equally destructive. Together, these films along with a few others (for example, *The President's Analyst*, 1967) take the cold war-era film into absurdist territory, bringing to mind *Duck Soup* in their treatment of the cold war as just another, though vastly more consequential, manifestation of the absurdity of human beings.

Director Stanley Kubrick's *Dr. Strangelove* establishes its tone immediately. After a prologue tells us that the Soviet Union has been developing a doomsday machine that will automatically and irrevocably trigger nuclear annihilation if the U.S.S.R. is attacked, the film shifts to a U.S. bomber being fueled in mid-air to the accompaniment of the lush and gentle strains of "Try a Little Tenderness." The scene is at once tender (the bomber is suckling the tanker), ironic (the very idea of a weapon of war being suckled), and even perhaps sexual (the two planes appear also to be having sex in flight). We then cut to the long, pointed prow of an aircraft on the ground, the first of scores of phallic references in the film—for *Dr. Strangelove* is a psychosexual black comedy in which that most basic of characteristics, sex, becomes the basis for the destruction of the world.

We are at the first of the film's three settings, Burpelson Air Force Base, a Strategic Air Command (SAC) facility, where General Jack D. Ripper (Sterling Hayden) has just directed that the base be closed after ordering, with no provocation, a nuclear attack on the Soviet Union by the bombers in his command. Ripper, a man of commanding voice and chiseled visage, is all authority and command. When a visiting British Royal Air Force officer, Group Captain Lionel Mandrake (Peter Sellers, in one of the three roles he plays in the film) learns of Ripper's order, he assumes it is merely an exercise "to keep the boys on their toes." But Ripper tells Mandrake it is no exercise: "This is a shooting war, Group Captain," and Mandrake quickly learns (via listening to a portable radio in violation of Ripper's order that all such radios be confiscated) that there is no justification for Ripper's order.

The cockpit of one of the B-52 bombers under Ripper's command is the second setting in *Dr. Strangelove*. We first meet the commander of the plane, Major T.J. "King" Kong (Slim Pickens), as he is looking at a magazine centerfold photo of a young woman with a banner reading "Miss Foreign Affairs" covering her breasts. Kong's reading is interrupted when he receives Ripper's orders to bomb the Soviet Union. His initial response is disbelief, but a careful by-the-numbers check confirms that the order is real. To the tune of "When Johnny Comes Marching Home," Kong prepares for his mission by donning a cowboy hat and telling his crew that, despite their understandable misgivings at what they are about to do, they must do it. There might even be some medals in it for them.

Air Force General "Buck" Turgidson (George C. Scott) learns of Ripper's order while dallying with his girlfriend (she turns out to be "Miss Foreign Affairs" from Kong's magazine) and rushes immediately to the Pentagon's War Room—*Dr. Strangelove*'s third main setting—where, with other military brass and President Merkin Muffley (Peter Sellers), he informs Muffley that only Ripper knows the code that will recall the bombers. The War Room is huge and dark; at its center is a round table, and above the table is a ring of light, an ironic halo beneath which sit the U.S. political and military elite. Like the other settings in the film, the War Room is enclosed, insular, an all-male environment. The incredulous Muffley cannot believe that an attack on the Soviet Union could be ordered without his knowledge. What about fail-safe procedures designed to prevent just such a circumstance? The president is told by Turgidson that the president himself approved the procedure, to be used when the president is disabled. The non-disabled Muffley is outraged, confused, and scared. Muffley concludes that Ripper must be insane, but Turgidson's response is to chastise the president. Facing nuclear war triggered by the actions of one man, Turgidson sanctimoniously cautions Muffley not to jump to conclusions "until all the facts are in." Turgidson concludes that it may be too late to recall the bombers and excitedly suggests that the president take advantage of the opportunity Ripper has presented them and completing the task of destroying the U.S.S.R. by sending in more planes—a doctrine known as preemptive war that was seriously advocated by some cold war-era strategists. Told by Muffley that the president will not go down in history as the greatest mass murderer since Adolf Hitler, Turgidson dismisses Muffley's concerns: "Mr. President, I'm not saying we won't get our hair mussed. I'm saying only ten to twenty million people killed, tops, depending on the breaks." Turgidson meanwhile finds time to take a phone call from his girlfriend, assuring her *sotto voce* that their relationship is not merely physical: "I deeply respect you as a human being. Some day I'm gonna make you Mrs. Buck Turgidson!"

By now the mix of power, sex, and insanity in *Dr. Strangelove* is established. All these men are powerful; they control other people as military men and as politicians, and they control weapons of mass destruction. Sex is no less present: the potent-and-proud-of-it Buck Turgidson's first name is slang for virile man; his last name means "swollen," and he treats the onset of nuclear war and a call from his girlfriend as equally important. Lionel Mandrake's last name refers to the mandrake plant, reputed to induce conception in women. President Muffley's name suggests slang for female genitalia, and General Jack D. Ripper, of course, brings to mind the series of murders of female prostitutes in late nineteenth-century Britain. And as for insanity, we soon learn the president is right—Ripper is quite mad.

This we suspect when the president in the War Room reads the transcript of a phone call Ripper makes to the outside just after sending the bombers and closing the base. The message in the screenplay by Stanley Kubrick, Peter George, and Terry Southern concludes: "God willing, we will prevail in peace and freedom from fear and in true health through the purity and essence of our natural fluids. God bless you all."

Ripper's madness is now confirmed, and its association with nuclear Armageddon and sex is established when we return to Ripper's office, where a desperate Mandrake is trying to get Ripper to reveal the code that will recall the bombers, which Ripper will not do. The base comes under attack from the U.S.

Army on orders of the president, in hopes of capturing Ripper and recalling the bombers. Ripper relishes the moment, pulling a machine gun from his golf bag and firing through his office window—a U.S. Air Force general shooting at U.S. Army troops even as he compliments them on their marksmanship: "That's nice shooting, soldier!" Kubrick photographs the battle for Burpelson Air Force Base in two distinct ways: in Ripper's office the camera is relatively motionless, while the external scenes are shot hand-held and are as jumpy as Ripper's office is serene, despite the machine-gun fire. Ripper may have caused this chaos but is himself at peace. During the battle for Burpelson we see signs bearing the Strategic Air Command's now ironic motto, "Peace is Our Profession," until the battle ends with the surrender of the base's defenders. The base is strewn with the bodies of U.S. Air Force men, killed by U.S. Army soldiers.

It is in the scene in Ripper's office that we learn the nature of the general's madness. Kubrick shoots Ripper in close-up from a low angle, a cigar jutting from his mouth. There is scarcely a shot in this scene without a phallic symbol: the cigar, a microphone, or the machine gun.   An increasingly horrified Mandrake listens as Ripper explains the theory that led to his sending the bombers. Pure water, Ripper explains to Mandrake, is essential to human life; people need "fresh pure water to replenish their precious bodily fluids." Fluoridation of public water began in 1946 ("How's that for your postwar commie conspiracy, Mandrake!"); and this for Ripper is nothing less than the sinister introduction of foreign substances into the human body ("Have you ever seen a commie drink a glass of water?"). Now, even more products are being fluoridated, including ice cream—"children's ice cream!" "Do you realize that fluoridation is the most monstrously conceived and dangerous Communist plot we have ever had to face?"[4]

The astonished Mandrake listens as calmly as he can and gently asks Ripper how he came to this conclusion. "I first became aware of it during the physical act of love," Ripper replies. A "profound sense of fatigue" came over him at the time, which Ripper was nonetheless able to interpret correctly as "loss of essence." Ripper assures Mandrake the problem has not returned: "Women sense my power and seek the life essence. I do not avoid women, Mandrake, but I do deny them my essence." Now entirely certain that Ripper is mad, Mandrake tries, again unsuccessfully, to learn the bombers' recall code. After professing his belief in an afterlife, Ripper calmly excuses himself, walks into the bathroom, and shoots himself dead. The comic madness of Ripper's speech nearly obscures the import of the scene: an insane general has blamed the U.S.S.R. and water fluoridation for his sexual dysfunction, setting in motion events that could lead to the end of all life on earth.

Mandrake eventually figures out the recall code but must next overcome the skepticism of Major "Bat" Guano (Keenan Wynn), one of the soldiers ordered to deliver the base from Ripper's control. Guano suspects that Mandrake is "some sort of deviated prevert" and is deeply reluctant to shoot a cola machine to enable Mandrake to get enough change to call the White House from a pay phone with the recall code. Guano finally relents, but he sternly warns Mandrake that if Mandrake is not telling the truth about the absolute need to shoot the machine, "you'll have to answer to the Coca Cola Company."

Prior to Mandrake's Coca-Cola-assisted phone call, however, President Muffley decides that the Soviets must be informed of Ripper's actions and concludes that the Soviets must also be provided the information to enable them to shoot down the planes. (This same idea of trading U.S. for Soviet casualties on a massive scale lies at the heart of the 1964 *Fail-Safe.*) Turgidson is livid at the idea. The Soviet ambassador, de Sadesky (Peter Bull, whose character's name is a reference to the Marquis de Sade, the man who lent his name to sadomasochism), is invited into the War Room where, after trying surreptitiously to photograph it, he ends up in a wrestling match with an enraged Turgidson. Muffley reproaches them both: "Gentlemen, you can't fight here. This is the War Room!" The ambassador helps Muffley locate Soviet premier Dimitri Kissoff (de Sadesky suggests the premier is with his girlfriend), and after warning Muffley that Kissoff is drunk, the president—sounding like a combination of a tentative suitor dealing with a lover and a careful parent dealing with a child—speaks via phone with Kissoff:

Fine, I can hear you now Dimitri, clear and plain and coming through fine. I'm coming through fine, too, eh? Good, then, well, as you say, we're both coming through fine. Good. Well, it's good that you're fine...and, and I'm fine. I agree with you—it's great to be fine. Now, then, Dimitri, you know we've always talked about the possibility of something going wrong with the Bomb...the Bomb, Dimitri, the Hydrogen Bomb. Well, now, what happened is that, uh, one of our base commanders, he had a sort of, well, he went a little funny in the head. You know, just a little funny. And he went and did a silly thing. Well, I'll tell you what he did. He ordered his plans to attack your country. Well, let me finish, Dimitri. Dimitri, how do you think I feel about it? Can you image how I feel about it, Dimitri? Why do you think I'm calling you? Just to say hello? Of course I like speaking to you...of course I like to say hello.

Soviet missiles intercept the U.S. bombers, and the bombers that are not shot down are recalled—except Kong's plane, which was damaged but not destroyed by a Soviet missile. The attack, however, has disabled the B-52's communications system and caused a loss of fuel. Kong's plane is now damaged but flying, and he elects to head for an alternative target. (Kong pronounces the name of the target as "Laputa." Laputa is the name of an imaginary flying island visited by Dr. Lemuel Gulliver in Jonathan Swift's [1667-1745] classic political satire *Gulliver's Travels,* whose mad-philosopher inhabitants engaged in useless and dangerous pseudoscientific activities.) Kong resourcefully orders the bomber to its new target and then, when the bomb door fails to open, crawls inside the belly of the plane, sits astride an atomic bomb and fixes the faulty door himself, the bomb between his legs. The target approaches, the bomb door opens, and Kong rides the bomb straight to its target, whooping and waving his cowboy hat as if the bomb were a bronco. But in the context of *Dr. Strangelove,* the bomb Kong rides seems, instead, to be the ultimate phallic symbol and its explosion, the nuclear rape of the earth.

The import of Kong's resourcefulness in dropping the bomb becomes clear back in the War Room, when Ambassador de Sadesky tells President Muffley of the Soviet Union's development of the doomsday machine, designed to deter any attack on the U.S.S.R. by guaranteeing an automatic and irrevocable retaliation against the aggressor. Muffley is appalled and asks one of his advisers if such a thing is possible, and it is here that we meet Dr. Strangelove (Peter Sellers) for the first time. Strangelove sits in a wheelchair wearing a black leather glove on his right hand. His hair is blonde, he speaks with a German accent, and we learn that, prior to serving the U.S. government, Dr. Strangelove was, as Turgidson says, "one of them Nazis." Strangelove explains to Muffley that there is no particular technological problem in creating a doomsday machine: it is "easily accomplished," he says. Such a machine requires "only the *vill* to use it." Word reaches the War Room that one plane—Kong's—is still unaccounted for.

The movie now becomes Strangelove's, and the comic madness that precedes it is further distilled as the military and political men discuss the possibilities of a postnuclear world. Strangelove suggests the use of deep mineshafts as dwellings in which to wait out the dissipation of nuclear radiation and concludes that it would, of course, be necessary for all the government's top military and political leaders to be protected. Warming to the task, Strangelove spells out the details: "Animals could be bred and *slaughtered*," for food, he says, adding that in order for the human species to survive it would be necessary to populate the mineshafts with a very high ratio of sexually attractive females for each male. Muffley raises a question or two about this scenario, but even the reasonable Muffley appears to be willing to consider it. The biggest concern is expressed by Turgidson, who suspects the Soviets might also retreat to their own mineshafts; he doesn't want the United States to be at a disadvantage when both sides emerge many years later from their shelters: "Mr. President, we cannot allow a mineshaft gap!" The image of powerful men escaping nuclear holocaust by seeking the shelter of womb-like mineshafts stocked with animals for food and women for breeding stock is at once deeply comic and deeply horrific.

Dr. Strangelove excitedly contemplates the post-attack world, in his growing enthusiasm almost addressing Muffley as "mein Fuhrer" instead of "Mr. President." So great is his excitement that Strangelove experiences his own internal struggle: his black-gloved right hand takes on a life of its own and attempts to strangle him. Several times his left hand saves him, but finally Dr. Strangelove can no longer resist his dark side, his true self. He rises from his wheelchair, takes a few steps, and his right arm snaps into a Nazi salute. He joyously cries, "Mein Fuhrer, I can walk!" Strangelove's body and arm are literally erect; they are, metaphorically, erections. The earth dies as Dr. Strangelove is reborn. It is difficult to watch the reborn Strangelove arise and not hear "mineshaft" as "mein shaft." It is the ultimate phallic reference, for it was Ripper's sexual problem that started it all and Kong's phallic bomb-drop that set off the doomsday machine and led to the talk of the mineshaft shelter.

After Strangelove's cry of triumph the film cuts immediately to a montage of nuclear explosions: the doomsday machine has been triggered. As scores of mushroom clouds arise, we hear Vera Lynn sing "We'll Meet Again," a World War II-era song of hope for the future: "We'll meet again, don't know where, don't know when, but I know we'll meet again some sunny day." But the suns in this final montage are the human-made suns of the bombs, and any future meetings will surely not be on earth.

For the audience that first saw it in 1964 there were many immediate references in *Dr. Strangelove* to the cold war rhetoric and personalities of the time. President Muffley is the mirror-image of Adlai Stevenson, the 1952 and 1956 Democratic presidential candidate, beloved of liberals but doomed to be thought weak and vacillating. General Turgidson and General Ripper, in their manner but especially in their strategic and military beliefs, bring to mind no one so much as General Curtis LeMay, the cold warrior who headed the Strategic Air Command and who, as a third-party vice presidential candidate during the Vietnam War offered the opinion that Vietnam should be "bombed back to the Stone Age."[5] Turgidson supports and Ripper causes the kind of preemptive war that was seriously argued by some cold war military strategists. And Dr. Strangelove himself recalls, if he recalls any one person, Dr. Edward Teller, the physicist whose research was instrumental in developing the hydrogen bomb and who remained thereafter a zealous cold warrior. One can also sense in Strangelove the echoes of two other cold war era writers, the establishment strategist Henry Kissinger and the more radical Herman Kahn.

There are also heroes of a sort in *Dr. Strangelove*. President Muffley is the only person of any power who appears reasonable, but he is ineffectual. Muffley is surrounded in the War Room by tough and certain military men (he is the only civilian authority in the film), and his phone conversation with Kissoff reveals him to be tentative and frail. Mandrake, in his brief role, is also something of a hero, but he is also British (the only non-American or Soviet in the film), a visitor, and not of great military rank or influence. Mandrake's fate is the fate of all the bystanders to the U.S.-Soviet conflict, for he has no real role in events. The biggest hero is Major Kong, the pilot of the B-52 that gets through. Associated throughout the film with the mythic American cowboy, it is Kong's dedication and resourcefulness that lead to his and his multiracial crew's catastrophically successful completion of their mission. The little guys triumph. The overwhelming import of *Dr. Strangelove,* however, is that everyone of any political or military power, Soviet or American, is mad or a fool.

All these human failings are magnified by the technological and human system of which the characters are a part and over which they appear to have control: Ripper, his air base; Muffley and the military men, their War Room; and Kong, his B-52. In this respect, *Dr. Strangelove* develops a theme common to many of Stanley Kubrick's films: *Paths of Glory* (1957), set in World War I, which examines a French general's efforts to scapegoat three enlisted men for a suicidal mission the general ordered; *2001: A Space Odyssey* (1968), a classic man-versus-machine fable placed in the context of the entire history of the human species; *A Clockwork Orange* (1971), a nightmare rendering of a society so fearful of violence that it wreaks violence; and *Full Metal Jacket* (1987), with its examination of the effects of military training and combat on soldiers. In all these films, Kubrick places people—sometimes quite mad, sometimes simply banally human—into a system that they ostensibly control but that finally controls and destroys them. In *Dr. Strangelove*, the combination of humans and the institutions they have created quite simply leads to the end of the world. Kubrick's Olympian stance in the film is that of cosmic laughter at the absurdity of it all. Klaatu would have understood.

Two years before the 1964 release of *Dr. Strangelove,* John Frankenheimer produced and directed *The Manchurian Candidate,* a film the equal of *Strangelove* as a cold war-era cautionary tale and, in its way, even more chilling. Both films tell a straightforward story, but while *Dr. Strangelove* does so in a direct narrative style, moving from setting to setting as events develop, *The Manchurian Candidate's* narrative is fractured emotionally and chronologically. We understand Ripper's madness at the outset of *Dr. Strangelove.* The madness at the heart of *The Manchurian Candidate* is not fully revealed until the film's end; but, like the detective story it essentially is, *The Manchurian Candidate* tells us all we need to know early on.

A prologue scene—"Korea 1952"—prior to the opening credits introduces us to Raymond Shaw (Laurence Harvey), a priggish and pompous soldier, and his comrades in a U.S. squad. In combat, the men are maneuvered into a position suggested by their Korean interpreter Chunjin (Henry Silva), whose dominance, despite his ostensibly subsidiary role, is made clear by his framing in the scene. In one of many deep-focus shots, Chunjin dominates the foreground while the U.S. troops in the background follow his advice. The squad is captured by the enemy and flown away in helicopters bearing a red star. The squad has been set up by its interpreter. The opening credits, dominated by an image of the Queen of Diamonds, follow. The narrative resumes two years later.

Raymond Shaw returns home a hero, a Congressional Medal of Honor winner, to an embarrassing welcoming ceremony and parade. His Medal of Honor citation credits him with saving his comrades from ambush, retaliating against the enemy attackers, and returning his comrades to safety—the same comrades we see in the prologue being taken away in Communist helicopters. His discomfiture with the ceremony turns to hatred when he is greeted by Mother (Angela Lansbury, whose character's name we never learn) and his stepfather, Senator John "Johnny" Iselin (James Gregory), and learns that Mother has organized it all to further her husband's political career. Raymond hates the welcoming ceremony, hates Iselin, hates his mother, and tells them so. Mother tries to soothe things. She wants, she says, only the best for both of them—"My boys, my two little boys." Aboard Iselin's campaign plane, Raymond, with great pleasure, tells Mother and Iselin he will be taking a job with Holborn Gaines, a newspaper columnist. "That Communist?" says his horrified Mother. "Mother, he's a Republican," Raymond replies, adding that he and Gaines have something in common: "We both loath and despise you and Johnny."

Now *The Manchurian Candidate* abruptly turns surreal. We see a woman give a lecture on the cultivation of hydrangeas at a garden club. The camera turns through a full circle and we see primly dressed middle-aged women listening to the hydrangea lecture, but we also see dazed-looking soldiers among them. The juxtaposition of soldiers and garden club members is as intellectually dizzying as the camera movement that shows it; on its next pass the camera shows us a large, bald, mustachioed Chinese man, Yen Lo (Kheigh Dheigh), talking about hydrangea-growing. Behind him are huge pictures of Joseph Stalin and Mao Zedong. The sequence becomes a bewildering mix of setting, character, voices, and dialogue. The setting changes from the garden club to a steeply-terraced operating theater as a group of men (we conclude from what several of them say that they are Chinese, North Korean, and Soviet Communists) listen to the lecture. The topic has changed from flowers to brainwashing.

Yen Lo lauds the virtues of brainwashing. A Soviet skeptic in the audience demands proof from the Chinese speaker, and we see Raymond Shaw compliantly strangle a U.S. comrade to death to prove the speaker's point. The film abruptly cuts to a screaming Bennett Marco (Frank Sinatra) as he wakes up from what has become a recurrent nightmare. Later Marco tells several military men, including the brass and his Korean comrade Al Melvin (James Edwards) about his dream; the strangled soldier in Marco's nightmare was one of the two soldiers reported killed in the action that won Raymond Shaw his Medal of Honor. And yet when Marco is asked about Raymond he immediately responds: "Raymond Shaw is the kindest, bravest, warmest, most wonderful human being I've ever met in my life."

Cut to Senator Iselin in a Senate hearing, berating the secretary of defense for security violations. He has, he says, a list bearing the names of 207 Communists knowingly employed by the Defense Department: "No cover-up!" The shouting match between Iselin and the defense secretary is televised, and the framing of the shot, with a television screen dominating the foreground while the actual event plays out in the background (another deep-focus shot), makes clear for what audience Iselin's charge is intended. Mother is pleased with the performance (she watches Iselin's image on the television screen though he is only a few feet away), but Marco, assigned to military public relations duties, later politely asks Iselin to verify just how many names are on the senator's list.[6] Iselin tosses out the numbers 104 and 275. Later, professing embarrassment at being hounded by "the boys" in the press for the precise number, Iselin complains to Mother, whose advice is cold and harsh: "Say what you are supposed to say!" Mother encourages Iselin to settle on a single number if it will make things any easier, and the senator finally decides on the number of 57, taken from the label of a ketchup bottle. He announces the number proudly on the Senate floor.

We return briefly to the brainwashing setting. This time we see Raymond kill a second soldier, the squad's boyish mascot, by shooting him through the forehead, and again we see it is a nightmare—this time Al Melvin's nightmare. Melvin's wife comforts him, and we hear Raymond Shaw described in familiar words, this time as the "kindest, bravest, warmest, most wonderful human being" Al Melvin ever met.

Raymond gets a phone call suggesting he play solitaire. He draws the Queen of Diamonds, then gets another call suggesting that he check into a sanitarium for a check-up. We see Raymond in a hospital bed (we learn it is in a Russian safe-house), victim of a hit-and-run accident, with two men: a Russian and Yen Lo, the advocate of brainwashing. It is here that we know for certain that Raymond has been brainwashed and that Marco and Melvin's nightmares are not imaginary. Both the Russian and the Chinese want to be certain that Raymond is properly programmed before he is turned over to his American operator. (In this and earlier scenes, the Chinese Communists are portrayed as the more clever and sinister of the two Communist powers.) The Russian wants a final test of Raymond's readiness, however, so for the third time Raymond is programmed to kill; this time it is his employer, newspaper columnist Holborn Gaines, whom Raymond shoots as Gaines lies in bed.

Marco is now convinced something is very wrong with Raymond. His and Melvin's nightmares are identical, and Marco's own recollection from Korea is that nobody ever liked Raymond Shaw: he is in reality the pompous young man we saw in the prologue, not the kind, gentle, and brave soldier of Marco and Melvin's brainwashed memories. Marco's suspicions are confirmed when he and Melvin, at different locations, identify the Russian and Chinese operatives from a series of photographs. Marco's insight about Raymond does not extend to himself, however; he is not quite able to comprehend how his own suspicions about Raymond fit with Marco's own praise of him, or with Marco's own presence in Raymond's squad in Korea.

An incomplete answer emerges when Marco, ordered to take some time off, travels to visit Raymond. On a train a very jittery Marco meets Rosie (Janet Leigh). After some small talk, they move to the space between the railroad cars, the countryside blurring through the window between them as we see Marco slumped on one side of the frame and Rosie in sharp profile on the other. Their conversation is nonsensical and cryptic. Rosie begins by observing that Maryland is a beautiful state and goes on to say that she was one of the Chinese workmen who built the railroad. When Marco replies, she gently corrects his response: he didn't get all the words quite right, she tells him. Throughout the scene Marco is rattled and gets more so; as he does, Rosie carefully observes him, her expression a combination of affection, bemusement, and cool detachment. Rosie boldly asks Marco if he is married and learning that he is not, gives him her address and phone number without his asking.

The suggestion is subtle: Marco, in search of the controlled Raymond Shaw, may himself be controlled by Rosie. (Rosie tells Marco her given name is Eugenie, the name of the ninetheenth-century empress of France and the wife of Louis Napoleon.) Raymond, we learn, has just hired Chunjin, the interpreter from his days in Korea and the man who set up Raymond's squad, as his valet and cook. Raymond, of course, has no recollection of Chunjin, but Marco does; and when Marco arrives at Raymond's apartment (Raymond is absent) and sees Chunjin, Marco immediately attacks him. "What are you doing here?" Marco screams. The meaning is clear but, like many things in *The Manchurian Candidate,* subtle: while both Marco and Raymond were brainwashed, Marco, unlike Raymond, has some recollection of the experience and is struggling to make sense of it, though his focus is on understanding Raymond's condition, not his own. Marco's understanding is incomplete.

Picked up by the police for attacking Chunjin, Marco is taken to a police station where he is immediately joined by Rosie, whom he tells that he must immediately find Raymond. With the same swiftness with which she gave Marco her phone number and address, Rosie now tells Marco that she has broken her engagement because of him. With their first meeting on the train and the second now in the police station, the closer Marco gets to Raymond, the closer Rosie gets to Marco.

Marco visits Raymond (Chunjin conveniently having the night off) and Raymond admits to Marco the basis of his deep hatred of Mother: she stood between Raymond and the woman he loved. As Marco listens to Raymond's tale of hatred for Mom, George Axelrod's screenplay (based on a novel by Richard Condon) has Marco casually mention Orestes and Clytemnestra. "Who's that?" Raymond asks. "Couple of Greeks in a play," the well-read Marco offhandedly replies. In classical Greek mythology, Clytemnestra and her lover, Aegisthus, kill her husband, Agamemnon, and both are in turn killed by Orestes, her son with Agamemnon.

The woman at the heart of Raymond's hatred for Mom is named Jocie (Leslie Parrish). She is young, blonde, pretty, and sweet. Jocie and Raymond met prior to Raymond's departure for Korea. In a flashback, Raymond is bitten by a snake in an Edenic country setting and Jocie tends his wound. She takes him to her family's cabin where Raymond meets Jocie's father, Senator Thomas Jordan (John McGiver). "The Communist?" Raymond asks. Asked by Senator Jordan where he comes from, Raymond replies the "red house from across the lake," the home of Mother and Iselin. That explains Raymond's characterization of Jordan as a Communist. Senator Jordan is the committed adversary of both Senator Iselin and Mother. Senator Jordan explains to the politically naive Raymond that Mother accuses anyone who disagrees with her of being a Communist. In fact, Senator Jordan explains with pleasure, he once had the satisfaction of successfully suing Mother for slander and donating the proceeds to the American Civil Liberties Union. Jocie and Senator Jordan tend to Raymond's snakebite and Raymond, basking in what is an entirely unprecedented warmth, promptly proposes marriage to Jocie. Raymond has found a family.

Returning from the flashback, Raymond bitterly tells Marco how Mother forbade him to marry what Mother called "that Communist tart."[7] "We are at war," she tells Raymond. "It's a cold war but it will get worse." As for Senator Jordan: "He is evil." Raymond tells Marco that he—or maybe it was his mother, Raymond is not sure—wrote a painful letter to Jocie ending their relationship. And soon after Raymond went off to Korea.

Now, after the war and Raymond's return, Mother has a change of heart. As she helps Iselin prepare for a television appearance ("I keep telling you not to think. Just keep yelling 'point of order, point of order,' and I'll take care of the rest"),[8] she concludes that Raymond should marry Jocie and plans a party to enable the two to meet again. The party is a costume affair, with Iselin dressed as Abe Lincoln (one of many ironic visual associations between Iselin and Lincoln) and Mother dressed as Bo Peep. Even Senator Jordan, wearing a tux rather than a costume, has been invited and attends what he calls this "Fascist rally" (we see a knife, wielded by Iselin, cut through a cake decorated as the U.S. flag) for the sake of his daughter.

Mother calls Raymond to the study and suggests he play solitaire; but she is called away, and, in her absence, Jocie enters the room, her costume dominated by the Queen of Diamonds—the Red Queen, but of (hard) diamonds, not of (loving) hearts—the symbol that triggers the programmed Raymond, as an increasing number of hints in the film indicate. Jocie and Raymond kiss. Mother, meanwhile, is trying to make a political deal with Senator Jordan. Senators Jordan and Iselin are both members of the same party—clearly the Republican party, though this is never said directly. Will Senator Jordan allow Senator Iselin to have a run at the vice presidential nomination without blocking him? Mother asks. Jordan replies that he despises Johnny Iselin and "Iselinism." He will do all in his power to stop Iselin, Jordan says, after which he delivers one of the central lines of dialogue in the film: "If he [Iselin] were a paid Soviet agent he could not do more harm to this country than he has done now." Rebuffed, Mom returns to the study to find Jocie's Queen of Diamonds costume card and Raymond and Jocie gone. At the same time, Marco has figured out the role the Queen of Diamonds plays in triggering Raymond and tells Rosie of his plans to free Raymond of the effects of the brainwashing.

Under the spell both of the Queen of Diamonds costume and his love of Jocie, Raymond marries Jocie and tells Marco of his great happiness. Marco urges Jocie to help him have Raymond "put himself under arrest." "He's sick," Marco tells Jocie, but Jocie persuades Marco to give them 48 hours together first. The marriage becomes public—a Romeo and Juliet political wedding—and simultaneously Senator Iselin charges Senator Jordan with treason and threatens Jordan's impeachment. Outraged at the actions of his hated stepfather, Raymond sends Jocie to her father's home and seeks out Iselin. At Mother and Iselin's home, observed by a bust of a stern Abe Lincoln, Raymond and Mother meet. "Darling, something important has come up," Mother says. "There is something you have to do." On those last few words the camera shows Mother's hands opening a drawer and reaching for a deck of cards.

Mother sends her son to kill his wife and her father. Obeying Mother, he does so, shooting them both—the fourth and fifth murders Raymond has committed. Marco learns of the killings and knows immediately who committed them, blaming himself for allowing the newly married couple to go away for a few days. Raymond is heartbroken at the murders though unaware he committed them. He calls Marco and tells him he's cracking up. When the two meet, Marco suggests solitaire, and, one after another, Raymond turns over Queens of Diamonds—Marco has a deck of 52 of them. Looking into Raymond's eyes, Marco tells Raymond what happened to him in Korea and since and asks Raymond what he has been programmed to do. Raymond does not know. Only Moscow and his U.S. operator know that. Whatever Raymond is to do, he is to do soon, he says, perhaps at the upcoming party nominating convention. Overwhelming Raymond with the deck of all Red Queens in an effort to purge him of the brainwashing, Marco tells Raymond, "It's over. You don't work anymore." The phone rings, Raymond answers, listens for a moment, then turns to Marco: "It's time for my American operator to give me the plan." Then he returns to the phone and says, "Yes, yes, I understand, Mother." Then turning to Marco once more: "She wants me to go." Marco gives Raymond a phone number to use when he knows his assignment and reminds him again: "The wires have been pulled. They can't control you any more. You're free." But Marco cannot be certain.

Raymond and Mother meet again. Her voice strong and cold, her face shot close-up from a low angle, Mother tells her son his assignment. Raymond will be dressed as a priest. Chunjin will supply him with a rifle. Raymond will station himself in a projection booth high above the convention floor and will shoot the presidential nominee in the head at a precise point in his acceptance speech. His running mate, Senator Iselin, covered with the nominee's blood, will deliver a rousing, defiant speech—a speech, Mother says, that has been worked on in Russia and the United States for the past eight years in preparation for this moment, a speech "rallying a nation of television viewers into hysteria to sweep us up into the White House with powers that will make martial law look like anarchy." Mother is the Red Queen; the television viewers, Bo Peep's sheep.

Mother moves close to Raymond. She didn't know it would be Raymond, she tells him. "I told them to build me an assassin," she says, but she did not know it would be her own son who would be the instrument of "winning for them their greatest victory." But Mother will get her revenge. "When I take power they will be pulled down and ground into dirt for what they did to you and what they did in so contemptuously underestimating me." With those words, Mother places both her hands on Raymond's head and pulls him toward her. She kisses him once on the forehead—a mother's kiss. Then Mother kisses him twice on the mouth—a lover's kiss.

Raymond stations himself in the convention hall as ordered while Marco waits anxiously for word from Raymond of Raymond's assignment. But Marco hears nothing from Raymond and finally rushes into the hall through the tumult of the delegates on the floor. Marco spots the light from the projection booth and rushes up the stairs toward it. As the climactic moment in the nominee's speech nears, Raymond trains his sights on the nominee, but as the nominee delivers the key line—"My life before my liberty"—Raymond swings his rifle away from the nominee and instead shoots and kills Iselin and then Mother. For the sixth and seventh time in *The Manchurian Candidate*, Raymond kills. Marco arrives at the booth in time to see Raymond place his Medal of Honor around his own neck, then kill himself. The echo of Raymond's final shot segues into a thunderclap and into the final scene, where we see a distraught Marco, Rosie sitting nearby, look out a window at the falling rain. Marco reads aloud from a book of Medal of Honor citations; he closes the book and speaks his own citation for Raymond Shaw: "Made to commit acts too unspeakable to be cited here, by an enemy which had captured his mind and soul. He freed himself at last and in the end heroically and unhesitatingly gave his life to save his country. Ah, hell . . . hell."

As with *Dr. Strangelove, The Manchurian Candidate* operates at both political and personal—especially sexual—levels. Politically, *The Manchurian*

Candidate is a film of the center, looking askance at both the political Left and Right, at both the Communist world and the domestic politics of anticommunism. In this, the movie is closely allied with *Dr. Strangelove, The Day the Earth Stood Still,* and *Invasion of the Body Snatchers* in its political suggestion that both the Right and Left are to be rejected, though each film has its particular emphasis. In the world of *The Day the Earth Stood Still,* both sides are to be feared because they possess new and dangerous weapons; their ideological differences are merely "petty squabbles." In *Invasion of the Body Snatchers,* both sides are dangerous because they foster dehumanization and spiritual death. The world of *Dr. Strangelove* is one of Soviet and U.S. fools whose sexual problems and personal weaknesses destroy the world. The world of *The Manchurian Candidate* likewise damns both Left and Right in the cold war, though in quite different ways.

The Soviets and Chinese are presented as evil and cunning; they know what they want and go after it using whatever means necessary. The U.S. anti-Communist Right, in the person of Senator Iselin, is by contrast merely foolish. Iselin is a boor and an amiable drunk. He takes Mother's directions agreeably, though one doubts he believes or cares much about what he says. Senator Jordan, by contrast, occupies the sensible political center. Jordan, like Iselin, is a Republican. Unlike Iselin, Jordan understands what harm Iselin and those like him can do. And Senator Jordan and his daughter provide the only loving family that Raymond Shaw has ever known. When Raymond kills Thomas and Jocie Jordan, love, reason, and the political center die.

Marco sorrowfully says of Shaw, "poor Raymond, poor, poor Raymond," and so he is. Programmed by the Chinese Communists and the Soviet Union, directed by his mother, he is programmed to kill five people including two of his comrades, his employer, his wife, and her father. When he finally frees himself of the brainwashing, that freedom leads him to kill his mother and her husband, and finally to kill himself. Marco's brief reference in the film to Clytemnestra is all too apt. The fates of Raymond, Iselin, and Mother precisely parallel the fates of their mythological precursors, Orestes, Aegisthus, and Clytemnestra. Raymond's story is an overwhelming tragedy: he bears the evils of family and circumstance. Raymond Shaw is by turns a victim (of Mother's hideous manipulation, of incest, of cold war politics, and finally of himself in his suicide) and a perpetrator of murder, especially those of his wife and her father—the only loving family "poor Raymond" will ever know. The reference to Clytemnestra is even more chilling, for Clytemnestra and her lover killed her husband, Agamemnon. Did Mother kill—or have killed—Raymond's father so she could marry the oafish Iselin and begin her drive for power?

Political extremism is not the only villain in *The Manchurian Candidate,* however, for the film also constitutes a hateful portrait of women, the best rendering we have in film of what was called "Momism," a term associated most forcefully with Philip Wylie's 1942 book, *Generation of Vipers,* a mean, broad-based assault on the alleged pathological effects of mothers on their children, especially their male children, an idea that took root in the same era that gave us *film noir*'s chilling portrayal of women. Wylie writes:

Freud has made a fierce and wondrous catalogue of examples of mother-love-in-action which traces its origins to an incestuous perversion of normal instinct. That description, of course, is sound. Unfortunately, Americans, who are the most prissy people on earth, have been unable to benefit from Freud's wisdom because they can *prove* that they do not, by and large, sleep with their mothers....

Mom is something new in the world of men...Usually, until very recently, mom folded up and died of hard work somewhere in the middle of her life...Nowadays, with nothing to do, and all the tens of thousands of men...to maintain her, every clattering prickamette in the republic survives for an incredible number of years, to stamp and jabber in the midst of man...The machine has deprived her of social usefulness...never before has a great nation of brave and dreaming men created a huge class of idle middle-aged women. (Wylie 1942, 185, 186-187; emphasis in the original)

Wylie, a reactionary social critic, anticipated the combination of animus toward women and the assertion of their power that is the central sexual element of *The Manchurian Candidate*. Virtually every male character in *The Manchurian Candidate* is weak: Raymond is destroyed by Mother and the foolish Iselin is manipulated by her—"my two little boys." The strong and loving Senator Jordan dies at Raymond's hands on Mother's orders, as does Jocie. In the nightmare recollections of the brainwashing scene, the male controller is recalled as a woman in a garden club surrounded by other women, Raymond politely responding "Yes, ma'am" to his orders. In the world of *The Manchurian Candidate*, strong women control and weak men follow. Men who do not follow or women who do not control die. Raymond's commits his original sin when he is bitten by the snake and meets Jocie, the loving and sexual woman.

There is a final relationship in the film that combines sexual and political elements and that appears to escape the tragedy that befalls the other couples: Marco Bennett and Rosie. What of them? The two are the most conventional male-female couple in the film. They meet and fall in love. They also both survive, the only male-female couple not to be killed by Raymond. But it is impossible to look at the final scene of the film, with Marco mourning poor Raymond and Rosie sitting contentedly nearby, and not realize that things are not that simple. At their initial meeting, Rosie's and Marco's cryptic conversation leads to the suspicion that Rosie is Marco's U.S. controller. Marco was, after all, also brainwashed in Korea. When Marco is taken to the police station, Rosie somehow knows about it and meets him there, and she forcefully approaches Marco sexually, giving him her phone number and address and breaking up with fiancé because of him. And then there is her name, Rosie. As *The Manchurian Candidate* ends, one suspects that Marco is next: he will be the next Raymond Shaw.

RAND

Most cold war era films were works of the political middle. A politically centrist film did not, in the cold war context, necessarily mean an ambiguous film; it could mean, as well, a film that was, instead, ambivalent, that would attack—or satirize—both the Left and the Right, a strategy that was simultaneously politically safe and likely to attract a larger audience. For a relatively brief period at the very beginning of the cold war, however, many films turned to the Right before they reacquired their typically centrist tendencies.

One such group of rightist films was born at the end of the World War II, nurtured by the Korean War, and produced in some measure to mollify a Congress some of whose members professed concern that films were doing to Americans what the Chinese, Soviets, and Mother did to Raymond Shaw. The same industry that had been praised, encouraged, and aided in producing films like *Mission to Moscow, Song of Russia*, and *The North Star* now found itself trying to cover its political right flank. It did so by making anti-Communist movies, and thus were produced *The Iron Curtain* (1948); *The Red Menace* (1949); *The Red Danube* (1949); *Red Snow* (1952); *The Steel Fist* (1952); *I Was a Communist for the FBI* (1951); *Big Jim McLain* (1952), with John Wayne as a House Committee on Un-American Activities investigator at work in Hawaii aided by his psychologist girlfriend; and what must be seen as the classic of the genre, *My Son John* (1952).

The domestic anti-Communist movement and the politics of the film industry met in the fascinating, though not very good, 1949 release *The Fountainhead* (directed by King Vidor), based on the best-selling novel of the same title by Ayn Rand. While Rand is known primarily for her fiction and her "objectivist" philosophy, she was additionally a screenwriter (she wrote the screenplay for *The Fountainhead*) and a vigorous Hollywood political activist for the political Right.

The Fountainhead is the story of Howard Roark (Gary Cooper), a young architect expelled from school at the beginning of the film because he refuses to go along with the crowd, because he is "too original." Professionally, Roark is proudly an extremist, convinced of his own genius, demanding independence, and prepared to pay the price for both. Urged by teachers, friends, and critics to compromise in his architectural designs, he refuses. The middle way is not his way. Roark finally gets his break, the design of the ironically named Security Bank Building, but the bankers think Roark's design is too radical and clutter his modern design with classical bits and pieces. "It's the middle of the road," Roark is told. "Why take chances when you can be in the middle?" Roark declines the commission for the building and instead finds work in a stone quarry, where he meets his love interest, Dominique Francon (Patricia Neal) in whose father's quarry Roark now works.

Dominique is at first asexual ("I'm a woman completely incapable of feeling. I'll never fall in love"), but when she meets Roark all changes. The symbolism is heavy and entirely without irony or satire: Dominique, echoing her name, sits astride a stallion, flicking her mount—and Roark—with her whip, and gazing in wonderment at Roark as he breaks hard rock with his phallic drill. After some resistance on Dominique's part, they consummate their relationship: Roark enters Dominique's bedroom one night and knocks her down. She rises and hits him; they struggle, then kiss. Dominique, conquered, passes out. Roark has dominated Dominique and she loves it; the scene is essentially a rape. She begs him to marry her: "I'll cook, I'll wash clothes, I'll scrub the floor," she begs. But Roark says no. He needs no one but himself.

Dominique marries Gayle Wynand (Raymond Massey), a millionaire newspaper publisher who also befriends Roark, perhaps because they have similar philosophies: "We have no choice but to submit or rule," Wynand says. For Roark there is no middle when it comes to his architectural designs; for Wynand there is no middle ground when it comes to power. Despite Dominique's history with both men, Roark and Wynand becomes fast friends, Wynand seeing Roark more frequently than he sees his wife, Dominique.

Roark gets another professional break: the design of the Enright House for yet another self-made millionaire. But Roark meets opposition from a newspaper architecture critic, a liberal who derides Roark's individualism and castigates him for building an apartment building for the rich while the poor go homeless. "I don't like geniuses," the critic says. "They're dangerous." The building is a great success but the critic manages to wreck Roarks' career anyway; once again he must begin anew, designing such humble structures as gas stations and small farmhouses. The design of such structures for the common folk is an obvious comedown for Roark, but he perseveres. Roark agrees to design a model housing project for the poor but only if his design is followed to the letter. When it is not, when others again meddle in his work and build the houses contrary to his plans, he dynamites them.

Having spurned society by rejecting its meddling in his work, Roark now takes one additional step by becoming an outlaw. In taking this step, he is joined by Dominique, whom Roark persuades to leave Wynand and join him in blowing up the homes. Dominique could not persuade Roark to marry her with promises of cooking and washing—commitments to him as a person and a husband—but to join Roark in the dynamiting of the houses is a commitment outside the laws of conventional society based on Roark's certainty of his own genius.

Roark is arrested and tried for the dynamiting. As with the trial in *Mr. Deeds Goes to Town*, the defendant becomes his own defense attorney. He attacks his enemies for making "robots" of men of genius like himself and defends the "individual against the collective." "The parasite follows the opinion of others," he says in his summation, though the collective, in this case the jury, acquits Roark. Wynand commits suicide, freeing Dominique to marry Roark, and in the final scene in the film, Dominique rides to the top of Wynand Building that Roark has designed, Roark having vanquished his friend and taken his wife for his own. "Where's Mr. Roark?" Dominique asks a construction worker. "He's way up on top," she is told, and she and the audience rise in an open elevator toward Roark, high atop his newly built phallic symbol, his genius and power confirmed. The solemn celebration of phallic, male power and Dominique's submission to it in the 1949 *The Fountainhead* would become the subject of savage derision in the 1962 *Dr. Strangelove*.

The uneasy ambivalence about the common man one sees in Frank Capra's films is entirely gone in *The Fountainhead*. The masses are fools, and those who celebrate them—moderates and especially liberals—are also foolish, for the role of the masses, by definition, is to thwart the will of men like Howard Roark. The question becomes not whether Roark is a great architect but whether he will prevail. The basis of his claim that he should prevail is his belief in his own greatness. The confirmation of that greatness is that the masses do not understand it and liberal elites fear it and demand compromise. Roark is an authoritarian, even a Fascist, hero. The messy politics of accommodation and compromise do not exist for him, for to accommodate or compromise is to acknowledge the legitimacy and judgment of those to whom Roark is convinced he is superior. While Ayn Rand's novel *The Fountainhead* was a best-seller, the film did considerably less well. Rand herself, however, remained politically active in the film industry as the cold war wore on.

Rand's concern was the ideological message of films. She was critical of the scene in *The Best Years of Our Lives* in which a banker is reluctant to give a loan to a recently returned soldier, which Rand saw as consistent with "the party line of making the returned soldier fear that the world is against him." Rand saw subtleties of Communist influence in movies of the sort that were quite invisible to others, even her own political allies, including Ronald Reagan, Robert Taylor, and Adolph Menjou, all of whom testified before the House Committee on Un-American Activities that they were unaware of any successes by the Communists to, as Reagan said, "use the motion picture screen as a sounding board for their philosophy or their ideology." (quoted in Whitfield, 1991, 130).

As part of her drive to keep collectivist and anticapitalist ideas out of scripts, Rand published *Screen Guide for Americans* (1950), which was aimed less at Americans in general than it was at those Americans who made movies. "The purpose of the Communists in Hollywood is *not* the production of political movies openly advocating Communism. Their purpose is *to corrupt our moral premises by corrupting non-political movies...*making people absorb the basic principles of Collectivism *by indirection and implication*" (quoted in Whitfield, 1991, 130; emphasis in original). As Rand's worldview was radically individualistic, virtually any form of collective action smacked to her of collectivism. The publication was distributed by the Motion Picture Alliance, a conservative anti-union group with strong ties to the studios. Among Rand's admonitions were: "Don't Smear the Free Enterprise System," "Don't Glorify the Collective," "Don't Smear Success," "Don't Smear Industrialists," "Don't Deify the Common Man." For Rand, the celebration of domination and power at the heart of *The Fountainhead* went hand in hand with her revulsion of the masses and her rejection of any form of altruism. Unlike the uncertain and imperfect democratic heroes of so many films before and after, Rand's Howard Roark derived his authority not from his being from the masses, like Tom Joad, or from his symbolic identification with them, like Jefferson Smith, but rather from an explicit rejection of any form of democratic legitimacy. The democratic hero, however flawed, derives his legitimacy by his association with the people; Howard Roark derives his legitimacy from his rejection of them, and their rejection of him.

The cold war in film subsided before the real cold war did. The production of cold war parodies, black comedies and satires signaled that the genre had played out. A small handful of films produced as the Soviet Union itself ceased to exist addressed the end of the cold war itself: John Frankenheimer, the director of *The Manchurian Candidate,* directed *The Fourth War* (1990), which centered on whether a renegade Army colonel, will single-handedly sabotage détente between East and West. The same story—the loose-cannon theme of so many mature cold war films—appears in *The Hunt for Red October* (1990), *Crimson Tide* (1995) and *Broken Arrow* (1996). In such films the precarious-balance theme of many cold war films is maintained despite fundamentally different political circumstances, for despite those different circumstances the result may still be war. An even smaller group of films focused on détente itself: *Star Trek VI: The Undiscovered Country* (1991), in which the Star Trek surrogate for the Soviet Union, the Klingons, begin to collapse after their own Chernobyl-style meltdown and move toward détente with the Federation (complete with script references to Richard Nixon and dialogue and title from Shakespeare), and the 1984 *Moscow on the Hudson,* which treats détente at the level of the individual rather than the state.

VIETNAM

The advent of Vietnam in film provided an opportunity for filmmakers who were denied an actual shooting war: a parallel, surrogate setting in which cold war themes could be played out. Vietnam appeared in U.S. films as far back as 1948 with *Saigon*, which used the city as a setting for post-World War II intrigue. For the mass film audience, however, Vietnam surfaced in the mid-1960s.

Several broad classes of movies emerged during this period. One involved traditional combat films, chief among them the 1968 John Wayne vehicle (he directed and starred) *The Green Berets.* It would be some time, however, before many films centered on combat appeared. A second class of Vietnam film focused on the returning Vietnam combat veteran, though these, like the combat films, would appear in even greater numbers—and quality—some years later. A final film reading of the war was more tangential to the war itself, with the production of movies that addressed the counterculture of the 1960s, a major but not exclusive aspect of which was the antiwar movement and the domestic political and cultural confrontation associated with it. Perhaps the most interesting aspect of the war in Vietnam in U.S. films was the extent to which the war was not confronted until it was over. The best films on Vietnam made in the United States were virtually all released after U.S. participation ended officially in 1975. The films that followed dealt with early U.S. involvement, with the war's effects on the U.S. home front, and, in a score of films starring Sylvester Stallone and Chuck Norris, with wish-fulfillment fantasies in which the outcome of the war was, on the screen, reversed.

John Wayne's intention in producing *The Green Berets* was explicitly political. Wayne wrote to President Johnson expressing his support for the war: It was, Wayne wrote, "extremely important that not only the people of the United States but those all over the world should know why it is necessary for us to be there" (quoted in Devine, 1995, 39). The Pentagon agreed to help, though there were restrictions: any references to South Vietnamese brutality were to be eliminated, as were any references to the war being a Vietnamese civil war. Rather, the conflict was to be seen as a war of external aggression, a continuation of cold war politics.

Early in the film a group of reporters questions Sergeant Muldoon (Aldo Ray): "Why is the United States waging this ruthless war?" Muldoon's reply is that of a soldier: "Foreign policy decisions are not made by the military. A soldier goes where he is told to go and fights whoever he is told to fight." George Beckwith (David Janssen), another skeptical reporter (all reporters in movies are at least skeptical and usually cynical), says, "A lot of people...believe this is a war between the Vietnamese people. Why not let them handle it?" Muldoon points to a display of Soviet, Chinese, and Czech weapons seized from the enemy: "What's involved here is Communist domination of the world."

The central lesson of *The Green Berets* is learned by the initially hostile reporter, Beckwith, via a journey to Vietnam with Colonel Mike Kirby (Wayne) as his guide. By the end of the film, Beckwith—the film's stand-in for the civilian public—is convinced the war is justified, even necessary; Beckwith even ends up toting a rifle. The critics largely hated *The Green Berets*. As would happen years later with the films of Oliver Stone, another explicitly political filmmaker, John Wayne's Vietnam effort was reviewed as much for its politics as for its quality, though the film did respectable business.

In retrospect, however, *The Green Berets* is a surprisingly prophetic film. Even in this early and politically focused film, ambivalence abounds. The easy racial stereotyping that characterized portrayals of Asians in World War II films is impossible to sustain; while the enemy was Vietnamese, so were the allies. Thus, the movie must distinguish between good and bad Vietnamese, which it does largely through substituting ideology for nationality. The controversial nature of the war is also acknowledged, though it is resolved in a way consistent with Wayne's own political preferences. Most interesting, however, is the extent to which *The Green Berets* suggests in its early scenes the schism between military and political elites, a schism that would reach its peak in the United States-wins-the-Vietnam-War combat fantasies of the *Rambo* films and their kin. Colonel Kirby is merely frustrated; John Rambo feels betrayed. Portraying military frustration with civilian leadership also constitutes an interesting contribution made by Vietnam films to the standard cold war mix: a reintroduction of civilian authority into their portrayals of the U.S. power structure. So long as movies dealt with U.S.-U.S.S.R. relations, the military was very much dominant. But in the cold-war-by-surrogate world of many Vietnam films—including *The Green Berets*—civilian leadership reappears, usually seen from the military viewpoint, and usually negatively.

If *The Green Berets* anticipated themes that were developed in later films more fully and artfully, another small group of Vietnam films followed the same path: the veteran-gone-wrong film. Most of these were drive-in movie fodder: their ancestor was *The Wild Ones* (1954), the archetypal biker movie. *The Angry Breed* (1968) and *Satan's Sadists* (1969) were others, set in the world of young, disaffected outlaw bikers. From such "B" films emerged the now-stock character of the confused, angry, and combative Vietnam vet. Closely related to the vet-gone-wrong film—because they sought the same young audience—were films that tapped the early stirrings of the youth counterculture, many of which placed Vietnam somewhere in the background. *Greetings* (1968) and *Hi Mom!* (1970), both directed by a young Brian De Palma, and both starring a young Robert De Niro, were comedic examinations of sex, the draft, antiwar politics, and a variety of other related counterculture themes.

While the vet-gone-wrong films were directed at a blue-collar audience (an audience likely to have fought in the war) and the counterculture films were aimed at a middle-class audience (an audience less likely to have fought) both are similar in the important respect that they treated the war as either something to avoid or something that, if one could not avoid it, left one damaged. In either case, the nature of the war itself was addressed primarily in terms of what it did to those in the United States. Many of the early Vietnam-era films thus have about them an out-of-time quality, examining as they do, with the notable exception of *The Green Berets*, the home front almost exclusively, as though the war itself were over—as though, it was time to produce, immediately, the Vietnam War's *The Best Years of Our Lives*.

The best Vietnam films were produced after the war ended; 1978 was an especially important year, with the release of *Coming Home, The Deerhunter, The Boys in Company C*, and *Go Tell the Spartans*. The first and last of these films illustrate what might be called mature Vietnam films, one dealing with the war itself and the other with its aftermath.

Go Tell the Spartans, though released in 1978, was set in 1964, when the U.S. military presence in Vietnam was officially limited to several thousand military advisers. The film, directed by Ted Post, is based on a book by Daniel Ford, *Incident at Muc Wa*, published in 1967, which was prophetic in its analysis of what was to come. Almost immediately after the book's publication, plans were made to turn it into a film, though many years of rewrites (with perhaps some studio caution) were required before a script (by Wendell Mayes) was approved for production; and thus the prophetic nature of the book appears, years later on the screen, to be simply perfect hindsight. Prior to the credits we see on the screen, "In 1964, the war in Vietnam was still a little war—confused and far away."

The film opens with Major Asa Barker (Burt Lancaster) saving the life of a Viet Cong prisoner who is being drowned by a vicious South Vietnamese interrogator, nicknamed Cowboy, assigned to U.S. forces. Barker receives an order to reconnoiter a hamlet known as Muc Wa. His forces undermanned, he instead manufactures a report to his superiors. He considers the request a waste of time; Barker is one of those soldiers whose concern for his men outstrips his desire for promotion. We are introduced to the rest of the cast, all U.S. advisers, as they arrive in Vietnam: Corporal Courcey (Craig Wasson), college-educated, a draftee who volunteered for Vietnam service; Lieutenant Hamilton (Joe Unger), with more military training than experience or judgment, and eager for action; Sergeant Oleonowski (Jonathan Goldsmith), a weary veteran; and

Abraham Lincoln (Dennis Howard), a burned-out drug-addicted medic. These character types recall the "ark movie" casting of so many combat dramas—with their mix of age, experience, and personality, but with a particular Vietnam twist in the presence of the sadistic Cowboy, the drugged-out Lincoln, and the bourbon-drinking Oleonowski.

The basic structure of *Go Tell the Spartans* is again that of a journey. In this respect it anticipates the more explicitly metaphorical journey of *Apocalypse Now* (1979), based on Joseph Conrad's *Heart of Darkness*. In *Apocalypse Now*, however, the journey leads to death and grandiose madness; in *Go Tell the Spartans,* a more conventional combat film less laden with symbolism, the journey leads simply to death and futility. Barker's journey begins when his faked report is discovered and he is ordered to Muc Wa. Barker feels the mission is pointless and dangerous, especially since, by virtue of his rank, the untested and gung-ho Hamilton will have nominal command.

In Muc Wa, Courcey finds a cemetery in which are buried the bodies of French soldiers, France having been the most recent colonial power in what was called Indochina. Above the cemetery is a sign bearing the inspiration for the film's title, "Go Tell the Spartans," from the Greek historian Herodotus's story of the battle of Thermopylae in 480 B.C. in which 300 Spartan troops died defending their ground:

Here is the place that they fought, four thousand from Peloponnesus [Athens], and here, on the other side, three hundred, ten thousands against.

That was the inscription over them all; but over the Spartiates there was a particular one:

Go tell the Spartans, stranger passing by, that here obedient to their words we lie.

This was for the Lacedaemonians [Spartans]; but for the seer there was this one:

Here lies Megistias; think on him, a brave man whom once the Persians
Killed when they crossed the [River] Spercheus and came to the other side.
He was a prophet who knew, right clearly, the doom coming on him,
But he had not in his heart to desert the leader of Sparta.

(Herodotus, 1987, 551-552)

While only the brief "Go tell the Spartans" passage appears on the cemetery sign in the film, the remainder of the scene resonates with the longer passage quoted above. Observing the arrival of the U.S. troops is an old, one-eyed Vietnamese man. He is the "seer," the prophet who knew "right clearly the doom coming on him." The cemetery is the central literal and figurative setting of the film, a place where the futility of death in battle reaches back not only to the French experience in Indochina but to the wars of which Herodotus wrote. The old man's one eye at once suggests an ironic wink; it suggests also that, even with one eye, the old man has seen and understood more about the place than the French and Americans ever did or ever will.

After a brief return to headquarters, where Barker endures a presentation on the latest Pentagon approach to systematizing the war (called the "incident flow priority indicator"), the men return to Muc Wa. The stoned Lincoln recites the Gettysburg Address during a mortar attack, and later, in an ambush, Lieutenant Hamilton is killed trying to rescue a wounded and pinned-down South Vietnamese farmer. Oleonowski, feeling guilt (because he escaped the initial ambush) and anger at Hamilton's death (because he has come to look at all Vietnamese as "dinks") expresses his bitterness and sense of futility about the war (it is "their war") to the less experienced Courcey. Not long after, Oleonowski kills himself.

With enemy activity increasing near Muc Wa and concerned for his men, Barker is forced to deal with a corrupt South Vietnamese military man, whom Barker bribes to secure men and equipment. At the same time, Barker learns that support from the U.S. side will not be forthcoming; rumors of a coup in Saigon have led the U.S. command to divert resources to the South Vietnamese capital. Only by calling in military IOUs does Barker get any help from his own commander. But none of this helps and Barker is ordered to evacuate Muc Wa. He helicopters to the hamlet to help in the evacuation; Courcey, having lost none of his idealism, is appalled to learn that the South Vietnamese with whom he has fought will not be allowed aboard the helicopter. Courcey refuses to board the chopper despite Barker's efforts to convince him otherwise. Barker reluctantly stays with Courcey as the chopper lifts off, and the two soldiers talk about the war.

Barker tells Courcey that unlike World War II, of which Barker is a veteran, Vietnam is a "sucker tour, going nowhere, just around and around in circles." The attack on Muc Wa continues, with everyone being killed or wounded. Courcey passes out, and when he wakes the next morning he finds the stripped bodies of the dead, including Barker. As Courcey stumbles past the cemetery, he sees again the one-eyed Vietnamese man, who appears for a moment to be planning on shooting the young soldier. But the old man lowers his gun, and Courcey, in the film's final line, says to him, "I'm going home, Charlie."

From going home to *Coming Home*, also released in 1978, the setting shifts from "in country" to the United States and from male characters to both male and female principals. The film is the story of who survives Vietnam and who does not, focusing on a politically charged love triangle involving Bob Hyde (Bruce Dern), his wife Sally Hyde (Jane Fonda) and Luke Martin (Jon Voight). Bob Hyde is the dutiful marine, Sally his loyal wife, and Luke a paraplegic Vietnam veteran. The opening sequence shows a diverse group of severely wounded veterans talking, trying to make sense of the war. Cut to Bob Hyde jogging, preparing himself to go to Vietnam, intercut with shots of the wounded veterans. Bob and Sally Hyde meet at the officers' club, Sally apprehensive, Bob and his male comrades no less so but nonetheless full of bravado.

On their last night together, Bob and Sally make love, almost literally by the numbers. Bob treats the encounter as a matter of military command and control between husband and wife, but Dern plays the scene in a way such that we understand that Bob is scared and has retreated into a military mode as a way of escape. For Sally the lovemaking is unsatisfying. As Sally says goodbye to Bob, she meets Vi Munson (Penelope Miford), who is saying goodbye to her boyfriend, Dink (Robert Ginty), a friend of Bob's. The women strike up an acquaintance that becomes a close friendship. Sally learns that Vi's brother Bob (Robert Carradine) is a Vietnam vet confined to the psychiatric ward of the base hospital, and Sally decides to fill her free time by volunteering there.

It is at the hospital that Sally meets Luke, whom we first see being wheeled through the hospital on a gurney holding a bag of his own urine. Sally and Luke collide, the contents of the bag spilling, and the humiliated Luke delivers a tirade against the overburdened hospital staff. Luke is restrained and drugged. When Sally visits Luke—lashed to his bed—she realizes she recognizes him from their high school days, Luke recalling Sally as a cheerleader and Sally recalling Luke as the high school's star football player. Sally's maiden name was Bender, and Luke tells her that the high schools boys referred to her as "Bend'er Over." The prim Sally is embarrassed, but the revelation about Sally's names in Waldo Salt and Robert C. Jones's screenplay makes a point that is developed throughout the film. At the beginning of the film Sally hides; later she bends. It is the bending that will allow Sally to survive.

Sally and Vi move off-base into an apartment near the beach. Sally buys a Porsche convertible and acquires a new looser, less severe hairstyle. In case the point is lost, Vi chides Sally about all these changes that follow Bob Hyde's departure. Sally continues to visit Luke, who presses her verbally about why Sally is not playing the usual role of officer's wife at the base golf course. When Luke clumsily jokes about Bob coming home in a body bag, Sally challenges him directly, and her emergence continues when she attempts to get the base women's club newsletter to address conditions at the hospital. Sally's suggestion is patronizingly rebuffed. By now she has sallied forth from the life of the base; her withdrawal from it is almost complete.

Sally and Luke—he is now more mobile but confined to a wheelchair—grow closer, and Luke admits to Sally hat he spends most of his time thinking about making love to her. She responds that she has never been unfaithful to Bob. Sally visits Bob, who is on leave, in Hong Kong. Their meeting is strained and distant; Bob is angry that Sally works in the hospital and she must struggle to convince him that they need time alone together. In their hotel room, Bob confesses that the war most Americans see on television is not the war he sees: "T.V. shows what [Vietnam] is like; it sure don't show what it is." Sally returns to her earlier hairstyle and covers her head with a scarf; as Sally and Bob walk around Hong Kong, Sally sees the world with a camera obscuring her face. She is hiding her new identity. Their physical contact is no more than a back rub from Sally; director Hal Ashby underlines the contrast by cutting to a scene with a happy Luke and a prostitute.

When Sally returns to the United States, she finds Luke flourishing. He drives a specially fitted Mustang and is no longer the bitter and angry veteran she first met. His emergence parallels hers. The further both are from Vietnam the more free—and sexual—both become. For Bob Hyde it is the opposite, and for Vi's brother it is even worse: Bill locks himself into a room in the hospital and kills himself with an injection of air into his vein as others helplessly watch.

An angry and despondent Luke drives to a Marine recruiting office and chains himself to the entrance. He is arrested and bailed out by Sally.

Sally and Luke return to Sally's apartment. As they do we see that the FBI has the newly politicized Luke under surveillance. Sally and Luke make love for the first time. Luke's confinement to the wheelchair require consideration and cooperation on the part of both lovers. It is difficult to avoid the film's conceit that, as *Ms.* magazine wrote, "doves are better than hawks in bed" (quoted in Devine, 1995, 157). This sexual mutuality is in stark contrast to Bob Hyde's by-the-numbers lovemaking in the earlier scene with Bob and Sally, and, unlike that earlier scene, Sally is orgasmic. There follows *Coming Home*'s music video-like interlude (to the tune of the Beatles' *Strawberry Fields Forever,* one of many contemporaneous rock songs used) in which the two lovers fly a kite, spend time with Vi, and see a slide show of Luke's pictures of Vietnam in which Luke talks of the beauty of the Vietnamese landscape and people. The audience, but not the characters, learn that all this is being observed by the FBI, and the lovers' brief period of bliss ends when they learn that Bob Hyde is coming home. Sally tells Luke she cannot leave her husband and Luke—who by now has developed into the prototype sensitive male—understands and accepts her decision.

Bob Hyde's first words to Sally—the two are initially separated by a fence, a recurring visual motif in the film that separates Bob and Sally—are to reproach her about her hairstyle. He does, however, like the Porsche. Bob has been wounded, but not particularly heroically: he shot himself in the leg (not quite the foot, but close) as he stepped from the shower. The war is for Bob embarrassing and meaningless. He wants nothing more than to spend time with his male friends, which he does in a drunken get-together, falling asleep afterwards with a revolver in his hands. Bob learns of Sally and Luke's affair and calmly confronts Luke (who is shown teaching children to swim at his apartment's pool). Bob tells Luke any decision about the future is up to Sally.

After Bob returns home to Sally, he becomes increasingly agitated. In uniform and holding his rifle, Bob rejects his entire life, saying he doesn't belong in their home, he didn't belong in Vietnam, and that he doesn't deserve the Purple Heart he got for shooting himself. Luke arrives and Bob becomes increasingly unhinged. Luke, in command and calm, tells Bob: "I'm not the enemy. The enemy is the fucking war. You don't want to kill anybody here. You have enough ghosts to carry around." Bob relents. The next day he endures his sparsely attended Purple Heart ceremony in a shabby office.

The film concludes with the immediate fates of the three members of the love triangle. At a student assembly in a high school (reminiscent of two similar scenes in *All Quiet on the Western Front*), a Marine recruiter delivers a pep talk to the gathered students. Luke follows with an emotional speech about the futility of the war:

I wanted to be a war hero and kill for my country, or whatever . . . and now I'm here to tell you that I don't feel good about it because there's not enough reason, man....I don't want to see people like you, man, coming back and having to face the rest of your lives with that kind of shit. It's as simple as that. I don't feel sorry for myself. I'm a lot smarter now than when I went, and I'm just telling you that there's a choice to be made here.

Intercut with Luke's speech, we see a nervous and uncertain Sally trying to mollify Bob and begin to put their two lives back together. Sally and Vi go off to the supermarket for the makings of a barbecue. After they leave, Bob goes to the nearby beach, strips naked, and drowns himself in the surf. The final shot of *Coming Home* shows Vi and Sally entering a Lucky supermarket through the exit door; as they walk in, the sign on the open door reads "Lucky Out."

The political moral of *Coming Home* is clear in the fates of Bob and Luke. Bob is trapped by the war and becomes its victim. He is not so much disillusioned by Vietnam as he is bewildered by it: Bob Hyde ultimately cannot hide from the war nor, unlike Sally, does he bend. He is a tragic figure, and brings to mind "poor, poor Raymond" Shaw of *The Manchurian Candidate*. Both are caught up in war, both are used, both do what they are told, both kill themselves. Luke escapes by rejecting the war and then moving beyond it. Sally Bender/Hyde does too, or at least one imagines that she will. Less directly affected by the war than either Bob or Luke, and with her husband gone and her lover gallantly withdrawn from the scene, Sally emerges triumphant, with neither the committed antiwar stance of Luke or the gung-ho military discipline of Bob. Sally is the sensible middle, the survivor, and she emerges also as a sort of reasonable feminist heroine. Sally has her lucky out.

The themes developed in *Go Tell the Spartans* and *Coming Home* were to dominate many Vietnam films: the circumstances of the Vietnam vet (*Taxi Driver* [1976]), his politicization *(Born on the Fourth of July* [1989]), the state of combat, including fear and drug use (*Platoon* [1986]), and the transition to and from combat (*The Deerhunter* [1978]). Vietnam films paralleled many cold war films in their emphasis on the domestic effects of a distant, controversial, and not well understood conflict. Whether the setting was the home front or the dynamics of a combat unit, the war was seen primarily in terms of its human costs, without references to the reasons for which it was being waged.[9] The metaphor of the journey that underlay *Apocalypse Now* and *Go Tell the Spartans* was especially powerful as these were journeys of futility or madness.

While such films were at one level antiwar, they were also profoundly conservative in their suggestion that wars had always been part of the human experience and would continue to be so. The final scene of *Apocalypse Now* underlines this: after Captain Willard (Martin Sheen) completes his journey and his mission by killing the insane Colonel Kurtz (Marlon Brando), Willard is hailed by Kurtz's followers. Director Francis Ford Coppola asked, "Will Willard become another Kurtz? Or will he learn from his experience and choose another direction?" (quoted in Devine, 1995, 193). One imagines the one-eyed man of *Go Tell the Spartans* asking a similar question.

Such musing did not occupy in the victory-fantasy films of the 1980s, which were set against the background of the Iranian hostage crisis, the election of Ronald Reagan, and the belief of some that many U.S. soldiers were still imprisoned in Asia. Taken together, these films were an affirmative answer to the question asked by John Rambo (Sylvester Stallone) in *Rambo: First Blood*

Part II (1985): "Do we get to win this time?" The *Rambo* films and their kin, including the *Missing in Action* films (1984 and 1985) starring Chuck Norris, spoke to the inconclusive and unresolved nature of the U.S. departure from Vietnam. The most interesting political aspect of these films is not their wish-fulfilling, revisionist nature but the manner in which "we win."

The hero in these films is something of a throwback to the loser-veteran genre of film—a loyal, working-class American male.[10] But where in those films the veteran was either a psychopath (the classic example is Travis Bickle [Robert De Niro] in *Taxi Driver*) or the tragic character of Bob Hyde in *Coming Home*, in the "we win" films of the 1980s the hero fights back. He may fight back against homegrown discrimination, as John Rambo does in his first movie incarnation, *First Blood* (1982), or engage in full-blown warfare against his former enemy. The heroes of these films typically combine technology—ranging from high-technology military hardware to Rambo's bow and arrow—with their own brawn. What is most interesting about them, however, is that they essentially do it alone, often in contradiction to their orders. In these films the enemy is not the enemy in a war that is officially over but rather the civilian and military leadership that failed to win the war. In many of these films the chain of command is reduced virtually to nothing; it is a case of one brave man righting past wrongs in the service of saving his imprisoned brothers-in-arms. The entire civilian and military superstructure is the enemy that the movies' vets fight, but this time it is their *own* country's leadership that is the adversary. Indeed, the heroes of these films no longer fight for their country or against their enemy: they fight only to free their imprisoned comrades and to rectify a past injustice. These heroes wear no uniforms—they are throwback warriors.

The cold war rationale for the Vietnam War expressed in *The Green Berets* becomes instead, a generation later, simple revenge. These films thus have more in common with the gangster, cowboy, and revenge films than they do with the melodramas and satires of most cold war-era films. It is a long way from the frustrated but obedient soldiers of *The Green Berets* ("Foreign policy decisions are not made by the military. A soldier goes where he is told to go") to the retaliation fantasies of the lone-wolf heroes of the "we win" movies. So well established did these characters become that they almost immediately became the subjects for parody in the two *Hot Shots!* movies (1991, 1993). The rapid arrival of the parodic stage signaled the rapid end of the "we win" films. It is a small irony that the cold war in film, which began with the sweeping warnings of Klaatu delivered to all the earth from his spacecraft, would end celebrating one man alone in a jungle brandishing a bow and arrow.

NOTES

1. In addition to such feature films as *The Man in the Gray Flannel Suit* (1956) set in corporate America, series television often dealt with the conformity issue, including many "Twilight Zone" and, later, "Star Trek" episodes.

2. Interestingly, very few films released after the end of the World War II portrayed directly the bombings of Hiroshima and Nagasaki; among those that did were *The Beginning or the End* and *Above and Beyond* (1953), which dealt with the crew that

dropped the atomic bomb on Hiroshima.

3. This was to have been the last scene as the film was initially edited, but the studio concluded it was too negative and added the present final scene in which Miles is taken to a hospital, where his message of warning is finally believed. Interestingly, the now-worried people at the hospital immediately call the FBI. The "You're next!" cry was reprised by Kevin McCarthy, playing a deranged street person, in his cameo appearance in the 1978 remake of *Invasion of the Body Snatchers*.

4. The belief that fluoridation of public water supplies was a Communist plot was, in fact, seriously asserted by several right-wing groups in the 1950s and 1960s, leading to a number of destructive local political battles throughout the United States.

5. In a great many films of this era, it was the Air Force that played the military villain, largely because it was the most technologically sophisticated of the services and because it was associated with the strategic bombers that delivered nuclear weapons.

6. The allusion to Wisconsin Republican Senator Joseph R. McCarthy is obvious. McCarthy made a similar charge, specific as to numbers, in a radio broadcast for which no transcript or recording was available. The press eventually picked up on his claims, but without ever securing from McCarthy specifics as to the number or employment of the alleged Communists.

7. Mother is not entirely wrong. Jocie is usually portrayed in some sort of semi-dress: when she first encounters Raymond she wears a swimsuit and takes off her blouse to use it as a tourniquet. Later she wears a revealing—for the time—costume at a party, and, after she and Raymond marry, she wears a man's shirt as a nightgown. Hardly risqué, but Jocie's portrayal as a sexual being is clearly something new for Raymond and threatening for Mother. To call Jocie a "Communist tart" suggests that Mother is as upset with Jocie's sexuality as she is with her assumed politics and sees both as threats.

8. This is another reference to McCarthy and McCarthyism: McCarthy frequently shouted the parliamentary objection "point of order" during hearings, and the phrase itself became the title for a 1963 documentary on the Army-McCarthy hearings. McCarthy's behavior during these televised and widely watched hearings was the beginning of his political and subsequent personal downfall.

9. A striking example is a film produced long after the height of the Cold War, *Testament* (1983), directed by a woman, Lynn Littman, which focuses entirely on the effects on a family of a nuclear attack. Here the usual point of view is reversed: the elites responsible for the destruction are distant, the victims immediate.

10. Rambo's first film appearance shows him a man out of place in his own country. Similar, and much less violent, treatments of the out-of-place or out-of-time male loner archetype may be seen in *Hud* (1963) and *Lonely Are the Brave* (1962), the latter dealing with a cowboy whose life has been rendered irrelevant.

7

ASPIRATION, DISILLUSIONMENT, AND AMBIVALENCE: POLITICS AND POLITICIANS IN FILM

It is difficult to imagine an area of human life more fraught with ambivalence than politics. It is not that we love politicians or hate them; it is that we love them *and* hate them. Political life embodies, simultaneously, great aspirations and great disillusionment, and this mix of aspiration and disillusionment is simultaneously individual and collective. The success or failure of an individual politician becomes the success or failure of the community from which that person comes and which that person, at some level, represents. Everyone is happy when Jefferson Smith wins.

The nearly complete focus on the individual in film, to the virtual exclusion of other elements of political life, is entirely consistent with the classical narrative style of movies, particularly U.S. movies. Bordwell summarizes this narrative style as follows:

The classical Hollywood film presents psychologically defined individuals who struggle to solve a clear-cut problem or attain specific goals. In the course of this struggle, the characters enter into conflict with others or with external circumstances. The story ends with a decisive victory or defeat, a resolution of the problem and a clear achievement or nonachievement of the goals. The principal causal agency is thus the character, a distinctive individual endowed with an evident, consistent batch of traits, qualities, and behaviors. (Bordwell, 1986, 18)

Films, like other media, tend to exaggerate and simplify these tensions—the good/bad and the individual/collective—for dramatic effect. As Alfred Hitchcock observed, movies are representations of life with the dull bits cut out;

as Hitchcock also noted, movies are not slices of life, they are slices of cake. The non-dull bits in movies—the slices of cake—tend to focus on individuals as representations of broader social, economic, and political phenomena, and those phenomena themselves are often simplified in the interests of storytelling. While scholars avoid writing of politics in terms of the actions of "great men" (and women), the creators of fiction do not. The story is better that way. The emphasis on the individual is not inevitable. The early Soviet cinema, for example, very much emphasized the collective, not the individual, and the early U.S. cinema did something of the same. This was in part a technical necessity: the camera was immobile and it was easier to film groups of people, not individuals; and in part economic: early film producers were resistant to celebrate individuals actors and then have to pay them more, as they eventually ended up doing. The star system fit nicely with the U.S. cultural emphasis on individualism. Here we will look at the political journeys of a small handful of singular political characters in film. Some are heroes, some are villains, some are both.

KANE

Citizen Kane is surely the most celebrated and analyzed of all English-language films and, arguably, the greatest—at least as measured by periodic surveys of critics and scholars. The film's considerable technique apart, much of this praise and attention derive from its juxtaposing of tensions between public history and private memory, between biography and political acts.

Orson Welles was twenty-five years of age when he directed *Citizen Kane* (1941), with an extraordinary career in theater and radio already behind him. Welles's Mercury Theatre group—his production vehicle for stage and radio work—had signed with RKO to produce two films with Welles to produce, write, direct, and star in both. Welles was given extraordinary control over the films, freedom unusual even for a seasoned filmmaker and unprecedented given Welles's age and his utter lack of experience in movies. After an abortive attempt to turn Joseph Conrad's novel *Heart of Darkness* into a movie (the novel later became the basis of *Apocalypse Now*) work began on what was to become *Citizen Kane.*

Citizen Kane's screenplay, virtually from the beginning, was the subject of great controversy, though there is no disagreement as to its inception: the first two drafts were written by Herman J. Mankiewicz, with Welles's associate, John Houseman, acting as sounding board and secretary, and with advice from Welles. Houseman was also charged with keeping the brilliant but alcoholic Mankiewicz on track. To reduce distractions, the initial work was done away from Hollywood in the small high desert community of Victorville, east of Los Angeles. There is likewise no disagreement as to the model for *Citizen Kane*'s protagonist: the story of Charles Foster Kane is the story of publisher William Randolph Hearst, though Welles often maintained otherwise (Carrington 1985, 15-18). The initial few drafts of the screenplay were largely montages of barely disguised events from Hearst's public life, along with material drawn from

Mankiewicz's own visits to Hearst's estate at San Simeon in California (the model for the film's Xanadu) and Mankiewicz's friendship with Marion Davies, Hearst's long-time mistress and the model for Susan Alexander Kane in the film. Partly on the basis of legal advice, subsequent drafts of the script involved removal of much of the overtly Hearst material. It is perhaps because of this weeding out process that Welles claimed the Hearst-Kane parallels were few because so many had already been removed. More than enough remain, however, to establish the connection.

By the time the seventh and final draft of the screenplay was completed and production was imminent it seemed clear to Mankiewicz that Welles planned to claim sole credit for the screenplay in a manner consistent with standard Mercury Theatre radio script practice, in which the writer was employed by the production company, which for legal purposes became the "author and creator" of the script. Mankiewicz, however, objected and threatened to sue; Welles relented, and the final screen credit attributes the screenplay to Mankiewicz and Welles in that order. The *Citizen Kane* screenplay controversy was revived years later by critic Pauline Kael (Kael, 1984), who argued vigorously for Mankiewicz's importance. After reviewing the available record, Carrington concludes:

Mankiewicz (with assistance from Houseman and input from Welles) wrote the first two drafts. His principal contributions were the story frame, a cast of characters, various individual scenes, and a good share of the dialogue....Welles added the narrative brilliance—the visual and verbal wit, the stylistic fluidity, and such stunningly original strokes as the newspaper montages and the breakfast table sequence. He also transformed Kane from a cardboard fictionalization of Hearst into a figure of mystery and epic magnificence. *Citizen Kane* is the only major Welles film in which the writing credit is shared. Not coincidentally, it is also the Welles film that has the strongest story, the most fully realized characters, and the most carefully sculpted dialogue. Mankiewicz made the difference. While his efforts may seem plodding next to Welles's flashy touches of genius, they are of fundamental importance nonetheless. (Carrington, 1985, 35)

Despite his successes in radio and theater, Welles was a neophyte at filmmaking, and much of the film's style is probably attributable to the free reign Welles gave to those more experienced than he was in filmmaking, especially the art direction of Perry Ferguson, the music of Bernard Herrmann, and the cinematography of Gregg Toland, whom Welles rewarded with a screen credit on the same title card as Welles' own director's credit. Prior to filming *Citizen Kane*, Welles repeatedly screened and studied John Ford's *Stagecoach*—it was Welles's version of film school—though in many respects *Citizen Kane* brings more forcefully to mind another Ford film, *The Man Who Shot Liberty Valance*, with its mingling of fact, fiction, history, and memory. As Bordwell observes, *Citizen Kane* establishes at the outset a basic tension: "objective fact versus subjective vision, clearness and superficiality versus obscurity and profundity, newsreel versus dream. By making us question the very nature of experience, this clash of forms and styles produces a tension between reality and imagination that is the film's theme" (Bordwell, 1976, 273).

Citizen Kane begins with a mood of foreboding and a visual joke about moviemaking. To the accompaniment of Bernard Herrmann's doleful and menacing score, the camera rises slowly up a fence from a "No Trespassing" sign, and despite the sign's warning, the camera continues over the fence toward Xanadu, the silhouetted hilltop castle of Charles Foster Kane (Welles), a single lighted window—Kane's bedroom—the only sign of light. The camera will not be deterred by the sign: it will trespass; the movie will go on. After lingering briefly on monkeys from Xanadu's zoo, Egyptian-style boats, and other peculiar details of the grounds, the camera takes us into Kane's bedroom, where the light is extinguished, then reborn. We see what appears to be snow falling, then a hand cradling a glass ball containing the model of a modest cottage. Now comes a close-up of a man's lips; he whispers "Rosebud!" and the ball falls to the floor and shatters, but it does so soundlessly: we are denied our sense of hearing in the scene. We see in the broken glass the distorted image of a nurse rushing into the room, then the deathbed of Charles Foster Kane, the nurse covering his body with a sheet. The camera returns to the lighted window, its point of access, and the scene ends.

The eeriness and silence of the opening sequence is shattered by a brutal cut to the brass-driven musical fanfare of the "News on the March" sequence, based explicitly on the "March of Time" newsreels of the day and edited for *Citizen Kane* by the RKO newsreel department for realism: the film scratched, the editing jerky, some of the footage overexposed, the announcer's voice stentorian. The opening sequence is Kane's private memory; the newsreel, his public life.[1] In a slam-bang chronology, we learn that Kane was a man of enormous wealth and power, a publishing tycoon whose wealth was based on a mining fortune founded on a seemingly worthless deed given his mother in payment for lodging at her boardinghouse. Kane, using some of his inheritance, took control of the destitute *New York Inquirer* as a young man and built it into the biggest paper in the city, then expanded his holdings into a hugely profitable empire. We learn that Kane's empire was nearly destroyed in the Great Depression. His first marriage, to the president's niece, and his political ambitions, both ended in failure. Kane's wife and young son were subsequently killed in a car accident. His final years, the newsreel tell us, were sad ones: his efforts to promote the opera career of his second wife failed; they were divorced, and Kane retreated to Xanadu, his vast, remote private estate. Two themes dominate the newsreel version of Kane's life—power and loss.

Kane's economic power is enormous. Indeed, the initial few minutes of the newsreel do not talk of Kane but of his possessions. He is defined in terms of them—"Xanadu's Landlord" the newsreel calls him—and we are told of Xanadu's gargantuan size and cost before we ever see Kane himself. Political power is no less obvious in the "News on the March" sequence, as we see in two substantial portions of newsreel footage. We see Welles as Kane skillfully blended into genuine newsreel footage, with British prime minister Neville Chamberlin, Adolf Hitler, and campaigning with Teddy Roosevelt.[2] We hear him confidently predict that there will be no war in Europe; we see him both praised and burned in effigy in mass rallies. During this montage we hear the narrator (using syntax that is a parody of the style used by *Time* magazine of the period) tell of Kane's time on the public stage:

Kane urged his country's entry into one war and opposed participation in another. Won the election for one American President at least. Fought for millions of Americans, was hated by as many more. For forty years appeared in Kane newsprint no public issue on which Kane Papers took no stand. No public man whom Kane himself did not support or denounce. Often support, then denounce.

Most tellingly, we hear three radically different versions of Charles Foster Kane's political identity. From Walter Thatcher (George Coulouris), the man whose bank managed young Charles Kane's fortune before Kane came of age to inherit it:

Mr. Charles Foster Kane, in every essence of his social beliefs and by the dangerous manner in which he has persistently attacked the American traditions of private property, initiative and opportunity for advancement is, in fact, nothing more or less than a Communist.

"That same month in Union Square," the announcer says, and we cut to an unidentified man addressing a crowd: "The words 'Charles Foster Kane' are a menace to every working man in this land. He is today what he has been and will always be, a Fascist." In the following shot, we see Kane's own characterization of himself quoted on a title card: "I am, have been, and will always be only one thing—an American."

The second sustained newsreel treatment of Kane's political life begins with a title card reading, "In Politics—Always a Bridesmaid, Never a Bride." The narrator is then heard:

Kane, molder of mass opinions though he was, in all his life was never granted elective office by the voters of his country. But Kane Papers were once strong indeed and once the prize seemed almost his. In 1916, as independent candidate for governor, the best elements of the state behind him, the White House seemingly the next step in a lightning political career, then suddenly, less than one week before election, defeat—shameful, ignominious. Defeat that set back for twenty years the cause of reform in the U.S. forever canceled political chances for Charles Foster Kane.

Kane's characterization of himself—"American"—is noteworthy when one considers that the working title for the *Citizen Kane* screenplay was "American." The newsreel stops abruptly in the middle of its concluding music: we are in a dark screening room, illuminated only by shafts of light from the projector slots high on a wall.[3] The abrupt end of the newsreel reminds us that it was only newsreel, an artificial construction of a life, not the life itself. This is underscored by the men in the room, who are skeptical about whether the newsreel gets to the heart of Kane's life, and is visually reinforced by the now-blank screen that forms the background of several shots: Kane's life is suddenly as blank as the screen. A reporter named Thompson (William Alland, who appears throughout the film but is rarely more than a shadow) is assigned to investigate further. Thompson's job is to uncover the meaning of Kane's last word, "Rosebud." With Thompson's quest, *Citizen Kane* becomes a mystery. Like many mysteries it begins with a death, but here Thompson's goal is to explain a life, not a death. The dream-like death scene followed by the literal newsreel footage delineate the private and public Kane; Rosebud is supposed to link the two. A single word is, in the context of *Citizen Kane,* the key to explaining the long, volatile life of Charles Foster Kane—Communist, Fascist, American.

As in countless films, the reporter, Thompson, becomes the audience's surrogate.[4] Thompson's job is to piece together Kane's life by talking with those who shared it with him; thus the film, like *The Man Who Shot Liberty Valance*, is series of flashbacks from multiple points of view. Unlike the great Akiro Kurosawa film *Rashomon* (1950), however, which examines the same discrete and relatively brief event (a rape and murder) from multiple viewpoints, *Citizen Kane*'s narrators are dealing with an entire life, and their participation in it is sequential. Each narrator's story will intercept Kane's life at different points; each story will partially overlap the others.

Thompson's first stop—via a long camera movement through a skylight into the interior of the El Rancho Club in Atlantic City—is to visit Susan Alexander (Dorothy Comingore), Kane's second wife. Susan is performing as a singer at the rundown club. She is drunk when Thompson arrives and does not want to talk about Kane, though a waiter tells Thompson that Susan says she has never heard of Rosebud.

Thompson next visits the cold, vault-like memorial library of Walter P. Thatcher, Kane's banker and onetime guardian. Thompson examines Thatcher's unpublished memoirs, leading to the first flashback, which is set in Kane's youth in Colorado. Kane's mother, Mary (Agnes Moorehead), and father (Harry Shannon) are concluding arrangements for Thatcher to become the eight-year-old Charles's legal guardian and to manage his considerable fortune until Charles is twenty-five-years old. Charles's father opposes the move; it is his mother's idea to send him away. But the now-valuable mine deed that is the basis of their new wealth was signed over to Mary only. She is photographed in sharp profile, dressed in black, her dark hair pulled severely back.

As the adults decide Charles Foster Kane's fate, the boy (Buddy Swan) is shown in the pure white snow playing with his sled, a tiny, happy figure framed by a window in the center of the frame, hemmed in on both sides by the looming foreground figures of his parents and Thatcher. Young Charles is trapped in the deep-focus shot. Told what is about to happen in his life, young Charles shoves his sled toward Thatcher, almost knocking him down. The scene ends with a shot of the sled covered with snow; then a cut to a new sled being unwrapped by Thatcher—he is shot from a very low angle and looms over young Charles. The new sled is a Christmas gift for the boy. In this and the preceding scene in Colorado, young Charles is grim and unsmiling; his only expression of joy comes as he plays in the snow. Thatcher wishes Charles a merry Christmas as he gives the boy his new sled; after Charles responds sullenly with his own "Merry

Christmas," there is an immediate cut to a much older Thatcher saying "and a Happy New Year." He is dictating a letter to Charles, who is now twenty-five and about to become independent of Thatcher and his bank. Thus, in a brief period of screen time, the film takes Kane from young child to young man, via both visual (the old and new sled) and aural (the holiday greetings) transitions. Almost all the elements in the mystery of Charles Foster Kane have now been presented.

Thatcher's holiday letter reminds Kane of the young man's impending inheritance, and he reproaches Kane for not being aware of the responsibilities that go with controlling the world's sixth largest private fortune; but in his reply Kane expresses interest in only one of his holdings, a failing newspaper, the *New York Inquirer*: "I think it would be fun to run a newspaper!" Thatcher scornfully says, quoting Kane's letter.

Thatcher's scorn is prescient, as the following montage of *Inquirer* headlines shows: "Traction Trust Smashed by 'Inquirer,'" "Landlords Refuse to Clear Slums," "'Inquirer' Wins Slum Fight," "Copper Barons Indicted," "Galleons of Spain off Jersey Coast.'" Kane's paper is attacking the economic and political foundations of Thatcher's life. In a scene in the newspaper's office, a young and cocky Kane introduces Thatcher to his newspaper colleagues Walter Bernstein (Everett Sloane) and Jedediah Leland (Joseph Cotten). Kane is read a cable from the paper's correspondent in Cuba:

Bernstein (reading cable): "Girls delightful in Cuba stop. Could send you prose poems about scenery but don't feel right spending your money stop. There is no war in Cuba. Signed Wheeler." [to Kane:] Any answer?

Kane: Yes. Dear Wheeler, you provide the prose poems, I'll provide the war.[5]

Kane hugely enjoys annoying Thatcher, flouting Thatcher's now-gone economic control over him and his own new-found power. Thatcher reminds Kane that Kane is himself the largest stockholder in a transit company the *Inquirer* is now attacking.

Kane: The trouble is, you don't realize you're talking to two people. As Charles Foster Kane, who owns eighty-two thousand three hundred and sixty-four shares of Public Transit Preferred—you see, I do have a general idea of my holdings—I sympathize with you. Charles Foster Kane is a scoundrel, his paper should be run out of town, a committee should be formed to boycott him. You may, if you can form such a committee, put me down for a contribution of one thousand dollars.
Thatcher: My time is too valuable for me to waste on such nonsense.
Kane: On the other hand I am also the publisher of the *Inquirer*. As such, it is my duty— I'll let you in on a secret—it is also my pleasure—to see to it that the decent, hardworking people of this community aren't robbed blind by a pack of money-mad pirates just because [Thatcher jumps up, Kane jumps up in response] they haven't anybody to look after their interests. I'll let you in on another secret, Mr. Thatcher. I think I'm the man to do it. You see, I have money and property. If I don't look after the interests of the underprivileged somebody else will—maybe someone without any money or property.

The scene establishes not just the young Kane's joy in his own power and his pleasure in annoying his former guardian but also his conception of his political role—the enlightened capitalist. Kane casts himself as a Progressive, a wealthy trust-busting champion of the underprivileged who also manages to sell newspapers to those he champions. Kane's reference to those without money or property suggests that his interests are not entirely idealistic; he understands—as one also sees in many Frank Capra films—that the poor are a potentially volatile political force, perhaps too easily led. Better that they be championed by a well-meaning and enlightened man of wealth than by someone without money or property.

The Kane-Thatcher relationship—the first one through which we see Kane—is one of conflict. It is Thatcher at whom Kane lashes out as child, pushing Thatcher with his sled; it is Thatcher whose censure about money Kane mocks and whose advice Kane rejects. Their conflict is not based entirely on Kane's animosity toward the man who took him from his boyhood home, nor is it based on wealth, for both are wealthy, but rather on what one does with wealth. Thatcher is not just older than Kane, he is old money; Kane is not just younger than Thatcher, he is new money. Thatcher's outrage is aimed at Kane's ingratitude and his lack of appreciation of the class and political responsibilities that go with wealth. Kane's newspaper crusades attacking everything Thatcher stands for define the difference between "sophisticated conservatives" represented by Kane and the Old Guard represented by Thatcher. When Kane notes that he has money and property, he is reminding Thatcher of the power of the politically dormant but large working class. Small wonder that Thatcher sees Kane, with his trust-busting newspaper stories, as a Communist. C. Wright Mills described this division among elements of the wealthy:

In the higher circles of business and its associations, there has long been a tension, for example, between the "old guard" of practical conservatives and the "business liberals," or sophisticated conservatives....They are "sophisticated" because they are more flexible in adjusting to such political facts of life as the New Deal and big labor because they have taken over and used the dominant liberal rhetoric for their own purposes and because...they have attempted to get on top of, or even slightly ahead of, the trend of these developments, rather than to fight it as practical conservatives are wont to do. (Mills, 1956, 122)

In a subsequent scene dealing with the Kane-Thatcher relationship, Kane, battered by the Great Depression, signs over much of his empire to Thatcher's firm and wearily contemplates his ambivalence about wealth in the company of Thatcher and Bernstein:

Thatcher: You know, Charles, you never made a single investment. You always used money to…
Kane: Buy things. To buy things. My mother should have chosen a less reliable banker. Well, I always gagged on that silver spoon. You know, Mr, Bernstein, if I hadn't been very rich I might have been a really great man.
Thatcher: Don't you think you are?
Kane: I think I did pretty well under the circumstances.

Thatcher: What would you like to have been?
Kane: Everything you hate.

The flashback ends with a return to Thompson in the library reading Thatcher's memoirs, no closer to the mystery of Rosebud.

Thompson next visits Walter Bernstein, Kane's general manager, now the retired chairman of the board, in his imposing office dominated by a portrait of Kane. Thompson asks about Rosebud; Bernstein's only response is to suggest that a "fellow will remember a lot of things you wouldn't think he'd remember." Bernstein dismisses Thompson's references to Thatcher's memoirs: "You take Mr. Kane. It wasn't money he wanted. Thatcher never did figure him out."

Bernstein suggests that Thompson visit Jedediah Leland, Kane's best friend since their college days—in Kane's case, there were many colleges, and he was expelled from all of them. Bernstein is the bridge to Leland. Leland and Bernstein were with Kane from the beginning at the *Inquirer*. Bernstein's recollections lead to the second extended flashback, from his and Leland's point of view, covering the period after young Charles leaves Colorado but before the period recalled by Thatcher. This period is the most joyous in Kane's life. He bursts into the sleepy *Inquirer*, making his office literally his home—he plans to sleep there and moves his bed and paintings into the office, the latter items anticipating his later massive art purchases. Kane remakes the paper. Meeting with his editors, Kane constantly revises the paper's front page and wants to know why the *Inquirer* is not covering the stories its competitors are. His appetite for food parallels his ambition:

Leland: "You still eating?"
Kane: "I'm still hungry!"

Demanding a headline as big as a competitor's, Kane tells the *Inquirer*'s long-time editor, "If the headline is big enough, it makes the news big enough."

In a scene with Leland and Bernstein, Kane writes a "Declaration of Principles," to be published on page one.[6]

Bernstein: You don't want to make any promises, Mr. Kane, you don't want to keep.
Kane: These'll be kept. I'll provide the people of this city with a daily paper that will tell all the news honestly. I will also provide them...
Leland: That's the second sentence you started with "I."
Kane: People are going to know who's responsible, and they're going to get the truth, quickly and simply and entertainingly. And no special interests are going to be allowed to interfere with that truth. I will also provide them with a fighting and fearless champion of their rights as citizens and as human beings.

As Kane bends forward to sign the declaration, he moves from light into deep shadow, an act that parallels an earlier one, when Kane tells Leland and Bernstein "I've got to make the *New York Inquirer* as important to New York as the gas in that light," then turns the light off. Both actions foretell the fate of

Kane's media empire and his idealism.

Still in flashback, a montage follows depicting the rapid rise of Kane's *Inquirer*: it surpasses all competitors in readership. Kane successfully raids his biggest rival for its entire staff, saying he feels like a kid in a candy store, and he calls his new staff his candy.[7] The *Inquirer* staff throws a party for Kane to celebrate the paper's success and to wish Kane bon voyage on a trip to Europe to buy yet more art.

Kane: I have promised my doctor for some time now I would leave when I could. I now realize I can.
Bernstein: Say, Mr. Kane, as long as you're promising, there's a lot of pictures and statues in Europe you ain't bought yet.
Kane: You can't blame me, Mr. Bernstein. They've been making statues for two thousand years, and I've only been buying for five.
Bernstein: Promise me, Mr. Kane.
Kane: I promise you, Mr. Bernstein.
Bernstein: Thank you.
Kane: Mr. Bernstein.
Bernstein: Yes?
Kane: You don't expect me to keep those promises, do you?

Questions about Kane's veracity and sincerity, expressed both in dialogue (about promises made and kept) and visually (movement from light to shadow, extinguishing the gas lamp), make clear that Kane does not necessarily mean what he says. A band and dancing girls sweep through the room, Kane dances with the women, and all join in a song ("Oh, Mr. Kane") celebrating Kane: "And for the poor you may be sure/ That he'll do all he can," but of whom the song also says, "He's still the same/ He's still the same."

Kane returns from his trip, his art acquisitions preceding him and filling the newspaper's offices. The staff gives him an ornate welcome-home cup, but Kane is preoccupied: he is about to get married, to Emily Monroe Norton (Ruth Warrick), the president's niece. "Before he's through," says Bernstein,"she'll be a president's wife." The flashback ends and we return to the present in Bernstein's office and Thompson's questions about Rosebud: Bernstein: "Maybe that was something he lost. Mr. Kane was a man who lost almost everything he had." Bernstein again suggests that Thompson visit Jedediah Leland, now elderly and living in a hospital. Leland's story is more personal than Thatcher's and Bernstein's. Leland is Kane's oldest friend, and his observations on Kane are at once more intimate and more analytical than Thatcher's and Bernstein's. Indeed, as we move from the first interview subject, Susan Alexander Kane, to Leland, the recollections become more detailed, personal, and revealing: Susan does not even want to talk about Kane. Thatcher sees Kane as a traitor to his class. Bernstein rejects Thatcher's analysis, and Leland wants to psychoanalyze him. Leland says:

I was his oldest friend, and as far as I was concerned he behaved like a swine. Not that Charles was ever brutal. He just did brutal things. Maybe I wasn't his friend, but if I wasn't he never had one. Maybe I was what you nowadays call a stooge, hmm?...He never gave himself away. He just left you a tip. Hmm? I don't suppose anyone ever had more opinions. But he never believed in anything except Charlie Kane. He never had a conviction except Charlie Kane in his life. I suppose he died without one. That must have been pretty unpleasant.

Leland's reminiscences about Kane lead to another extended flashback, this one dealing with the early years of Kane's marriage to Emily, the president's niece. The marriage's deterioration is traced in one of the film's best known sequences, set at the couple's breakfast table: the initially loving Charles and Emily sit increasingly farther apart, Emily's clothing and hair grow more severe, and their conversation goes from the suggestively amorous ("Oh Charles, even a newspaperman has to sleep") to Kane's deliberately provocative comments about Emily's uncle the president ("he's still a well-meaning fathead who's letting a pack of high-pressure crooks run his administration")[8] to near-silence. In the last shot of the sequence, Kane harshly finishes Emily sentence:

Emily: Really, Charles, people will think...
Kane: What I tell them to think.

The camera slowly tracks back in the final shot of the sequence, revealing the now-great distance between Kane and Emily at the table, with Emily pointedly reading the *Chronicle*, Kane's chief competitor, in complete and defiant silence.

Back in the present, Leland expands his analysis of Kane:

He married for love. Love...that's why he did everything. That's why he went into politics. He wanted all the voters to love him, too. All he really wanted out of life was love. That's Charlie's story. How he lost it. You see, he just didn't have any to give. Oh, he loved Charlie Kane, of course. Yeh. Very dearly. And his mother. I guess he always loved her.

Now comes another flashback, to Kane's accidental meeting with Susan Alexander—Kane is splattered with mud, anticipating what will soon happen to him in politics. On a table in Susan's tiny room is the glass ball containing the model cottage we see in Kane's hand in the death scene that opens *Citizen Kane*. When Kane and Susan meet he is on his way to go through some of his mother's old things placed in storage after her death—"sort of a sentimental journey," he tells her, "in search of my youth." But now having met Susan, he decides to stay. The connections between Susan and Kane run through their mothers and their pasts. These connections become more explicit when Susan talks about her dreams of becoming a singer:

Kane: What happened to the singing?
Susan: Well, Mother always thought—she always talked about grand opera for me. Imagine! Anyway, my voice isn't that kind. It's just—well, you know what mothers are like.
Kane (Pause): Yes.

The meeting with Susan dissolves directly into Kane's political career.

Leland introduces Kane for a campaign speech:

There is only one man who can rid the politics of this state from the evil domination of
Boss Jim Gettys. I am speaking of Charles Foster Kane, the fighting liberal, the friend of
the workingman, the next governor of this state, who entered upon this campaign to point
out and make public the dishonesty, the downright villainy, of Boss Jim Gettys's political
machine now in complete control of the government of this state.

Behind Kane as he speaks is a huge portrait of Kane himself (the image is
greater than the man), a motif used countless times since. Kane promises, if
elected, to prosecute the evil Gettys (Ray Collins), who watches the speech from
the balcony. After his speech, Kane is taken by Emily to Susan's apartment
where they are met by Gettys, who has told Emily about Susan. Gettys threatens
to expose Kane and Susan's relationship if Kane does not quit the race. The
scene is shot from both very low and very high angles, the disorientation
paralleling Kane's own emotions. The characters move from light to shadow and
back again, and from large to small presences in the frame, the framing and
lighting tracing the rapidly changing personal dynamics among the four
characters as what are essentially political coalitions are formed, then reformed.
In an early shot, a lighted Emily is framed by the deeply shadowed Kane and
Gettys—two powerful men, one an unfaithful husband, the other a politician
who will do anything to win, each competing for her support. In a later shot,
Kane and Susan, in the background, are dominated on one side by Gettys and on
the other by Emily, both now in control. But Kane refuses to withdraw from the
election, even when Emily urges him to and Susan reminds him of what a
scandal will do to his young son:

Emily: If you don't listen to reason, it may be too late.
Kane: Too late for what? For you and this public thief to take the love of the people of
    this state away from me?
Susan: Charlie, you got other things to think about. Your little boy, you don't want him to
    read about you in the papers.
Kane: There's only one person in the world to decide what I'm going to do, and that's me.

Gettys exposes Kane and Susan's relationship (the rival *Chronicle* headline
reads, "Candidate Kane Caught in Love Nest with 'Singer'") and Kane loses the
election, the loss defiantly reported in Kane's own newspapers with the "Oh, Mr.
Kane" song from the office party playing softly and mockingly: "Fraud at
Polls!" reads the *Inquirer* headline. Kane's meeting and affair with Susan, his
refusal to withdraw from the race—even at the cost of embarrassment to himself
and his family—and his election loss link the personal and the political in Kane's
life and underscore the extent to which Kane's idealistic politics—the "fighting
liberal, the friend of the workingman"—are subservient to ambition and ego.
With Kane's defeat love, loss, and politics and their interconnection are clarified
when Kane's equates electoral victory with "the love of the people of this state."
Later, Leland (now drunk) drives the point home after the election when he and
Kane talk:

Kane: I've set back the sacred cause of reform, is that it? All right, if that's the way they want it, the people have made their choice. It's obvious the people prefer Jim Gettys to me.

Leland: You talk about the people as though you owned them. As long as I can remember, you've talked about giving the people their rights as if you could make them a present of liberty, as a reward for services rendered.

Kane: Jed.

Leland: You remember the workingman?...He's turning into something called organized labor. You're not going to like that one little bit when you find out that means your workingman expects something as his right and not your gift. Charlie, when your underprivileged really get together—oh boy, that's going to add up to something bigger than your privilege, and then I don't know what you'll do. Sail away to a desert island, probably, and lord it over the monkeys.

Later in the scene, Leland declares, "You don't care about anything except you. You just want to persuade people that you love them so much that they ought to love you back." Finally Kane proposes "A toast, Jedediah, to love on my terms. Those are the only terms anybody ever knows—his own."

There follows a cut to a scene of Kane and Susan's marriage. A reporter asks Kane whether he is really through with politics, and Kane replies, "Am I through with politics? I would say vice versa. We're going to be a great opera star."

The "we" signals Kane's takeover of Susan's life in which he humiliates them both. Susan is no opera singer; her performances are a disaster. Kane does not care. His papers shamelessly praise her; he builds her an opera house; he demands that she continue. Her career is about his control, not her singing. She attempts suicide, and Kane finally relents and allows her to retire. Kane's failure to fashion Susan into what he wishes her to be signals his final loss, and his persistent and public humiliation of her finally leads a disgusted Leland to send Kane the original version of the "Declaration of Principles," which Leland had kept from the early, hopeful days of the *Inquirer*.

Kane and Susan retreat to Xanadu, where they are overwhelmed by is enormous scale—it is the desert island to which Leland referred, where Kane may "lord it over the monkeys," the phrase bringing to mind the shot in the death sequence when we see the monkeys in Xanadu's zoo. Life at Xanadu is grotesque and isolated. Susan works endlessly on jigsaw puzzles, a metaphor for the puzzle of Kane. Kane organizes a huge and joyless picnic, a funeral-like convoy of cars required to support it. Kane, now an old man, walks stiffly through the Great Hall at Xanadu, reflected in a series of mirrors. (Which Kane is real? How many are there?) When Susan finally leaves him, an enraged Kane destroys her room, finding there the glass ball seen twice earlier, and pausing in his rampage to hold the ball and say quietly, for the second and final time in the film, "Rosebud." Kane is left only with his staff and his cynical, indifferent butler Raymond (Paul Stewart). The details of Kane's life sketched in the newsreel have now been filled in, except for the meaning of Rosebud. This we—but not Thompson or anyone else in the film—learn at the end, before a final shot which precisely reverses the film's opening shot and returns us to the "No Trespassing" sign with which *Citizen Kane* began.

At the end of the film, as the search for Rosebud ends, we again hear skepticism as several other reporters and Thompson talk:

Eddie: Did you ever find out what it [Rosebud] means?
Thompson: No, I didn't.
Walter: What did you find out about him, Jerry?
Thompson: Not much, really.
Walter: What have you been doing all this time?
Thompson: Playing with a jigsaw puzzle.
Louise: If you could find out what Rosebud meant, I bet that would've explained everything.
Thompson: No, I don't think so. No. Mr. Kane was a man who had everything he wanted, and then lost it. Maybe Rosebud was something he couldn't get or something he lost. Anyway, it wouldn't have explained anything. I don't think any word can explain a man's life. No, I guess Rosebud is just a piece of a jigsaw puzzle, a missing piece.

Skepticism from Thompson aside, however, the conclusion of *Citizen Kane* is precisely that a man's life *can* be explained in a single word, or in the private meaning of that word. Welles himself called the Rosebud device "a gimmick, really, and rather dollar-book Freud" (quoted in Cowie, 1971, 111), and it is a testimony to the film's craft that it works so well. Some years after the film was released, Welles made a deposition in a plagiarism case in which he acutely summarized the personal dynamics underlying *Citizen Kane*:

We postulated a fairly classical psychological set-up involving the loss of a mother, the failure to make what psychoanalysts speak of as a "transference" to any other woman and the need to wield power as an expression of ego. Kane was a spoiled child, but spoiled without benefit of human affection. In other words, we wished to show a man with an urge to assume positions of responsibility in public affairs but having himself no sense of responsibility, only a series of good intentions, fuzzy sentiments and numb, undefined yearnings...his failure in public life and the transference of his efforts from his own broken political career to those of an untalented woman, a singer at whom audiences laughed, all this grew out of the initial character set up. Kane's retreat to one of those enormous imitation feudal kingdoms, which his type of public man tends to construct for himself, was another natural result of the character as conceived. If the world did not behave the way he wanted it to behave, then he would build a world where all the citizens were his subjects and on his payroll. Such men as Kane always tend toward the newspaper and entertainment world. They combine a morbid preoccupation with the public with a devastatingly low opinion of the public mentality and moral character. (Quoted in Callow 1995, 497.)

At its most accessible level, *Citizen Kane* is simply the well-told life story of a powerful public figure, but it is more than that.[9]

Kane as Power.   As Welles's comments above suggest, Kane's life is fundamentally about power, political and otherwise, and *Citizen Kane* is ultimately about why he seeks it and what it does to him and others. The film's answer to the puzzle of Kane's life is psychological, and the culprit in the mystery of Kane's life is his childhood loss of maternal love and its replacement by the compensatory drive for power.[10] In its psychological analysis of Kane's drive for power, *Citizen Kane* perfectly parallels a classic work of political psychology, Harold D. Lasswell's *Personality and Politics,* and both in turn essentially parallel Freud. As Lasswell writes: "Our key hypothesis about the power seeker is that he pursues power as a means of compensation against deprivation. *Power is expected to overcome low estimates of the self,* by changing either the traits of the self or the environment in which it functions" (Lasswell, 1962, 39; emphasis in original).

For Kane, it is the environment he attempts to change, not himself. Rosebud anchors Kane throughout his life, from his days as a happy boy to his deathbed. As the "Oh, Mr. Kane" song says, "He's still the same/ He's still the same." The film traces Kane's psychological constancy as he seeks love in the form of power in a variety of settings: as the zealous, iconoclastic newspaperman; as the media baron involved in great world and national events; as the political candidate; as Emily's husband; as the cruel ringmaster of Susan's singing career; as the master of Xanadu. All these things Kane loses, except Xanadu, which finally imprisons him and which is the newsreel's first characterization of him—"Xanadu's Landlord."

Throughout the film, the scope of Kane's power narrows: rejected by the voters, Kane focuses on Susan's career; rejected by Susan he retreats to Xanadu. The environment that Kane manipulates includes the beliefs he espouses and with which he is associated in the newsreel sequence—Kane the communist, the Fascist, the American.[11] Kane's reformist political beliefs are not entirely unprincipled, but much in the film suggests that Kane's animosity toward old wealth derives from his youth, his drive to build newspaper circulation, but also from his displaced anger at Thatcher, who takes him from his childhood home. As Welles observed, Kane was "raised by a bank" (Welles and Bogdanovich 1992, 54). Ultimately, beliefs for Kane, including political beliefs, are purely adaptive: as Leland says of Kane, "I don't suppose anyone ever had more opinions. But he never believed in anything except Charlie Kane." Political beliefs for Kane are means, not ends.

Kane as America. The very variety of political positions attributed to Kane suggests a broader meaning to the character, the one Kane gives himself in the film and the one given to the working title of the screenplay: American.[12] Charles Foster Kane may be seen as America itself: wealthy, young, powerful, idealistic, and comprised of great contradictions. The scope of Kane's power, the depth of his ambition, the size of his ego, and the variety of beliefs attributed to him remind one of passages from Walt Whitman's (1819-1892) "Song of Myself:" "I celebrate myself, and sing myself, And what I assume you shall assume, For every atom belonging to me as good belongs to you" and, later, "Do I contradict myself? Very well then contradict myself, (I am large, I contain multitudes.)"

Kane as the Left. Kane's political tragedy is the tragedy of wealth and idealism gone wrong, turned from good purposes to bad, from helping the weak to abusing the poor, talentless Susan—a woman of the working class whom the rich Kane absurdly and blindly tries to make into something she is not. Susan is the only direct contact Kane has with the working classes he championed as a young man. Having rejected old wealth (Thatcher) in favor of his own brand of reform politics, Kane directs his energies toward seeking the love of the people through his newspapers and through politics, both times portraying himself as their champion. Rejected by the voters who "denied" him their love, he then redirects his energies toward the working-class Susan. Rejected by her, he retreats to Xanadu. His failure to control the voters or Susan, and their rejection to him, brings to mind Leland's comments to Kane after Kane has lost the election: "You talk about the people as though you owned them." The speaker who calls Kane a Fascist in the newsreel segment is obviously a member of the working class. Kane retreats from youthful idealism to pathology, from using his wealth in the service of his "Declaration of Principles" to purchasing art works that will never been uncrated, opera houses for Susan, and the estate to which he retreats.

The entire progress of Kane's life is one of alienation and distancing. As Bordwell observes:

The intimacy of the honeymoon supper yields to the distance of the long breakfast table and, eventually, to husband and wife shouting across the halls of Xanadu. The movement is from crowdedness (The busy *Inquirer* office) to emptiness (the hollow vaults of Xanadu); from cheerfulness (Kane as a young editor) to despair (after Susan has left); from true friendship (Leland and Bernstein) through gradually materialistic relations (Emily and Susan) to sheerly materialistic relationships (Raymond); from a quick tempo (the liveliness of the *Inquirer*'s office) to a funereal one (the picnic cortege and Kane's final, deadened, walk. (Bordwell, 1972, 280)

Kane's personal alienation and failure move in lockstep with his retreat from progressive political idealism. As Welles—a lifelong supporter of left/liberal causes—once observed:

What's so bad about the American left is that it betrayed itself in order to save its swimming pools. There was no American right in my generation. Intellectually it didn't exist. There were only leftists and they actually betrayed each other. The left was not destroyed by McCarthy; it demolished itself, ceding to a new generation of Nihilists. That's what happened. (Cabos, Rubio, and Pruneda, 1971, 117)

The youthful, enlightened capitalist idealism of Kane is killed by Kane himself. For Kane, politics is an entirely expressive activity, the arena in which he plays out his "dollar-book Freud" substitution of power for love. The view of politics and of power-seeking that lies at the heart of *Citizen Kane* is profoundly negative. It is also profoundly limited insofar as it conceives of politics as solely the working out of private demons on the public stage.

NIXON

The character—in both senses of that term—of Charles Foster Kane has become an archetype for the dramatic treatment of political personality in its portrayal of political motivation as based on psychological projection. The Travis Bickle character played by Robert DeNiro in Martin Scorsese's *Taxi Driver* (1976), for instance, also displaces his murderous rage on women and a political candidate, his targets in this respect very similar to Kane's targets. We also see displacement in the 1995 Oliver Stone film *Nixon*. The fall from power of Richard Nixon in 1974 in the wake of Watergate—indeed Nixon's entire life—has often been treated by academics in terms of its pathological qualities (Brodie 1981). In Kane, as with Nixon, character is destiny, the stuff of classical tragedy.

Stone's treatment of Nixon is heavily based on Nixon scholarship, and much of that scholarship involves an analysis of the connection between early childhood experiences—especially emotional deprivation—and adult political behavior. In the case of *Nixon*, the fall of a powerful politician is explained in terms very similar to those of *Citizen Kane*, though in greater detail. In *Nixon*, political events are central to the title character's life; for Kane, politics is only a part, though a revealing part, of the character's drive for power. The political personality analysis of *Citizen Kane* is rooted in the brief early scene of young Charles's separation from his parents, especially the mother, whose decision it is to send him away. The analysis of *Nixon* is more nuanced and detailed, though expressed cinematically the same way—through flashbacks to the subject's early years. The prologue to *Nixon* begins, in words that the reporter Thompson might have used to describe his goal: "This film is an attempt to understand the truth of Richard Nixon."

The portrayal of Richard Nixon does not entirely parallel that of Kane, however. The most obvious difference is the thinly disguised but nonetheless fictional nature of Charles Foster Kane; that fictionalization serves to make Kane a more mythic character. Nixon, by contrast, remains Nixon, the purely political animal for whom the drive for power is played out solely on the political stage. *Nixon*'s portrayal of political events is accordingly more detailed: campaigns, Congressional hearings, foreign policy—all are addressed in considerably more detail than comparable political events in Kane's life. The explanation for these events offered by both films, however, is similar and so, therefore, is the view that politics is essentially driven by an individual's private demons.

Nixon, like *Citizen Kane*, begins with a mystery of sorts, in this case an opening scene of the Watergate burglary in June of 1972, the event whose unraveling drives the action and leads us to examine not just historical events but the mind and personality of the principal character. In *Nixon*, however, the action is tracked not just by newspaper headlines, newsreels, and television and audio montages as it is in *Citizen Kane* but by the voice of Nixon (Anthony Hopkins) as he replays the infamous White House tapes. In the film as in real life, Nixon becomes his own accuser, and *Nixon*'s Nixon is portrayed as considerably more self-aware than Kane. *Nixon* shows its central character's political life in detail and variety. *Nixon* likewise offers a more fully developed explanation of that behavior, though at its heart the film Nixon's motivations are the same as Charles Foster Kane's: childhood experiences, especially those centered in the family. This is a theme common in Oliver Stone films, which often feature young men choosing between alternative ways of functioning as adults by confronting different, older male role models, as in *Wall Street* (1987), *Born on the Fourth of July* (1989), and *Platoon* (1986), or by falling victim to horrible childhoods, as in *Natural Born Killers* (1994).

Nixon, especially in its early stages, is a continual mix of the personal and the political, with the personal elements shown in flashbacks to Nixon's early youth and later elements mixing political defeat with personal observations about Nixon by those in his life. Often this is done by his wife, Pat (Joan Allen), an unusually full and well-drawn female character for Stone, who wrote the screenplay with Stephen J. Rivele and Christopher Wilkinson. In an early scene set in Los Angeles after Nixon's narrow loss to John F. Kennedy in the 1960 presidential election, Richard and Pat Nixon reflect on political defeat, honesty, and family history:

Nixon: We lost...
Pat: I know.
Nixon: It's hard to lose.
Pat: It makes us human.
Nixon: It's not fair, Buddy. I can take the insults. I can take the name-calling. But I can't take the losing. I hate it.
Pat: We don't have to put ourselves through this again, Dick.
Nixon: What do you mean? We worked for it. We earned it. It's ours.
Pat: It is. We know that. And it's enough that we know. Just think of the girls. They're still young. We never see them. I lost my parents. I don't want them to lose theirs. I don't want them to grow up without a mother and a father.
Nixon: Maybe I should get out of the game. What do you think, Buddy? Go back to being a lawyer and end up with something solid, some money at the end of the line....You know I keep thinking of my old man tonight. He was a failure, too.
Pat: You're not a failure, Dick.
Nixon: You know how much money he had when he died? Nothing. He was so damned honest. But I miss him. I miss him a hell of a lot.

Later, after Nixon loses the 1962 California governor's race, he and Pat talk in a scene reminiscent of *Citizen Kane*'s allusions to Charlie Kane's promise-keeping:

Nixon: Buddy, look at me—just look at me. Do you really want me to quit?
Pat: We can be happy. We really can. We love you, Dick. The girls and I...
Nixon: If I stop, there'll be no more talk of divorce? [She agrees silently.] I'll do it. No more.
Pat: Are you serious?
Nixon: Yeah. I'm out.
Pat: Is that the truth?
Nixon: I'll never run again. I promise.

Inevitably—as the audience well knows—Nixon decides to run again in 1968, the year he finally won the presidency:

Pat [Resigned to her husband's running again]: You should be going. The primaries are
   soon, aren't they? New Hampshire...
Nixon: They [the voters] love you, Buddy. They need you, too.
Pat: I don't want *them* to love me.

And a little later:

Pat: Do you really want this, Dick?
Nixon: This. Above all.
Pat: And then you'll be happy?
Nixon: Yes. You know it. I will. Yeah!
Pat: Then I'll be there for you.

The screenplay later has Pat Nixon talk about her husband in terms that
sharply recall Jedediah Leland on Charles Foster Kane. Leland tells Kane: "You
don't care about anything except you. You just want to persuade people that you
love them so much they ought to love you back."

Similarly, Pat Nixon tells her husband:

Pat: I just wish...you knew how much I love you, that's all. It took me a long time to fall
   in love with you, Dick. But I did. And it doesn't make you happy. You want *them* to
   love you.
Nixon: No, I don't. I'm not Jack [Kennedy].
Pat: But they never will, Dick. No matter how many elections you win, they never will.

Both these conversations come after the principal character has lost an
election, Kane's fictional race for governor in 1916, Nixon's real one for
president in 1960.
   As with Kane, the Nixon character's personality is traced to childhood
emotional deprivation, in Nixon's case portrayed in the film as at the hands of a
hard-working, harsh father and a deeply religious mother who tries to mediate
between her sons and her husband. The script has Frank Nixon (Tom Bower) tell
his family: "Charity is only gonna get you so far—even with saints like your
mother around. Struggle's what gives life meaning, not victory—struggle. When
you quite struggling, they've beaten you, and then you end up on the street with
your hand out."
   But the "saintly" mother, as portrayed in *Nixon*, has her own, damaging role
to play in the early life of Richard Nixon. In a subsequent flashback, after the
death of Richard's young brother, Harold, Nixon's mother Hannah (Mary
Steenburgen) moves toward Richard—ominously casting him in shadow—and
tells him that he can now attend law school. She speaks in characteristic Quaker
"plain talk:"

Hannah: It's a gift, Richard. This law school is a gift from your brother.
Nixon: Did he have to *die* for me to get it?
Hannah: It's meant to make us stronger. [She kneels.] Thou art stronger than Harold,
   stronger than Arthur [another Nixon brother who died young]. God has chosen thee to

survive.

Nixon: What about happiness, mother?

Hannah: Thou must find thy peace at the center, Richard. Strength in this life, happiness in the next.

Nixon's kinship with *Citizen Kane* is clearest in two scenes, one communicated primarily visually and the other through dialogue. The first scene is set in the Nixon White House during the Watergate investigation. Richard and Pat Nixon sit silently at the dinner table in a scene that ends when Pat, unable to communicate with her sullen and preoccupied husband, tells him, "Dick, sometimes I understand why they hate you." The two sit apart at opposite ends of the table, the visual echo of *Citizen Kane*'s tracing of the erosion of Charles and Emily Kane's marriage unmistakable. The second scene has Henry Kissinger (Paul Sorvino) watching a televised Nixon making a last-minute and futile attempt to explain away his role in Watergate. Kissinger muses on Nixon's character in a manner entirely reminiscent of Jed Leland's thoughts on Charles Kane, with Kissinger saying of Nixon, "Can you imagine what this man would have been had he ever been loved?"

There is a straight line between the attribution of childhood emotional deprivation and its replacement by a drive for power—a pathological drive for power—in both *Citizen Kane* and *Nixon*, an attribution, it is important to note, that is consistent with much of the scholarship on both Richard Nixon and William Randolph Hearst, Kane's prototype. But that scholarship also regularly examines the role of other, nonpsychological, factors in the lives of both men. Such factors, however, are difficult to write into a screenplay; they have little dramatic force; they are, worst of all, boring to an audience. The lives of the powerful are almost always portrayed in film as deriving fundamentally from formative childhood experiences. Such experiences may be for good, as in the case of Jefferson Smith's idealized parents, or ill, as in the case of Kane's and Nixon's damaging ones. The classical hero wins; the classical hero overcomes and does great and good things. In films with the tragic cast of *Citizen Kane* and *Nixon*, the central character's tragedy is that he is ultimately unable to overcome himself, his greatest adversary. As with Kane, the Nixon character defines a deeply pessimistic view of politics and politicians.

STARK

Kane and Nixon in film are trapped by their pasts. They do not change. They damage politics because they were themselves damaged. Willie Stark, the central character of *All the King's Men*, experiences the precise opposite: politics changes and damages him.[13] Released in 1948 and produced, directed, and written by Robert Rossen, the film (remade with a change in setting in 1996 as *City Hall*) was based on the novel by Robert Penn Warren, which in turn was based on the life of Huey P. Long of Louisiana, who founded a political dynasty that extended to Huey Long's son, Democratic U.S. Senator Russell Long.

Almost inevitably, *All the King's Men* begins with a reporter, Jack Burden (John Ireland), receiving an assignment to cover the Kanoma City political campaign of Willie Stark (Broderick Crawford). Burden has been told that Willie is that rare thing in politics—an honest man. Burden first sees Stark as Willie is giving a speech attacking the county commission's corruption in awarding a school building contract to relatives of commission members. Only the presence of Burden prevents the sheriff from breaking up Stark's speech. Burden and Stark go to the Stark home to conduct an interview, where a rock is thrown through Stark's window and his son, having been beaten, returns home from school. Despite the pressure, Stark refuses to quit the race.

Burden, impressed by Stark, files his story, then takes a vacation at his parent's home on Burden's Landing, an isolated retreat for the wealthy separated from the mainland by water. We meet Burden's family: his alcoholic mother (Katharine Warren), Jack's stepfather, Lloyd McEvoy (Grandon Rhodes), whom Jack's mother has married for his money, to maintain her social status and ties to the Old South-old money atmosphere of the Landing. Lloyd, by contrast, is a self-made man. He has little patience with or understanding of the remnants of the Old South that Burden's Landing represents. We also meet Jack's friends, Adam Stanton (Shepperd Strudwick), a wealthy doctor; Adam's sister and Jack's love interest, Anne Stanton (Joanne Dru); and their uncle, Judge Stanton (Raymond Greenleaf), Burden Landing's symbol of justice and rectitude. Jack's visit to the Landing underscores his alienation from it and all it represents—genteel, upper-class decay, the remnants of a South that is nearly gone. Burden's Landing is its last outpost, and that is why Jack left it. Anne tells Jack that she will wait for him, but he must make something of himself. Jack is caught between his family and class past, which he rejects, and his own future, which is uncertain. As Anne tells Jack she will wait for him, they are watched by the portrait of Anne and Adam's father, a revered former governor. When Jack returns from his trip home, he learns that Willie Stark has lost the election. So much for Willie Stark's political career, it seems.

Willie decides to get a law degree. Studying hard at night, he succeeds and becomes a populist lawyer, working in the interests of his poor clients even if it means working for fees that arrive late or not at all. Thus, we see several elements of the American South in transition: the traditional, genteel but dying Southern aristocracy (Jack's mother); the self-made but crude new economic aristocracy (Lloyd); the upcoming generation, educated and ambitious (Adam Stanton) but with elements of tradition (Anne will wait for Jack), uncertainty (Jack Burden, whose burden when we first meet him is how to reconcile all these elements of his personal and collective past into his own future); and the power and ambition of the "hicks" (Willie Stark), which will dominate them all.

The shabbily built school's fire escape collapses, killing several children. At the funeral one of the parents raises Willie Stark's hand and cries, "I am struck down for voting against an honest man!" Willie's facial expressions during the funeral are a mix of contempt and finally revelation: he is learning about people and how to manipulate them. Willie leads a campaign to bring the corrupt commissioners to justice. The campaign brings Jack Burden back to Kanoma City for an update. The state political bosses are also interested in Willie Stark's new campaign, fearing it might cost their candidate the upcoming gubernatorial election. They want someone to split the hick vote, thereby assuring a win, and decide Willie Stark is the man to do it. As Burden interviews Stark, a small convoy of cars, sirens wailing and tires screaming, arrives at Willie's modest home, carrying the bosses' henchmen with a political invitation for Willie. Initially reluctant, Willie agrees to run for governor.

As with *Mr. Smith Goes to Washington*'s Jefferson Smith and *Meet John Doe*'s Long John Willoughby, Willie Stark is being set up: the plan is for Willie to divert enough votes to permit the political establishment's candidate to win but without himself winning. Willie is given a deadly dull stump speech to deliver; he delivers it in a deadly dull fashion, watched over by Sadie (Mercedes McCambridge), a political operative as tough as her name, a much tougher version of Clarissa Saunders in *Mr. Smith Goes to Washington*. As Saunders falls for Jeff Smith, Sadie falls for Willie. She hates the way he is being used and finally, with help from Jack Burden, Sadie admits that Willie is being used by the bosses. Willie learns of the plan and gets drunk—once again, *in vino veritas*.

Willie passes out, then delivers, with a hangover, his first great speech of the campaign. Willie proudly identifies himself as a hick, just as his audience is a bunch of hicks, and tells them how he has been used by the bosses, just as the audience has been used: "Listen to me you hicks! This is the truth. You're a hick, and nobody ever helped a hick but a hick himself." Now liberated, Willie travels throughout the state repeating his message attacking the economic and political establishment, championing the hicks. Willie is a threat. Retaliations follow, including one aimed at Jack Burden, who is fired by his newspaper when it ends its support of Willie. Stark narrowly loses the election, but the education that began at the funeral is now complete: now Willie knows how to win.

As Willie Stark finds his direction, Jack Burden loses his, drifting from job to job, as aimless as Willie is committed. Willie builds a political organization, systematically making his own deals with the state's economic establishment. He hires Jack Burden to do research, which means uncovering information on those who might get in Willie's way; thus does Willie Stark get Jack Burden to prostitute his skills as a reporter, including providing information on Judge Stanton's distant past, which will finally lead to the judge's suicide. Jack takes Willie to Burden's Landing in pursuit of the things only the Landing can bestow: money, support, and establishment legitimacy. Willie's trip to the Landing unites all the elements of the state represented by the characters; but this time these elements are brought together in the service of Willie Stark's ambition. Stark tells them he will make a deal with the devil if he has to: "Good comes out of bad, because you can't make it out of anything else. You didn't know that, did you?" Stark's strength and certitude overwhelm his genteel but weak hosts. His ambition is thrilling. With this scene, the rest of Willie Stark's career and life— and the lives of the rest of the characters—are set. Tragedy follows for all of them: corruption, assassination, suicide; the betrayal of Willie's wife, his son, his lovers, of everyone who comes into contact with him including, finally, himself.

Charles Foster Kane and the film portrayal of Richard Nixon are psychologically constant: their drive for power never ceases; they corrupt politics.

Willie Stark is corrupted by politics. If Kane and Nixon are driven by their psychological demons, Stark is driven by class as well as personal resentment, a theme common in Robert Rossen's screen work (see, for example, Neve, 1992, 14-27). Power seduces him, dominates him, and finally kills him and virtually everyone around him. Like Long John Willoughby in *Meet John Doe*, Willie Stark sets in motion forces that unite the poor with the rich in a nightmare of domestic fascism, but unlike, Willoughby, Stark is nobody's errand boy. His triumph is the triumph of the hick, governing in the name and the interests of the hicks, by playing both ends of the social and economic scale against each other. In this Stark is very much unlike the political heroes of Capra films, who are manipulated by the wealthy. Stark governs in his own class interest by making common cause with his putative enemies, the wealthy.

Once Willie learns that he has been used by the bosses, he takes control. Like those of Willoughby and Jefferson Smith, Stark's journey is one from the country to the city, but, unlike them, he lives in the city; his wife and son remain in the country. Stark goes from weakness to power, from naïveté to cunning, from monogamy to infidelity, from teetotaler to drunk, from white clothing to grey and black. In this Willie Stark has more in common with gangster heroes like Rico of *Little Caesar* than with protagonists like Jefferson Smith or Long John Willoughby. Stark's destructive political life serves, however, as an ironic conformation of his political principles, of his willingness to make a deal with anyone to get what he wants—for the result of his political life is the creation of roads, hospitals, and schools for the hicks of his state, accomplishments as impressive as his corruption. There is no more clearly defined treatment in film for the proposition that, as Willie says, in politics "Good comes out of bad," and (to Judge Stanton), "You want to pick up the marbles but you don't want to get your hand dirty." Willie Stark sacrifices himself and everyone around him. After surviving impeachment, Willie addresses an audience of hicks:

They tried to ruin me, but they are ruined. They tried to ruin me because they didn't like what I've done. Do you like what I've done? Remember, it is not I who won but you. Your will is my strength and your need my justice and I shall live in your right and your will and if any man tries to stop me from fulfilling that right and that will I'll break him...for I have the strength of many.

The biblical rhythms of Stark's speech, its rhetorical merging of Stark and the hicks, its prominent use of "will"—all these invoke a crucifixion averted, a vestigial form of Jean-Jacques Rousseau's notion of the General Will, and out-and-out fascism. Willie's assassination at the hands of Adam Stanton (who himself makes a Faustian bargain with Willie) is a form of ritual sacrifice, Willie's own crucifixion. Willie's accomplishments and his treachery are both outsized: *All the King's Men* confronts the audience—starkly—with the issue of the price of success as a series of Faustian bargains. In the final ironic analysis, Willie Stark gives his hicks what he promised them, but at the price of corruption, treachery and death. Of those close to Willie, only the ambivalent Jack Burden—the political and moral center—survives relatively unharmed.

McKAY

Not all film portrayals of politicians and power seekers are as celebratory as *Mr. Smith Goes to Washington,* as psychologically predestined as *Citizen Kane* or *Nixon,* or as tragic as *All the King's Men.* A relative few such portrayals present a more nuanced and ambivalent view of the political life. One such is *The Candidate*, released in 1972, directed by Michael Ritchie and centered on Bill McKay (Robert Redford). Part of the film's particular approach to political life derives from its screenplay, written by Jeremy Larner, who before he began writing for film worked as a speechwriter in the 1968 Eugene McCarthy presidential primary campaign that so wounded Lyndon Johnson. Unlike Charles Foster Kane and Richard Nixon, politics changes McKay: it is not for him primarily a way of working out his personal past. But unlike Willie Stark, politics does not entirely dominate him either. In *The Candidate*, Bill McKay does what these other characters do not do: he makes an accommodation both with politics and his own past.

When we first meet McKay, he is an idealistic liberal lawyer working near the Mexican border of California. In this McKay is atypical of movie politicians because of the specificity of his situation: a concrete political circumstance, set in a real state and featuring a character with real political beliefs. McKay is alienated from his father, a former governor of California. When Bill McKay decides to run for office, his father does not immediately endorse him, and Bill does not seek his father's endorsement. The audience is to conclude that Bill McKay's life is a partial rejection of his father: Bill McKay has turned his back on politics but not political action, a Democratic son of a Democratic politician father whose relationship represents generational, ideological, and personal separation.[14]

McKay is approached to run for the U.S. Senate by political consultant Marvin "Luke" Lucas (Peter Boyle), who is attracted by McKay's good looks and political lineage—but attracted also by the prospect of a new client. Initially dismissive, McKay is also flattered and finally agrees to run. His opponent will be incumbent Republican senator Crocker Jarmon (Don Porter), conservative, smooth, calculatingly charming, *The Candidate*'s Ronald Reagan stand-in. McKay wins the Democratic primary, then the general election, and in the film's final line asks, barely audibly, *The Candidate*'s payoff question: "What do we do now?" McKay is finally not so much corrupted by seeking power as he is befuddled by it. But the process does change him.

McKay's nearly inaudible question underscores the prime technique of the film—its use of sound—and the film's dominant tone of sly irony. Repeatedly throughout the movie, McKay and others cannot be heard and cannot themselves hear. The characters duck into tiny spaces—an airliner's cockpit, a bathroom, an elevator—to escape the din of politics. We see their mouths move but hear little; when we do hear them they are all talking at once. "It's just noise," McKay says at one point; he complains later to his advisers that he can't hear himself think. What the characters do say is often sly. At a political banquet, McKay is condescendingly introduced by the master of ceremonies (Pat Harrington, Jr.), who mispronounces unequivocally as "unequivocably"; after

McKay speaks a few sentences, we hear an off-screen television reporter tell his camera operator to stop, "We've got all we need." When McKay visits a brush fire in search of publicity, he is adroitly trumped by Jarmon; over the din, McKay is barely audible as he looks at Jarmon and says, "The son of a bitch" in admiration. All these bits of sound and dialogue are easily missed on first viewing. Redford's acting underscores the irony: he plays McKay with a combination of bemusement and detachment, as though the candidate understands the truth of what one of his former associates from his legal aid days tells him during the campaign: "Look, you and I know this is all bullshit, but the point is they're buying it." Whether by design or by accident, there is also a small, ironic visual joke: McKay stands with his back to a wallpaper-covered wall and very briefly cocks his head to one side; the wallpaper's starburst pattern frames his head and turns the candidate into the head of the Statue of Liberty.

McKay's journey is one in which he moves closer to power—and to his father's political world—even as he attempts to keep some distance from it. Much of this is done stylistically—McKay collapses into helpless laughter while trying to tape a television statement; he mocks his own stump speech—but some is substantive as well. Advised to cut his hair, he does. His early straightforward stands on issues—on abortion rights he is pro-choice, and when he hasn't thought through an issue he says so—give way to ambiguity. In one of the movie's cleverest bits of dialogue, McKay is advised by his campaign handlers to blur his clear position on abortion rights by saying he is considering what his position should be. McKay's response to his advisers is to tell them, "O.K., I'll think about it." But does this mean that McKay is considering whether to take his advisers' advice, or that "I'll think about it" has now become his position on abortion rights? The audience doesn't know, and we suspect McKay doesn't either.

McKay's journey was begun at the behest of Lucas, and the candidate's compromises continue at the urging of his campaign staff, including Lucas and McKay's media adviser Klein, who plays on McKay's sex appeal and youth in his commercials. It is Klein's character who first raises the essentially male, sexual character of politics that underlies *The Candidate*. Jarmon is "soft as an old banana"; Klein tells McKay that by contrasting him on television with the older Jarmon, people will conclude that "the Croc can't get it up any more." Indeed, Klein is a constant source of sexual/political references: "beating his [Jarmon's] meat;" "balls in both hands," "unzip himself." Klein's view of politics is to portray the contest between Jarmon and McKay as the simple choice between youth and age, virility and impotence. This Klein does while smashing a bag of nuts with a small hammer. The candidate has turned over part of his life and his future to relative strangers, his campaign advisers; as the campaign wears on, McKay's old allies from his storefront lawyer's days recede. McKay's new circumstances are illustrated in a shot with witty allusions to two other films: McKay struggles in the distant middle of the frame with a balky cola machine (reminiscent of the machine in *Dr. Strangelove*) while two advisers in the foreground frame him on both sides (as young Charles Foster Kane was dominated by his mother and Thatcher).

McKay's father, John J. McKay (Melvin Douglas), representative of the old politics, is also identified with traditional male characteristics: he is a football fan and hunter (something the younger McKay views with great distaste when the two meet to affect a personal and political reconciliation). To the elder McKay, Bill McKay's wife is a "beautiful female creature," and his son is Bud, not Bill. The reconciliation the two have, including a political reconciliation in which the father endorses his son's candidacy, begins after Bill confronts a labor leader—an old supporter of his father's—before accepting labor's endorsement; the reuniting culminates when Bill McKay defeats Jarmon. In victory, the elder McKay looks at his son, and, with a menacing smile—his teeth are made up into a hideous yellow, making John McKay look like a happy old vampire—growls, "Son, you're a politician."

McKay confronts the labor leader—the new Democrat challenging the party's old order—immediately after arriving late for their meeting because of what, the film suggests visually, is a brief sexual tryst between the married Bill McKay and an admirer. Thus there is a personal compromise for the candidate and an association between sex and power, which anticipate McKay's display of courage in telling the labor leader "We don't have shit in common."

The chaos of campaigning is relayed largely visually, much of it via hand-held cameras: McKay giving a speech in a mall to indifferent or bewildered shoppers; McKay's film crew trying to shoot footage to be used in commercials; a planning session for a rally in San Francisco that mutates into a discussion of who ordered what for lunch; a McKay speech to a nearly empty hall; a televised debate between Jarmon and McKay shot and edited to emphasize its intensity and confusion. In these scenes, we also see a good deal of the voters whom McKay and Jarmon are trying to persuade—usually in brief shots of individuals, such as a woman who applauds Jarmon, pauses to sneeze, then resumes applauding. While Jarmon's audiences are portrayed less flatteringly than McKay's, neither candidates' supporters are spared visually, and it is clear that some of McKay's support is based on what John McKay's says of his son: "He's cute." As shown in *The Candidate,* the voters are neither entirely idealized nor ridiculed.

Virtually every element in the lives Charles Foster Kane, Richard Nixon, and Willie Stark is present also in the life of Bill McKay: family life, especially a flawed relationship with the protagonist's parents; the mingling of personal history and political ambition; the element of pathology, often sexual; and the deeply ambivalent view of power. But McKay differs from the others in the extent to which the usual tendency for films to exaggerate these things—to be hyperbolic—is muted.

The Candidate understates its political case. Its stance toward political life is skeptical, not cynical; ironic, not tragic. McKay is imperfect to begin with and becomes less so; but he is surely no Kane or Nixon or Stark, each of whom goes from childhood innocence to adult tragedy. Bill McKay is an adult when we first meet him, not a child, as are the other characters. McKay has a flawed relationship with his father, but this is dwarfed by Kane's abandoning mother and Nixon's harsh parents. McKay wants to be elected, but his ambition is not overweening, as is Kane and Stark's; he compromises but does not betray, and his opponent is fatuous, not evil. McKay's political journey is much more gentle than those of Charles Foster Kane, the film version of Richard Nixon, and Willie Stark, though it is largely the same journey from innocence and idealism through compromise to—what? The audience learns the fates of Kane, Nixon, and Stark; their stories take them to the ends of their mortal and political lives. Bill McKay's political life begins as *The Candidate* ends, when he asks, "What do we do now?"

NOTES

1. Welles's first words as Kane in the newsreel are a clever reference to Welles' famous 1938 "War of the Worlds" radio broadcast, many of whose listeners concluded that the United States was being invaded by Martians: "Don't believe everything you hear on the radio."

2. This technique became the heart of the 1983 Woody Allen film *Zelig*, though the technique is used to say quite different things about the title character of Zelig than it does about the title character in *Citizen Kane*. Kane belongs with the prominent and powerful, Zelig merely adapts to them.

3. This scene, the first one shot for the film, was filmed in an actual screening room at RKO and prefigures much of *Citizen Kane*'s visual and aural style: high-contrast lighting, visible light sources, many characters operating in shadows, overlapping dialogue. The scene also indicates the financial constraints under which the movie was made. The initial budget was rejected as too high and many revisions were made to reduce the number of costly sets and to minimize the construction costs of sets that would be used. One way of doing this was to place portions of the sets in shadow—black velvet drapes were often used to assure that the areas were deep black—so that space and detail were implied but never actually seen. Set details not seen were set details not built.

4. There is a difference in tone, however, in Thompson's manner. Thompson is neither especially cynical nor especially driven to find the truth, as are so many movie journalists. He accepts his assignment with resignation at best. And as Pauline Kael observes, the contrast between Thompson and Kane also reflects different styles of journalism: the lone press baron of Kane and the corporate, collective journalism Thompson represents, as reflected by the group of men in the screening room and the corporate origins of the newsreel itself, whose real-life model was the Time, Inc., newsreel "The March of Time" (Kael, 1984, X).

5. This exchange is based on a story told about William Randolph Hearst in which illustrator Frederick Remington, sent by Hearst to Cuba, cabled Hearst: "Everything is quiet. There is no trouble here. There will be no war. I wish to return.—Remington." Hearst cabled back: "Please remain. You furnish the pictures and I'll furnish the war.—W.R. Hearst" (quoted in Swanberg 1971, 127).

6. William Randolph Hearst published such a "declaration" as a paid ad in competing newspapers, headlined "The Hearst Papers Stand for Americanism and Genuine Democracy."

7. Kane's comment brings to mind Welles's own comments about his first look at the RKO studios: "This is the biggest electric train set any boy ever had!" (quoted in Bazin, 1991, 53).

8. The allusion here is to President Warren Harding and the Teapot Dome oil scandal.

9. The 1933 *The Power and the Glory*, directed by William Howard and written by Preston Sturges, for example, is remarkably similar to *Citizen Kane* in structure but

without the psychological examination of the central character.

10. Mothers seem to bear an especially heavy burden in many films. Kane's mother's decision to turn him over to Thatcher is the key moment in his life, and one thinks also of "poor Raymond's" mother in *The Manchurian Candidate*. Fathers, on the other hand, especially in Frank Capra films, get better treatment in the context of politically charged films, though it is interesting to note that many biographers of William Randolph Hearst take a somewhat different approach to explaining Hearst by emphasizing Hearst's very long and close relationship with his mother. (See, for instance, Swanberg 1971, 422-26.) The suggestion is that Hearst was indulged by his mother, whereas the suggestion of *Citizen Kane* is that Kane was denied the love of his.

11. William Randolph Hearst was himself associated with a wide range of political beliefs that roughly parallel those of Kane, beginning as a champion of the urban working class, espousing—indeed largely creating—U.S. participation in the Spanish-American War—successfully running for the House of Representatives from New York as a reformer, losing a race for mayor of New York City running as a reformer, playing a key role in the 1931 nomination by the Democrats of Franklin D. Roosevelt, and ending his career as a political reactionary and rabid anti-Communist.

12. Orson Welles himself displayed none of the variety of political positions manifested by William Randolph Hearst or attributed to Charles Foster Kane. Welles was a life-long supporter of left/liberal causes and himself flirted with running for office. The politics of Herman Mankiewicz, *Citizen Kane*'s coauthor, however, were more like those of Hearst in their apparent contradictions: until the outbreak of World War II, the Jewish Mankiewicz, by some accounts, was both pro-German and anti-Semitic (Callow 1995, 482; see also Kael 1984, 28-29, on Mankiewicz's politics).

13. The title of Robert Penn Warren's novel *All the King's Men* is a direct reference to Huey Long's nickname, "Kingfish," and to his best-known political slogan, "Every man a king," as well as to the nursery rhyme's reference to the inability of all the king's men to put Humpty Dumpty back together again—that is, to disarray and collapse. It is this latter allusion that is most apt for Willie Stark.

14. Redford's character brings to mind a composite of California politicians of the time: his look is that of John Tunney, a U.S. senator from California, and a young Edward Kennedy; McKay's relationship with his father is roughly that of Jerry Brown to his father, Edmund G. "Pat" Brown, both two-term governors of California.

REFERENCES

Affron, Charles. 1982. *Cinema and Sentiment*. University of Chicago.

Ambrose, Stephen E. 1987. *Nixon: The Education of a Politician 1913-1962*. Simon and Schuster.

Andrew, Dudley. 1978. *Andre Bazin*. Oxford.

Bach, Steven. 1985. *Final Cut: Dreams and Disaster in the Making of* Heaven's Gate. William Morrow.

Bazin, Andre. 1971. *What is Cinema? Vol. II*. Ed. and trans. Hugh Gray. University of California.

Bazin, Andre. 1991. *Orson Welles: A Critical View*. Acrobat Books.

Bergman, Andrew. 1971. *We're in the Money: Depression America and Its Films*. Harper Colophon.

Bogdanovich, Peter. 1976. *John Ford*. University of California.

Bordwell, David. 1976. "Citizen Kane." In Nichols, 1976.

Bordwell, David. 1986. "Classical Hollywood Cinema: Narrational Principles and Procedures." In Rosen, 1986.

Brady, Frank. 1989. *Citizen Welles: A Biography of Orson Welles*. Charles Scribner's Sons.

Brodie, Fawn. 1981. *Richard Nixon: The Shaping of His Character*. W.W. Norton.

Callow, Simon. 1995. *Orson Welles: The Road to Xanadu*. Viking.

Capra, Frank. 1971. *The Name above the Title: An Autobiography*. Macmillan.

Carrington, Robert L. 1985. *The Making of "Citizen Kane."* University of California.

Ceplair, Larry, and Steven Englund. 1980. *The Inquisition in Hollywood: Politics and the Film Industry, 1930-1960*. Anchor.

Champlin, Charles. 1987. "Hollywood's Dark Days—And the Lingering Lessons." *Los Angeles Times*, Calendar section, 18 October 1987.

Cobos, Juan, Miguel Rubio and J.A. Pruneda. 1971. "A Trip to Don Quixoteland: Conversations with Orson Welles." In Gottesman, 1971.

Cowi, 1971. "The Study of a Colossus." In Gottesman, 1971.

Culbert, David, 1980. *Mission to Moscow*. University of Wisconsin Press.

Devine, Jeremy M. 1995. *Vietnam at 24 Frames a Second: A Critical and Thematic Analysis of Over 400 Films about the Vietnam War.* McFarland and Co.

Durgant, Raymond. 1974. *Jean Renoir.* University of California Press.

Ebert, Roger. 1989. *Roger Ebert's Movie Home Companion 1990 Edition.* Andrews and McMeel.

Ebert, Roger. 1994. *Roger Ebert's Video Companion 1995 Edition.* Andrews and McMeel.

Faulkner, Christopher. 1986. *The Social Cinema of Jean Renoir.* Princeton University Press.

Fielding, Raymond. 1972.*The American Newsreel 1911-1967.* University of Oklahoma Press.

Forman, Henry James. 1933. *Our Movie Made Children.* Macmillan.

Frank, Robert. 1979. *The Americans.* Aperture.

Friedrich, Otto. 1986. *City of Nets: A Portrait of Hollywood in the 1940's.* Harper and Row.

Gabler, Neal. 1988. *An Empire of Their Own: How the Jews Invented Hollywood.* Anchor Books.

Gallagher, Tag. 1986. *John Ford: The Man and His Films.* University of California Press.

Gehring, Wes D., ed. 1988. *Handbook of American Film Genres.* Greenwood Press.

Giannetti, Louis, and Scott Eyman. 1986. *Flashback: A Brief History of Film.* Prentice-Hall.

Gomery, Douglas. 1986. *The Hollywood Studio System.* St. Martin's.

Gottesman, Ronald, ed. 1971. *Focus on* Citizen Kane. University of California.

Grant, Barry Keith. 1986. *Film Genre Reader.* University of Texas Press.

Haskell, Molly. 1987. *From Reverence to Rape: The Treatment of Women in the Movies.* 2nd ed. Chicago.

Hecht, Ben. 1954. *A Child of the Century.* Simon and Schuster.

Herodutus. 1987. *The History.* Trans. David Grene. University of Chicago.

Higham, Charles. 1975. *Warner Brothers.* Charles Scribner's Sons.

Hirsch, Foster. 1983. *Film Noir: The Dark Side of the Screen.* Da Capo.

Hofstadter, Richard. 1967. *The Paranoid Style in American Politics and Other Essays.* Vintage.

Jowett, Garth. 1976. *Film: The Democratic Art.* Little, Brown.

Kael, Pauline. 1984. *The "Citizen Kane" Book.* Limelight.

Kael, Pauline. 1994. *For Keeps: 30 Years at the Movies.* Dutton.

Kauffmann, Stanley. 1966. *A World on Film: Criticism and Comment.* Harper and Row.

Kauffmann, Stanley. 1989. "Concurrent Lives." *The New Republic,* 6 November 1989, 88-90.

Kilday, Greg. 1989. "The Industry: The Eighties. " *Film Comment,* November-December 1989.

Koppes, Clayton R., and Gregory D. Black. 1987. *Hollywood Goes to War: How Politics, Profits and Propaganda Shaped World War II Movies.* Free Press.

Kracauer, Siegfried. 1957. *From Caligari to Hitler: A Psychological History of the*

German Film. Princeton University Press.

Lasswell, Harold D. 1962. *Power and Personality.* Viking.

Leff, Leonard J., and Jerrold L. Simmons. 1990. *The Dame in the Kimono: Hollywood, Censorship, and the Production Code From the 1920s to the 1960s.* Grove Weidenfield.

Litwak, Mark. 1986. *Reel Power: The Struggle for Influence and Success in the New Hollywood.* William Morrow.

MacCann, Richard Dyer. 1973. *The People's Films: A Political History of U.S. Government Motion Pictures.* Hastings House.

Maland, Charles. 1988. "The Social Problem Film." In Gehring, 1988.

Mast, Gerald, ed. 1982. *The Movies in Our Midst: Documents in the Cultural History of Film in America.* University of Chicago.

Mathews, Jack. 1989. "Children of the Blacklist." *Los Angeles Times Magazine,* 15 October 1989, 10.

McBride, Joseph. 1992. *Frank Capra: The Catastrophe of Success.* Simon and Schuster.

McClintick, David. 1982. *Indecent Exposure: A True Story of Hollywood and Wall Street.* William Morrow.

Michaelson, Judith. 1987. "The Blacklist Legacy." *Los Angeles Times Calendar,* 18 October 1987, 3.

Michaelson, Judith. 1988. "Blacklist Spirit Still Alive, Entertainment Leaders Warn." *Los Angeles Times,* 23 June 1988, Pt. VI, 1.

Miller, Mark Crispin. 1990. "Hollywood: The Ad." *The Atlantic Monthly,* April 1990, 41-68.

Mills, C. Wright. 1956. *The Power Elite.* Oxford.

Mitchell, Greg. 1992. *The Campaign of the Century: Upton Sinclair's Race for Governor of California and the Birth of Media Politics.* Random House.

Mitry, Jean. 1963. *Esthetique et psychologie du cinema. I. Les structures.* Trans. Charles Affron. Editions Universitaires.

Moldea, Dan E. 1986. *Dark Victory: Ronald Reagan, MCA, and the Mob.* Viking.

Moley, Raymond. 1938. *Are We Movie Made?* Macy-Masius.

Moley, Raymond. 1945.*The Hays Office.* Bobbs-Merrill.

Mordden, Ethan. 1988. *The Hollywood Studios: House Style in the Golden Age of the Movies.* Knopf.

Motion Picture Association of America. 1988. *Incidence of Motion Picture Attendance among the Adult and Teenage Population, July 1988.* Motion Picture Association of America.

Motion Picture Producers and Distributors of America. 1930. *The Motion Picture Production Code of 1930.* MPPDA.

Navasky, Victor. 1980. *Naming Names.* Viking.

Neve, Brian. 1992. *Film and Politics in America: A Social Tradition.* Routledge.

Nichols, Bill, ed. 1976. *Movies and Methods: Vol. I.* University of California.

O'Connor, John E., and Martin A. Jackson. 1975. *American History/American Film: Interpreting the Hollywood Image.* Frederick Ungar.

Phelan, J.J. 1919. *Motion Pictures as a Phase of Commercialized Amusement in Toledo,*

Ohio. Little Book Press.

Powdermaker, Hortense. 1950. *Hollywood the Dream Factory: An Anthropologist Looks at the Movie-Makers.* Little, Brown.

Riesman, David. 1961. *The Lonely Crowd: A Study of the Changing American Character.* Yale.

Rejai, Mostafa, ed. 1971. *Decline of Ideology?* Aldine-Atherton.

Rhode, Eric. 1976. *A History of the Cinema from Its Origins to 1970.* Da Capo.

Roffman, Peter, and Jim Purdy. 1981. *The Hollywood Social Problem Film: Madness, Despair and Politics.* Indiana University.

Rogin, Michael. 1987. *Ronald Reagan, the Movie, and Other Episodes in Political Demonology.* University of California.

Rosen, Philip. 1986. *Narrative, Apparatus, Ideology: A Film Theory Reader.* Columbia University Press.

Rosenfield, Paul. 1989. The Inside Man. *Los Angeles Times,* Calendar section, 3 December 1989.

Rosten, Leo C. 1941. *Hollywood: The Movie Colony and the Movie Makers.* Harcourt Brace.

Sarris, Andrew. 1968. *The American Cinema: Directors and Directions.* E.P. Dutton.

Sarris, Andrew. 1975. *The John Ford Movie Mystery.* Indiana University.

Sarris, Andrew. 1978. *Politics and Cinema.* Columbia University Press.

Sayre, Norah. 1982. *Running Time: Films of the Cold War.* Dial Press.

Schatz, Thomas. 1981. *Hollywood Genres: Formulas, Filmmaking, and the Studio System.* Random House.

Schatz, Thomas. 1988. *The Genius of the System: Hollywood Filmmaking in the Studio Era.* Pantheon.

Schickel, Richard. 1975. *The Men Who Made the Movies: Interviews with Frank Capra, George Cukor, Howard Hawks, Alfred Hitchcock, Vincente Minnelli, King Vidor, Raoul Walsh, and William A. Wellman.* Atheneum.

Schickel, Richard. 1989. *Schickel on Film: Encounters—Critical and Personal—with Movie Immortals.* Morrow.

Schlesinger, Arthur M., Jr. 1963. "When the Movies Really Counted." In Mast, 1982.

Schlesinger, Arthur M., Jr. 1975. "Introduction," In O'Connor and Jackson, 1975.

Schwartz, Nancy Lynn. 1982. *The Hollywood Writers' Wars.* Knopf.

Sesonske, Alexander. 1980. *Jean Renoir: The French Films, 1924-1939.* Harvard University Press.

Sherry, Michael S. 1995. *In the Shadow of War: The United States since the 1930s.* Yale University Press.

Shuttleworth, Frank K. and Mark A. May. 1933. *The Social Conduct and Attitudes of Movie Fans.* Macmillan.

Sinclair, Upton. 1962. *The Autobiography of Upton Sinclair.* Harcourt, Brace and World.

Sklar, Robert. 1975. *Movie-Made America: A Cultural History of American Movies.* Vintage.

Somerville, John, and Ronald E. Santoni, eds., 1963. *Social and Political Philosophy.* Doubleday Anchor.

Spoto, Donald. 1976. *The Art of Alfred Hitchcock: Fifty Years of His Motion Pictures.* Doubleday Dolphin.

Spoto, Donald. 1983. *The Dark Side of Genius: The Life of Alfred Hitchcock.* Ballantine.

Stowell, Peter. 1986. *John Ford.* Twayne Publishers.

Stowell, Peter. 1986. *John Ford.* Twayne.

Suid, Lawrence H. 1978. *Guts and Glory: Great American War Movies.* Addison-Wesley.

Swanberg, W.A. 1971. *Citizen Hearst: A Biography of William Randolph Hearst.* Bantam.

Sylbert, Richard. 1989. "Dialogue on Film: Richard Sylbert." *American Film*, December 1989, 22-26.

Taylor, John Russell. 1983. *Strangers in Paradise: The Hollywood Emigres 1933-1950. Holt Rinehart.*

Thomson, David. 1994. *A Biographical Dictionary of Film.* 3rd ed. Knopf.

Trevelyan, John. 1973. *What the Censor Saw.* Michael Joseph.

Truffaut, Francois. 1983. *Hitchcock.* Simon and Schuster.

Warshow, Robert L. 1964. *The Immediate Experience.* Doubleday.

Waxman, Chaim. 1969. *The End of Ideology Debate.* Simon and Schuster.

Welles, Orson, and Peter Bogdanovich. 1992. *This Is Orson Welles.* Harper Collins.

Whitfield, Stephen J. 1991. *The Culture of the Cold War.* Johns Hopkins.

Whyte, William H. 1956. *The Organization Man.* Simon and Schuster.

Wilder, Billy. 1989. Interview, Michael Jackson program, KABC-AM, Los Angeles, 26 September 1989.

Wills, Garry. 1987. *Reagan's America: Innocents at Home.* Doubleday.

Wylie, Philip. 1942. *Generation of Vipers.* Farrar and Rinehart.

INDEX

About the Author

PHILLIP L. GIANOS is Professor of Political Science at California State University, Fullerton.